ADVANCE PRAISE FOR *ASK QUESTIONS, SAVE MONEY, MAKE MORE*

"If you want to be more financially savvy, powerful, and confident, this essential guide for navigating sometimes-tricky money questions offers expert advice and valuable tools such as fill-in-the-blank scripts."

—Laura Adams, author of *Money-Smart Solopreneur*

"Take the worry out of managing your money. The practical advice, compelling testimonials, and easy-to-follow scripts in this book can help you conquer your financial fears with ease."

—Lauren Cook, PsyD, author of *Generation Anxiety*

"I've read dozens of books that offer financial tips, but none of them go as deep into specific communication strategies for reducing bills and debts as this one does! . . . If you're looking for a practical guide to help you cut costs and negotiate better terms with your service providers, this is it."

—Yanely Espinal, author of *Mind Your Money*

"This book offers everything you need to get better deals from airlines, banks, health insurance companies, and more. The advice is actionable and easy to execute—and, most importantly, it works. If you want to save more money, this book is for you."

—Catey Hill, author of *The 30-Minute Money Plan for Moms* and *Shoo, Jimmy Choo!*

"Matt Schulz has created the ultimate guide to asking for what you want in practically every financial situation. *Ask Questions* will help you become your own best advocate when it comes to your money."

—Cameron Huddleston, author of *Mom and Dad, We Need to Talk*

"This book is my new go-to guide to set financial grownups up for success. Schulz not only shares strategies on negotiating bills and salaries, but he also tackles sticky social situations that we tend to avoid because we simply don't know how to ask uncomfortable questions. It's not just about the money, it's about approaching those we care about in a way that preserves and strengthens our relationships with friends and family."

—Bobbi Rebell, CFP, founder of Financial Wellness Strategies and author of *Launching Financial Grownups*

"Engaging, accessible, and expertly written, this guide can help you build self-confidence and courage in your financial life and remove guesswork from the equation. Matt Schulz gives you all the tools you need to champion yourself as a consumer and get the responses you want from your money requests." —Selena Rezvani, author of *Quick Confidence*

"This is a must-read for anyone looking to save money every day. Clear and actionable advice makes somewhat scary tasks, such as negotiating with your doctor's office or talking to your parents about their finances, seem more manageable. The scripts make it easier to navigate those awkward conversations, and the book reads like you've got a good friend sitting on the sidelines, cheering you on. Real people can save real money, and what's better than that?"

—Lindsey Stanberry, author of *Refinery29 Money Diaries*

"This book is for everyone who has ever wondered, *Can it really hurt to ask?* . . . Matt Schulz has given us the ultimate guidebook on how to save more and stress less while getting exactly what we want."

—Kathryn Tuggle, coauthor of *How to Money*

ASK QUESTIONS,
↳ SAVE MONEY,
↳ MAKE MORE

How to Take Control
of Your Financial Life

MATT SCHULZ

Countryman Press

An Imprint of W. W. Norton & Company
Independent Publishers Since 1923

To Dad

Copyright © 2024 by Paul Matthew LLC

Image Credits: Pages 12, 19, 25, 30, 35, 38, 42, 47, 52, 56, 65, 70, 74, 78, 82, 87, 92, 96, 101, 105, 111, 117, 123, 128, 132, 137, 141, 145, 149, 152, 157, 162, 166, 171, 177, 181, 189, 198, 206, 211, 217, 227, 234, 239, 246, 252: iStock / isiddheshm; pages 12, 166: iStock / fonikum; pages 30, 102, 190: iStock / yalcinadali; pages 47, 58, 78, 149, 171, 234: iStock / Victor Metelskiy; page 70: iStock / Neonic_Flower; page 87: iStock / Esra Sen Kula; page 111: iStock / Maksym Rudoi; page 123: iStock / vector; page 149: iStock / Sudowoodo; page 165: iStock / Alex-White; page 178: iStock / Hiranmay Baidya; page 210: iStock / Andrii Tokarchuk; page 211: iStock / Anton Porkin; page 227: iStock / panom73; page 246: iStock / appleuzr; page 252: iStock / 4zevar

For information about permission to reproduce selections from this book, write to Permissions, Countryman Press, 500 Fifth Avenue, New York, NY 10110

For information about special discounts for bulk purchases, please contact W. W. Norton Special Sales at specialsales@wwnorton.com or 800-233-4830

Manufacturing by Lakeside Book Company
Production manager: Devon Zahn

Countryman Press
www.countrymanpress.com

An imprint of W. W. Norton & Company, Inc.
500 Fifth Avenue, New York, NY 10110
www.wwnorton.com

978-1-68268-840-3 (pbk)

10 9 8 7 6 5 4 3 2 1

"The most common way people give up their power is by thinking they don't have any."

—Alice Walker

CONTENTS

FOREWORD

MATT SCHULZ HAS SPENT his career helping people improve their relationship with money and work toward financial security. He has done the legwork and found hacks to help you speak up and save. In this book, he walks you through how to empower yourself and how not to shy away from your importance as a consumer. He wisely guides you through asking the right questions, steering your way to success by sharing real-life examples of how other people effectively maneuvered through life's biggest challenges for the best ways to save and earn more.

As the senior consumer investigative correspondent at NBC News, I've interviewed him many times for his practical advice on how to make your money work for you. Good journalism asks tough questions and deals responsibly with uncomfortable confrontations. In many everyday situations, those skills have helped me advocate for myself and, by extension, my money. Years ago, my husband and I were in the market for an SUV. Our family was expanding, and we needed cargo space for strollers and bulk grocery purchases, not to mention extra seats for transporting grandparents. It was the largest car we'd purchased and our biggest investment at the time. I cared about only one feature. The car needed to have as many cameras as possible so that, when behind the wheel, I could see everything around the vehicle. We found a model with that technology and ordered it with a safety package that included a 360-degree camera.

Months later, the car arrived—with all-wheel drive. A nice feature, sure, but we didn't order it, and it cost several thousand dollars more. The dealer tried to charge us for the extra feature, but we pushed back. We argued that we shouldn't pay for their mistake. They insisted that they couldn't sell us the car if we didn't pay for the upgrade, but we held the line. We said that we'd walk away if they didn't honor the agreed-on price for what we ordered. After some back and forth, we got the car with the extra feature for the original price. If we just accepted the dealer's attempt at upselling us, we'd have spent thousands more than we wanted.

If the first answer you receive is "No," my father always taught me to ask more than one person, but we as consumers too often accept scenarios presented to us, whether it's an extra fee on a travel booking or the sky-high interest rate on a credit card. No one wants to leave money on the table, but a lot of us don't have the knowledge or confidence to advocate for ourselves. This book—full of inspiring stories of people who bettered their lives through common-sense discipline and smart saving practices—shows how they overcame those obstacles. Let their stories inspire your own savings journey.

From small daily habits to more substantial long-term methods, *Ask Questions, Save, Money, Make More* provides a range of tips and techniques for you to use in a wide array of situations. If you think negotiating at work is tough, you're right! But with detailed guidelines and sample scripts for how to do it, you can grow your skillset and learn how to unlock better opportunities for yourself. Plus, understanding how to negotiate successfully will give you a powerful tool that can improve all areas of your life. Often a sensitive subject, money can get complicated, particularly with a significant other, family, or friends, so this book explores the intricacies of lending and gifting, managing expectations, and setting boundaries. By comprehending the dynamics of those financial connections, you can maintain healthy relationships while safeguarding your own well-being. Travel can enrich and transform, but it often comes with a hefty price tag. In that chapter, you'll discover lots of insider info on how you can find the best deals, travel smart, maximize your experiences, and save along the way. From budget-friendly accommodation options to creative ways to save on transportation, you can see the world without breaking the bank.

Money doesn't buy happiness, but it sure does offer more choices in life, and it can help ease stress. Knowing how to navigate the complex landscape of personal finance by saving and spending effectively is an essential skill. If you care about achieving financial stability, you should read this book—often.

Whether you recently graduated, are a seasoned professional, or simply are looking to take better control of your hard-earned funds, this book can help you build your financial fitness. By recognizing your strength as a consumer, you can gain the confidence to make the right requests and informed decisions about your future. You also will understand how to master the art of negotiation, learning valuable insights and strategies to maximize your chances of securing desired outcomes in all areas of your life: requesting a salary increase, buying a vehicle, or just haggling for a good deal at a flea market. Negotiating can save you thousands and boost your earning power.

Establishing healthy habits and embracing a growth mindset can help increase your control of your money, reduce anxiety, and pave the way for long-term success. But on your journey to empowerment, remember the importance of paying it forward. The lessons in this book can improve your life profoundly, but they also can benefit others. Share your newfound wisdom, inspire others to take better control of their finances, and create positive ripples in your community.

By reading this book, you're embarking on a transformative journey. The practical tools that it contains can help you make confident decisions, save money, understand your worth, build wealth, and achieve long-lasting financial happiness. There's no time like the present to get started!

—*Vicky Nguyen*
Senior consumer investigative correspondent, NBC News

INTRODUCTION

YOU HAVE MORE POWER OVER YOUR MONEY THAN YOU REALIZE

IN ALMOST A DECADE of answering media questions about credit cards for a living, I probably have said, "You have more power over your money than you realize" as often as my name and title. But that simple statement often takes people by surprise. Over the years, more than a few friends and relatives have rolled their eyes in response, as have journalists, podcasters, and bloggers. I get it. The idea that the average person has any sway over the megabanks seems absurd, given how much power those multinational conglomerates have.

Yet studies show that about 76 percent of people who ask for a lower interest rate on their credit cards get one, and many of those rates drop by 10 percentage points or more, say from 25 to 15 percent.[1] Surprising, right? Those same studies show that you have an even better chance of success when asking for a higher credit limit, a waived late fee, or reduced annual fee. Plus, these success rates have stayed high through booming economies and even the lows of the most recent pandemic. Do I have your attention now? Suddenly the absurd feels a little more plausible, doesn't it?

But here's the thing. You don't have power over just card issuers. You have it when securing a mortgage or car loan. Same with your student loan company and the bank that holds your savings. It's not even just financial institutions. You have it over furniture stores, cable companies, gyms, and so many other companies that you pay for goods and services. You even have it over medical providers and colleges. When requesting these breaks, deals, and discounts, your chances for success can vary, depending on who you are, what you're asking, and whom you're asking, but more often than not, they're a lot better than zero. Add it all up, and my original statement, the title of this introduction, doesn't go far enough.

You have *way* more power over your money than you realize.

Read that line again, this time aloud: "I have *way* more power over my money than I realize."

Now, don't misunderstand. As with a casino, the house always wins in the long run. But that doesn't mean that you can't come out on top from time to time and put some real money back in your pocket in the process. Sometimes it requires nothing more than a phone call. Here's the simple reason: Most companies view customers in terms of *lifetime* value. The longer they have you as a customer, the more money they can make from you. Companies want you to stick around, and they often will work with you to make sure that happens. We saw exactly that happen during the Great Recession from 2008 to 2009, when banks worked with millions of cardholders and mortgage and auto borrowers to help them weather that relatively short-term financial crisis. We saw it again during the COVID-19 pandemic.[2]

Sure, during both those crises, we also saw banks close accounts and shrink credit limits for millions of cardholders.[3] But most of the cards they closed already lay dormant or little-used. When you don't use a card, the bank doesn't make any money from it, unless it comes with an annual fee. When the bank doesn't make money off an asset, that asset becomes expendable, and expendability often leads to closure. But if you use your card regularly and pay your bill consistently, banks have a vested interest in keeping you happy.

You don't even have to have spectacular credit. If you're a good customer and help make the bank money, they want to keep you around so they can sell you credit cards, investment accounts, mortgages, and other financial products, which allows them to make more money from you. That's what it's all about: making more money. Banks aren't charitable organizations. They don't want to keep you happy out of the goodness of their hearts. They want to make more money. That's it. Over the years, they've realized that, every once in a while, it's worth it to give a little money back to customers if it means they'll stick around. For a bank, waiving an $89 annual fee doesn't even amount to a rounding error on a rounding error. It's one grain of sand on a beach. But the goodwill it can engender can create a loyal customer for decades, allowing the bank to make more money in the long run—and much more than just $89.

The same math holds true with so many other companies. The longer you belong to that gym, subscribe to that streaming service, or shop at that department store, the more money they make off you. In many cases, it's worth it for them to give you that free logo hoodie, 30-day free trial, or extra 5 percent off your purchases if that means you keep spending your money with them. Understanding the relationship from the companies' side should change your perspective. You're not coming to them on bended knee, asking for mercy. You're approaching them from a position of power. You matter to them, and that's a big deal.

Still, most people don't ask. Why? One of the biggest reasons is simple: Asking feels scary. It feels that way for me and for most people all the time. Even when you know that you probably will succeed, asking seems daunting. It makes you vulnerable in front of someone else, no easy situation, especially if you feel like you're facing a heartless, profit-thirsty megabank.

Plus, so many of us have learned all our lives *not* to ask. Long-outdated gender norms teach women that asking makes them appear bossy and disrespectful and men that it makes them look weak. Our parents and countless self-help books tell us to be happy with or grateful for what we have. We also feel like the deck is stacked against us. Sure, some folks might succeed, but systemic sexism, racism, homophobia, and other vulgar biases, overt and covert, mean that other people may not have the same advantages, opportunities, or luck.

Then there's the old saw that everyone's fighting a battle that you can't see, and asking feels like just another struggle, another box to check on that never-ending to-do list. "That all impacts you," says Rita-Soledad Fernández Paulino, a former public-school math teacher who runs WealthParaTodos .com (wealth "for all"). "It impacts you mentally, emotionally, and it drains your capacity to feel like you can advocate for yourself because, at the end of the day, it's like, *I'm advocating for myself daily at work, at home, simple places. Now I'm going to call somebody and ask to reduce my interest rate? I'm tired!"*

That's why I never shame anyone who doesn't ask, and nor should you. Shame only makes people feel bad, and that's the last feeling anyone needs. What people need is help. They, meaning *you*, need practical, concrete, actionable advice about how to ask and when. You need proof that asking can work, and you need to know what to do when it doesn't. You need to know when it's better to run for the exits instead, and, no matter what happens, you need empathy.

Ask Questions, Save Money, Make More does all of that and much more. It guides you through asking big and not-so-big money questions that can improve your finances. Money touches virtually all aspects of our lives, so the book casts a wide net. It covers lowering credit card fees, interest rates, and medical bills. It shows you how to ask for a promotion or a higher salary—and when it's better not to ask. It teaches you how to lower your mortgage costs, how to talk to a mechanic about vehicle repair, and how to get a cash refund for a cancelled flight instead of a voucher or credit. You don't ask all-important money questions just of businesses and strangers, though. Coworkers, friends, and relatives can prove trickiest of all to face. This book walks you through how to talk about money with your significant other, how to ask your parents about their financial situation, and what to do if any of them don't like that you're asking. You'll learn how to talk to brides or grooms about how insanely expensive joining their wedding party can be. It even shows you how to split the bill for a group gathering without getting stuck paying more than you owe.

To make the book quick to navigate and easy to revisit, each ask features ratings from 1 to 5 in three categories:

POSSIBLE IMPACT

How much does the ask matter? In most cases, we're talking financial impact, so negotiating a lower interest rate on a mortgage has a higher impact than lowering your cable bill. But sometimes results go beyond the bottom line, such as when you talk about money with your significant other for the first time or ask the billing administrator at your doctor's office to explain the cost of a service or procedure before you approve it.

CHANCE OF SUCCESS

How likely is it that asking will work? Some asks are slam dunks, such as having a credit card late fee waived for a first-time missed payment. Others are dicier, including talking about wedding party costs with a bride or asking real estate agents to lower their commission. For many of these asks, it's hard to quantify the odds precisely, but it's still important to have a rough idea of your chances before you try.

SIMPLICITY

How easy is it? Some asks don't require much more than "Who can I speak with about waiving a late fee?" Other cases can prove more challenging. You typically don't request a promotion, talk to your parents about money, or negotiate mortgage closing costs with just a phone call. First you need to research, strategize, and practice. The goals also could have a million variables to consider, which the simplicity ratings illustrate.

These ratings not only help demystify the process, but they also present the unvarnished truth. Despite the adage, sometimes it *can* hurt to ask, and the results can prove far worse than simply hearing "No." Plenty of people who try to negotiate higher salaries or better titles with outside job offers stumble when the other companies revoke those offers. Women, people of color, and other groups often face discrimination simply for being who they are.

This book embraces reality rather than ignoring it. That's one reason that it features a diverse array of voices. The privilege and experiences of being a middle-aged white male differ vastly from those of lots of others, and people learn best from those to whom they can relate best. With that in mind, you'll find lots of viewpoints and perspectives in the pages that follow, all gathered through more than 100 interviews conducted specifically for this book.

For each ask—in addition to ratings on potential results, prospects of success, and ease—you also will review crucial information, including: Does asking pose any risks? How do you do it? What if you don't succeed?

What do you do if your ask is rejected? and more. For each request, you'll find one or more fill-in-the-blank scripts that tell you exactly what to say.

Along the way, you'll see lists, charts, graphs, success stories, and more to make the message more engaging. I want this handbook to pay for itself out in the world, but that won't happen if you read it just once and set it aside. The book is about what happens when you read it the second or ninth time and act on it. It's about saving $89 from your credit card's annual fee. It's about trimming $10 off your phone bill, allowing you to keep an extra $120 a year in your pocket. It's about getting that $5,000 raise at work. All that makes the sticker price of the book seem like a bargain, right?

No one attends funerals or weddings every day. We're not applying for mortgages, asking for promotions, or facing sky-high medical bills that often, either. You won't be able to implement all the strategies immediately. I'll explain them and show you how to do them now, but the opportunity to enact them might not arise for a while. That's why this book plays the long game. Yes, you're going to save money or earn more right away, but it also helps prepare you to split the bill on that group brunch or dinner next month without overpaying. It's about knowing, in six months, what to do when seeking a promotion at work. It's about having the confidence, next year or the year after, to handle those fraudulent charges on your credit card. In short, it's about helping you pay less and earn more today, tomorrow, and for years to come.

It all starts with an ask.

BEFORE YOU BEGIN

LET'S LAY SOME NECESSARY GROUNDWORK. Every ask is different, in part because everyone asking is different. You bring your own strengths, experiences, biases, and weaknesses to every conversation you have, whether negotiating a six-figure salary or haggling for a pair of kids' pajamas at a garage sale. Conducting the hundred-plus interviews for this book revealed commonalities among successful requests and those who make them. Once you understand them, you can apply them to pretty much any request you make. This entire book stands on the foundation of these basic beliefs, clear concepts, and simple themes. You don't need an advanced degree to grasp them nor special talents to execute them. Some may seem obvious to you but not others, and vice versa, which is why they all are in here. Even if you've heard some of them many times, reading them again is still worth your time.

YOU CAN DO IT

It all starts with this belief. It won't always be easy. You won't always say perfectly what you meant to say. You won't always get your way. But that's OK. We learn by trying, sometimes failing, realizing that it isn't the end of the world, and trying again. There's nothing in this book that you can't do if you try your best and, if necessary or appropriate, keep trying.

THERE'S POWER IN SHARING YOUR STORY

Don't be afraid to share it. If you're struggling with paying your mortgage this month because your company laid off you and 99 other people, tell your lender. If your daughter has plastered her bedroom with posters of Alex Morgan, Carli Lloyd, and Megan Rapinoe and she wakes at 5 a.m. every day to kick the ball around but you can't afford a travel league for her because you're drowning in medical bills, tell the head of the league. If you'd love to go on that three-night bachelorette trip to Nashville but you have to take care of your sick mother, tell the bride. Most of the time, people want to help when others are struggling, but they won't know that you are unless you tell them. Nothing connects people quite like a story.

"Nobody will advocate for you better than you will," says Mori Taheripour, a negotiation expert whose clients include the National Football League, Goldman Sachs, and Google.[4] The best way to do that, she says, is by telling your story. But that requires you to be vulnerable with others, which can be hard, Taheripour says, because "we don't value ourselves enough." We don't think our stories matter or are that bad. They even may embarrass us. But your story matters and probably to more people than just you.

IT'S OK TO BE NOT OK WHEN YOU ASK

If the thought of sharing your story or asking these questions makes you break out in a cold sweat, you're not alone. Intense physical reactions indicate that you're "doing something unfamiliar, and unfamiliar things sort of change our bodies," says financial therapist Amanda Clayman.[5] "Our bodies and brains have particular ways of gearing up for that kind of event, so we're going to feel the adrenaline. We're going to feel our hearts race. We might get clammy. We'll notice all these physiological symptoms."

The key, Clayman says, is recognizing those reactions as they happen and telling yourself that, even though your body is behaving as though you're in danger, you're OK. "Sometimes what feels safe in the moment is in opposition to our long-term safety and security. So it requires not necessarily the ability to react that much better but to be able to note the reaction, let it exist, and then focus more on moving ourselves into that space where we can reintegrate and not let that physical process run away with us."

In that moment, it can feel like a case of easier said than done, especially for people with anxiety and other mental health conditions and concerns. For some, repetition can vanquish the fear: doing the scary thing repeatedly and realizing that they survive it every time. Others might need the professional help of a therapist or even medication. Those steps can serve you well beyond just helping you feel comfortable when asking for a lower interest rate on your credit card.

ROLE-PLAYING MAKES GREAT PRACTICE

Steph Curry takes hundreds of shots every day to make sure he's ready for his next basketball game. Adele warms up her voice before every show. The person who gave that moving, inspiring TED Talk rehearsed her presentation many times. Practice can help you, too, and experts say one of the best ways to do that is through role-play, acting out the conversation with a friend or relative before you do it for real.

Clinical psychologist Lauren Cook says that just saying the request aloud to someone else can help ease people's minds.[6] "They realize when they do it, *Oh, that wasn't so bad*, and then they start to build confidence from there." Picking the right people for practice is key. You should feel comfortable with and trust them. Once you've chosen someone, run through it multiple times, starting with a best-case scenario, says Jacki Carlson, confidence coach with the Confident Girl Hotline.[7] "You want to build the person up who's trying it, and then you do the call again with someone making it difficult on you." Selena Rezvani, author of *Quick Confidence*, says the second time through should be "more adversarial," with pushback that you might hear in a real conversation.[8] "Maybe poke holes in your argument. Say, 'I don't think you're ready for a promotion. What makes you think you're ready for it?' Oftentimes it can boost your confidence to feel like you've already been in that conversation. You've already blocked and tackled, conversationally speaking, in ways that don't make it feel brand new when you actually get there and you're talking to your boss or that authority figure."

Carlson recommends making the role-play experience feel as much like the real-world conversation as possible. For example, if the conversation will take place over the phone, so should the role-play. "You need to practice how you're going to play it," she says.

YOU HAVE MORE NEGOTIATING EXPERIENCE THAN YOU REALIZE

You negotiate every day, regardless of whether it feels like it. Here are some examples:

- the temperature of the thermostat
- the best time for a work meeting
- which parent takes which kid to which activity
- what to buy at the grocery store for the week
- what to listen to while making dinner or driving somewhere
- convincing your roommate, significant other, or child to do the dishes or take out the trash
- what TV or movie to watch with a friend or relative
- what time your kid needs to come home
- where to have dinner with a friend or relative
- what dessert to split
- where to go for your next family or group vacation
- who brings what to a holiday meal

In many or most of these activities, you probably don't feel like an inexperienced scaredy-cat, right?

NEGOTIATION CHOICES SHOULD MATCH YOUR VALUES

Most of us probably should negotiate more, but you don't always have to, and sometimes you shouldn't. No one-size-fits-all rules apply across the board. Much of the choice comes down to what you value. With that in mind, here are some examples from interviews for this book.

Artists

"A lot of artists undervalue themselves, and it's hard to have a business," says Barbara Sloan, author of *Tipped* and the founder of Tipped Finance, a site devoted to teaching service industry professionals about money.[9] "I don't buy a ton of art, but if it's something I'm going to buy, then I want the person who is going to create my lifelong enjoyment of this piece of art to feel valued."

Small Businesses

Many people make a point of not haggling with small businesses. "Only with big companies," says Rita-Soledad Fernández Paulino of Wealth para Todos.[10] "I always pay small businesses what they ask." Larger companies likely have more wiggle room on their bottom line, but this strategy also values and shows respect for the small businessperson and the challenges of entrepreneurship.

Businesses with Which You Want to Have a Long-Term Relationship

Do you tip more at a favorite restaurant? In the same way, you may choose more leniency in negotiating with a business that you want to stay in business. "Something my dad really instilled in me was that you pay people for good work," says Jacki Carlson of Confident Girl Hotline. "You don't haggle with them because you want them to come back if something were to happen." That guideline holds especially true with service-industry folks, such as personal hygiene providers (haircutters, pedicurists, waxers), contractors, and repair people.

Charities or Religious Organizations

Even if you think the cost of that sweater at your church's thrift shop or the shelf at the Habitat for Humanity Re-Store is running high, don't haggle. Just pay the sticker price. If you're in the store, chances are that you support the organization, so you know that the full amount will further a good cause.

Also, don't haggle if it's not worth the effort, money, or time. For example, spending 30 minutes on the phone or driving across town to recoup a $1.37 overcharge might not make the best use of your day.

MAKE THE NEGOTIATION A WIN-WIN SITUATION

Sometimes you need to play hardball to get what you want—but not always. Many times, the best way to approach a situation is by making sure that you're offering the other side something in return for helping you.

"I'm big on asking and negotiating, but I always make sure I also am adding value," says Sunitha Rao, real estate investor and chief sanity officer at Afford Anything.[11] "I don't ask just for the sake of asking. I will push back against my contractors at times. I will push back against certain people who I've worked to develop relationships with. But I know that over time I've made their lives easier by working well with them. I've brought them business. I add value to their lives."

You can add value in lots of ways. You can refer your friends and family to a particular business, or you can post glowing reviews on review sites or social media. If you're a renter, you can sign a longer lease in exchange for a lower monthly payment. If you're buying a vehicle, you could finance it through the dealership, rather than a third party, in exchange for a lower price. It's not always just about the bottom line, either. "If you can be likable and easy to work with, people will be willing to cut you a break sometimes just because it's easier," says Rao. "There is a price to mental anguish."

THREE IS A MAGIC NUMBER

Throughout this book, various experts and I recommend getting estimates or quotes from multiple businesses before you decide on one. Whether you're looking for a better deal on a mortgage, car repair, or even a funeral, shopping around can help ensure that you get a good deal. But how many estimates should you get? "The magic number is three bids," says Kristin McGrath, senior editor at RetailMeNot.[12] "If you've got the time for multiple quotes, you can see the lay of the land."

You always can get more if you have the time, if the standard three estimates vary widely or if you just want another opinion. But most experts agree that three bids should give you a sense of the marketplace and help you frame any future negotiation.

GET IT IN WRITING

As you apply what you read in this book, you likely will come to many verbal agreements. You'll strike a deal with the person on the other end of the phone, feeling proud of yourself for achieving your goal. But the deal's not done unless you have it in writing. You don't need written confirmation for haggling at a garage sale or splitting the bill for brunch, but in many other cases, it's absolutely essential. Confirmation in writing offers concrete proof of the terms to which you agreed, and it can protect you if the other party tries to backpedal. Most of the time, you won't need a lengthy contract, notary, or lawyer. A simple email outlining the agreed terms usually will cover you.

Written notes from your conversations can prove useful as well. You don't need a transcript verbatim, but taking the time to note the date and time of your call, the name of the person you spoke with, the topic of conversation, and anything you agreed to can make future discussions easier. It also helps guard against a company saying one thing in one call but claiming later that they said something else.

THE CLOSER TO POWER, THE GREATER THE CHANCE OF SUCCESS

The fastest way to doom any negotiation is speaking to people with no power. You can connect with them deeply, dazzle them with knowledge gleaned from hours of research, and offer them tons of convincing reasons that you should get what you're requesting, but if they don't have the authority to help you, all your efforts ultimately mean nothing.

If you do find the right person who can make the decision you want, just asking nicely could work. That's why experts say that smaller businesses—independent pharmacies, family-owned furniture and appliance stores, boutique clothing shops—can offer the most fertile ground for negotiation. In those places, you more likely will find someone empowered to give you a lower price in the right circumstances. The person behind the counter could be the owner herself or close enough to the owner to influence the decision to give you a lower price. In some ways, it's like a garage sale or flea market, where you deal directly with the proprietor. That still doesn't guarantee success because small businesses need to make a profit, too, but at least you have a chance. In a giant chain store, corporate policies, bureaucracy, and paperwork might tie the hands of the retail associates, rendering them powerless to help.

Just because you may be more likely to succeed in negotiating with a small business doesn't mean that you should. As you read earlier, several experts interviewed for this book don't negotiate with small businesses specifically because of their often-lower profit margins and other reasons. But if you just want a lower price, a smaller, locally owned business can provide a real opportunity for savings.

OPEN-ENDED QUESTIONS MAKE IT HARDER TO SAY NO

A simple "no" can stop any negotiation dead in its tracks. Those two powerful little letters can make people cower, and even the possibility of hearing them keeps a lot of folks from asking for a better deal. You can ensure that you hear it less often, however, and one of the best ways is to use open-ended questions.

Open-ended questions can't be answered by a simple yes or no. Used skillfully, these can help you avoid someone shutting down a negotiation before it starts. The scripts in this book feature lots of open-ended questions. Look at these examples of closed and open questions.

- Splitting the bill at a group gathering:
  Closed: "Can we split the bill evenly?"
  Open: "How can we split the bill so that we all pay our fair share?"
- Negotiating vehicle repair:
  Closed: "Can I get a lower price on this repair?"
  Open: "What can we do to lower the price for this repair?"
- Escalating a conversation to a manager:
  Closed: "May I speak with someone else on your team?"
  Open: "Who else on your team can I ask about this?"

In the examples above, the open-ended questions avoid a conversational dead end. They don't guarantee a positive response—because the other side still can respond that they can't do anything about it—but open questions make it virtually impossible to kill the request with a "no." That's a big deal because, if you never hear "no," you might keep pressing forward with your request. If you do, you never know what could happen.

A PHONE CALL ALSO MAKES IT HARDER TO SAY NO

Many people hate phone calls. "Especially for Millennials, we don't like talking on the phone if we don't have to," says travel blogger and social media manager Samantha O'Brochta.[13] "We'll probably try to find an Internet way to do it instead." Not just Millennials feel that way, though. Millions of people of all ages prefer to use their phones for anything other than making phone calls. Chatbots, social media–based support, apps, and other avenues make negotiating and asking for help online easier, but that ease doesn't always make those tools the best way to go.

It seems downright old-fashioned, but this book preaches the power of phone calls. Hearing another voice can bind people together in ways that text-based communication can't. Your voice makes you more real. It humanizes you, which means that it can make it harder for someone to tell you, "No." It's one thing to type that word onto a screen but something else entirely to say it to someone whose voice is trembling with nerves, with kids playing and a dog barking in the background. Social media proves this truth every day. Millions of people around the world post cruel, hurtful comments about others that never in a million years would they say over the phone.

But phone calls don't always feel easy. It can seem almost impossible to get to a real person on the other end of the line. Once a human is listening, the conversation can involve a greater level of vulnerability than a text message or online chat does. That's why most people tend to shy away from them. But again, nerves are normal. You can work through them, and once you do, you can use the power of phone calls to your advantage.

BEING NICE GOES A LONG WAY

Successful negotiations don't have to involve icy stares and pounding on tables. That looks great for the movies, but experts agree that, in most real-world cases, an honest smile and a kind word can take you every bit as far. Want proof? In the interviews for this book, many people said, "You catch more flies with honey than vinegar," an old-fashioned dictum meaning that it's easier to get what you want by being nice.

"Being nice is a big part of it," says shopping expert Trae Bodge.[14] "You're going to go a lot further if you're kind to a person versus rude." That approach works far beyond shopping, too. It holds true when talking with your parents about their finances, a bride about the costs of attending her wedding, a credit card company about a late fee, and countless other examples.

Kara Pérez, who runs financial education website Bravely Go, says, "When it comes to a negotiation specifically, I always start with, 'Thank you so much for thinking of me' or 'Thank you so much for the service you provide,' right? If I'm calling to get a fee knocked off my credit card, I'm always like, 'I love being a Capital One customer. I've been with you for a long time, and I've always had a good experience with the company.' It's about not seeing a negotiation as an antagonistic conversation where you need to be the hero and they need to be the bad guy."[15]

But kindness doesn't mean weakness. It's still important to be firm and not let the other person push you around, but that doesn't mean you have to be a jerk about it. Remember, everyone's fighting a battle that you can't see, so when in doubt, be kind. It's the right thing to do, and it can help you get what you want.

———

Everything that follows depends on the preceding thirteen principles, so take your time with them. For example, think through your story and make a few notes about what details you feel comfortable sharing if necessary. Consider which friends or relatives you might enlist to help with role-playing practice. Determine who should go on your "No Negotiating" list and what you need to do to prepare to take control of your financial life.

Now let's get started.

I. CREDIT AND DEBT

Don't Pay the Bank a Cent More Than Necessary

How to ask for:

A LOWER INTEREST RATE ON A CREDIT CARD

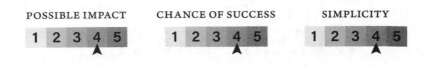

POSSIBLE IMPACT   CHANCE OF SUCCESS   SIMPLICITY

1 2 3 4 5   1 2 3 4 5   1 2 3 4 5
          ▲   ▲   ▲

Q *What are you asking?*
A You're requesting a lower interest rate on your credit card.

Q *How big a deal is it?*
A Potentially huge, depending on how much debt you have. If you owe $5,000 on a credit card with an interest rate of 24 percent and make monthly payments of $200, you'll pay $1,832 in interest, and it will take you 35 months to pay the balance. If you drop the interest rate 5 percentage points to 19 percent and leave everything else the same, you'll pay $1,301 in interest and take 32 months to pay the balance. Saving more than $500 and paying off your debt three months faster just by making one phone call?[16] Yeah, that's a big deal!

In the past year, 76 percent of people who asked for a lower credit card interest rate received one. (LendingTree)

Q *How likely is it that you will succeed?*
A It might surprise you, but very likely. A 2023 LendingTree survey showed that 76 percent of folks who asked in the past year were successful, and the average reduction clocked in at 6 percentage points.[17] That's huge! This isn't just a blue-moon event, either. For years, surveys from other companies have shown high success rates, too. A CreditCards.com survey from

2017 showed a 69 percent success rate. That number means that not just people with long credit histories and perfect scores get what they request.[18] It's great news for cardholders, but it won't always work. The better your credit, the better your chances of success. Plus, if you've asked successfully in the recent past, it's unclear how likely it would be that an issuer would reduce your rate further—though of course it's worth asking.

Q *Does asking pose any risks?*
A Yes, but if you have good credit and have paid your bills on time for a while, the risks are small. When you ask for the lower rate, an issuer could do a hard pull on your credit. That means that they'd request your credit report and review it as if you were applying for a new loan. That hard pull likely will drag your credit score down a little, but the hit typically is small and temporary. The benefit of the lower interest rate should far outweigh the temporary ding to your credit score, so it's generally not a big deal.

But here's the big exception that proves the rule. If you're planning to apply for a vehicle loan or a mortgage, you may want to delay asking for the lower interest rate on your card. Even that small, temporary decrease in your credit score can have a significant impact on the rate you secure for that mortgage or auto loan, and those loans typically are big. Even a slightly higher interest rate can translate to significantly more money out of your pocket.

This situation assumes that your credit looks good. If it doesn't—say, if you've missed a payment or run up balances recently and lowered your score a bit—your lender likely will notice that activity during the hard pull. If your score has fallen enough, it could prompt them to *raise* the interest rate on the card instead. But they'd have to give you 45 days' notice before doing so, and the potential increase could apply only to future purchases.

Q *Does not succeeding pose any risks?*
A If it doesn't work, your credit score will have taken a small hit, and you'll have nothing to show for it; that's about it. The hit to your credit won't last long. Plus, given the high success rates, it's likely worth the risk—

again, unless you're planning to apply for a mortgage or auto loan in the near future. If so, do that first before negotiating your credit card's interest rate.

Q   *How do you do it?*

A   First, make sure that you're current with your payment on the card. If you recently have missed payments, this negotiation is much less likely to work. Also, be patient. It's probably best to wait until you've had the card for at least six months before asking for a lower rate. This negotiation works particularly well if you have offers from other card companies that you can use to frame the conversation. For example, many new credit cards come with a range of possible interest rates for applicants, based on their creditworthiness. Generally speaking, the better your credit score, the better your chance of getting a rate at the lower end of the range. If the issuer's website says your card comes with a range of rates from 15.99 to 24.99 percent and your rate is 24.99 percent, call the customer service number on the back of the card and request the lower rate. Even if they counter with a smaller reduction, you still win.

Alternately, if you've received a card offer in the mail, tell your own card company about it and ask if they can match the terms. Offers on websites—a card issuer, Bankrate, NerdWallet, LendingTree—can work, too. It also never hurts to mention how long you've been a customer, that you use the card regularly, and have paid the bill late never or rarely. Finally, be nice. The person on the other end of the line is just a person doing a job. Being a jerk will make that person less likely to want to help you.

SCRIPTS

"Hello, I'm calling to request a lower interest rate on my credit card. I've had the card for ____ years and have never been late with payment in _____ [time period]. I received an offer for a card from _____ [name of issuer] for ____ percent. Right now, my rate with you is ____ percent. Who can I speak with about getting that lower rate on my card?"

OR

"Hello, I'm calling to request a lower interest rate on my credit card. I've had the card for ____ years and have never been late with a payment in

_____ [time period]. I saw [on your website/online] that you're offering some people a rate as low as ____ percent on the card, while mine is ____. Who can I speak with about getting that lower rate on my card?"

From here, multiple scenarios could play out.

Scenario 1: *They agree to the rate you requested.*

"That's great. I'll take that rate. Thank you for working with me. Please send a confirmation email to me at [your email address]."

OR

"That's great, thank you. Would it be possible to go a point or two lower?"

If they refuse to lower the rate another point or two, which is the most likely response . . .

"I understand, and I appreciate you working with me. I'll take the new rate that you quoted me. Please send a confirmation email to me at [your email address]."

If they agree to lower the rate a little more . . .

"That's fantastic. Thank you so much. I'll take that new, lower rate. Please send a confirmation email to me at [your email address]."

Scenario 2: *They offer a lower rate but not as low as you requested.*

"I appreciate you working with me on this, but I think ____ percent is a reasonable rate, based on [my research/offers from other issuers]."

If they still won't budge after the second request . . .

Graciously accept.

"OK, thank you. I would've liked a lower rate, but I'll accept this one. Please send a confirmation email to me at [your email address]."

OR

Escalate the issue.

| "Who else on your team can I speak with about a lower rate?"

When they connect you with another representative, return to the start of the script to begin the new conversation.

Scenario 3: They refuse to change your rate at all.

| "That's disappointing. I think the rate I'm requesting is reasonable, based on [my research/offers from other issuers]. Who else on your team can I speak with about this?"

If they continue to refuse to negotiate . . .

| "I hear you, but, again, the rate I'm requesting is reasonable based on [my research/offers from other issuers]. Who else on your team can I speak with about this decision?"

At this point, consider asking them to lower your rate temporarily rather than permanently.

If they refuse to connect you . . .
    Politely end the call.

| "Thank you for your time." [Hang up.]

Then call back in a few days and repeat the process.

OR

Ask about closing the card.

| "I hear you. In that case, who on your team can I speak with about closing my credit card?"

If they still won't budge and you're comfortable with closing the card, start the process. If you don't want to close it yet, thank them for their time, hang up, and call back in a few days.

Scenario 4: They refuse to lower your rate, instead offering other perks, such as a waived annual fee, extra rewards points, or a higher credit limit.

> "Thank you for that offer, but what I want is a lower interest rate. Based on my research, I've requested a reasonable rate. Who on your team can I speak with about lowering my rate?"

If they continue to refuse to lower your rate . . .
Accept the counteroffer.

> "I would have preferred a lower rate, but I appreciate your flexibility. I accept. Please send a confirmation email to me at [your email address]."
> > **OR**

Counter their counteroffer.

> "I hear you. You offered me ____ percent. If you can offer me ____ percent, I would accept that rate. Can you do that?"
> > **OR**
>
> Escalate the issue. "I hear you. Who else on your team can I speak with about getting a lower rate?"

When they connect you with another representative, return to the start of the script to begin the new conversation.

Q *What if they deny your request?*
A Don't take no for an answer. It's OK to ask to speak to the manager of a customer service representative. If that fails, wait a day or two, call back, and ask again. Phone reps are human, too, and sometimes you can catch one on a bad day. On that second or third call, the voice on the other end of the line might be willing to give you a break that others wouldn't. You also can ask what else the issuer can do for you beyond just lowering rate.

"It's really important to call your credit card companies and say, 'Hey, what other programs are available? If you can't lower my interest rate, what can you do for me?'" says Tiffiny Williams, an entrepreneur in San Antonio, Texas, who successfully has requested breaks from banks several times. They could lower your interest rate temporarily rather than permanently, increase your credit limit, or perhaps allow you to skip a payment during a difficult time. If you haven't already, you can offer to sign up for automatic payments. Sarah Potter, who runs *Dopamine Deficient*, a mental health podcast, says that, when she called to ask for a lower interest rate, her issuer said they would if she signed up for automatic payments.[19] It's a relatively easy step to take, and it shows commitment on your part to paying the bill on time.

If all else fails, consider threatening to close the card. If you've been a good customer, a bank probably won't want to lose you over a few percentage points on an interest rate—though it does happen. Make sure that you understand what it would mean to follow through on that action, including the impact on your credit. You don't want to damage your credit in a fit of frustration over 2 percentage points. But if you think that the bank has treated you unfairly and you no longer want to do business with them, closing your credit card can send a powerful message. It doesn't have to be your only move, however. Consider complaining formally to the Consumer Financial Protection Bureau, a federal agency that serves as a watchdog over the financial services industry. It also may be worth contacting a not-for-profit consumer protection group such as Consumer Action. In extreme cases, you might need to hire a lawyer.

REMOVING A FRAUDULENT CHARGE
FROM A CREDIT OR DEBIT CARD

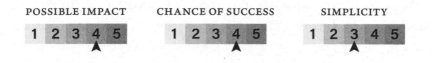

POSSIBLE IMPACT	CHANCE OF SUCCESS	SIMPLICITY
1 2 3 **4** 5	1 2 3 **4** 5	1 2 **3** 4 5

Q *What are you asking?*
A You want to eliminate an illegally purchased item from your debit or credit card.

Q *How big a deal is it?*
A Potentially quite big, depending on the amount and the number of transactions. Security.org estimates that more than 151 million American adults have experienced a fraudulent charge on a credit or debit card.[20] Some cases can run as small as a dollar or two, but in others, fraudsters can go on spending sprees to the tune of hundreds or even thousands. It's a big problem if someone does it with your credit card, but it's even worse with your debit card because those charges take real money from a real account, which can cause real headaches when bills come due.

151 million
Americans have experienced credit card fraud. (Security.org)

Q *How likely is it that you will succeed?*
A Highly. Banks often waive fraudulent charges without too much questioning. That can change for a large amount, a transaction from a long time ago, or a large number of recently reported cases of fraud. (Don't cry wolf about card fraud. Banks are pretty good at sniffing out when people are trying to pull one over on them.)

Q *Does asking pose any risks?*

A In most cases, no, but there's always the possibility that, in looking into the supposed fraudulent activity, you could uncover something you didn't want to know about a friend or loved one. For example, your child, who might've had easy access to your account, could've made that charge without your knowledge. That could lead not only to not getting the charge waived but also to some intensely uncomfortable conversations. It may be worth asking those closest to you, "Hey, you didn't buy anything from Retailer X with my credit card, did you? I'm trying to figure out this strange charge and covering all my bases," before you report the fraud.

Q *Does not succeeding pose any risks?*

A The biggest risk is getting stuck paying for a purchase that you didn't make. For folks on a budget, living paycheck to paycheck, every cent counts. Paying hundreds or thousands for something that you didn't buy can prove absolutely devastating.

Q *How do you do it?*

A It all starts with discovering the fraudulent charge. Receiving text alerts from your card issuer every time your card is used can help you quickly know when someone has used your card without your permission. You also should check your statements on a regular basis to see whether anything looks unusual—at least once a week. The more often you do it, the easier it becomes, because you have fewer transactions to review.

Once you've discovered the problem, report it immediately. If the questionable charge is just a billing error, such as being overcharged or perhaps double-billed, first call the merchant. If the charge is legitimately fraudulent, contact your credit card issuer first. Tell them about the specific charge(s) in question, adding any relevant details to make your case. (For example, "The charge was at a gas station in Oklahoma City, but I've never been to Oklahoma City.") Experts also recommend that you consider filling out a police report detailing the incident.

Many banks and credit unions allow you to report a charge as fraudulent online or through an app. You also can call your bank or card issuer to report

Event	Credit Card	ATM or Debit Card[21]
If you report your card as lost **before** someone uses it . . .	you aren't responsible for any charges that you didn't authorize.	you aren't responsible for any charges that you didn't authorize.
If you report your card as lost **after** someone uses it . . .	you could be responsible for a maximum of $50.	your responsibility level depends on how quickly you reported it.
If your card isn't lost or stolen but someone uses the account number . . .	you aren't responsible for any charges that you didn't authorize.	if you report the loss within 60 calendar days from the date of your statement, you aren't responsible for any transactions that you didn't authorize.

If you report your ATM or debit card as lost or stolen . . .	your maximum loss will be
before any unauthorized transactions	$0
within 2 business days of discovering the loss or theft	$50
more than 2 business days after discovering the loss or theft but within 60 calendar days from the date of your statement	$500
more than 60 calendar days from the date of your statement	all the money taken from your account and any accounts linked to that account

it. Tell them that the purchase was fraudulent and that you don't want to pay it. Federal law says that credit cardholders can't be liable for more than $50 in fraudulent charges, whereas debit card laws allow for more cardholder liability, depending on how long it takes to report the fraud.[22] (If you wait 60 days or more after the charge, you could be stuck paying all of it.) But most card issuers have so-called zero liability policies that go beyond what the law requires. These policies mean that the bank won't require you to pay a penny of a charge that it deems fraudulent. But experts suggest following up on your report with a written letter, detailing any relevant information about the disputed charge.

With credit card fraud, the issuer, in most cases, simply will waive the charge, wiping it from the bill so the cardholder never has to worry about it again, usually issuing a new card with a new number, for safety's sake. Debit-card fraud isn't as simple because, after the charge is wiped, the money needs to be replaced. The bank generally has 10 business days to investigate your claim, though that number rises to 20 for a new account. If the investigation goes longer than that, the bank generally must provide a temporary credit for the amount in question. Some banks may provide that temporary credit at the time of initial reporting, but a short period of time may pass before that money goes back where it belongs.

SCRIPTS

> "Hello, I just noticed a fraudulent charge on my account that I'd like to have removed."

Then provide the specific details of the transaction and any other information to support your case. For example:

> "The charge was for _____ [amount] at _____ [name of business] in _____ [location] on _____ [full date, including year]. I have never set foot in _____ [name of retailer or location]."
>
> OR
>
> "I shop frequently at _____ [name of website], but I didn't buy _____ [item or items] on _____ [full date], and I'd be happy to provide documentation from my account showing that the purchase didn't come from my account."

In most cases, that's all you'll need to do. The bank usually will waive the charge. If the transaction took place with a credit card, check online in a few days to make sure the company removed the transaction from your account. If the charge took place on a debit card, you should have a few more questions.

> "Thank you for handling this. How quickly can I expect to see the money returned to my account?"

It's often a matter of hours. If there's going to be a significant delay, consider asking the bank for written confirmation of the fraudulent transaction. That way, if the missing money causes you to pay a bill late, you can provide that confirmation to the creditor when you ask for leniency.

Q *What if they deny your request?*

A They won't reject your ask immediately, but sometimes an issuer will push back, refusing to waive the charge right away. This can happen for lots of reasons: a large disputed charge, a charge from a long time ago, or a large number of recent reports of fraud. But the law requires the bank to investigate a report of fraudulent charges before they can reject it altogether. For a credit card transaction, the issuer must either acknowledge your report within 30 days and wrap up the investigation in two billing cycles or no more than 90 days.[23] For a debit card transaction, the law says that the bank typically has 10 days (or 20 for newer accounts) to investigate and report back to you.[24] In either case, they typically will contact the merchant in question and go from there. If, after the investigation, they still refuse to acknowledge the charge as fraudulent, you can escalate the issue with calls to the card issuer and the merchant, complain to the Consumer Financial Protection Bureau, or even retain a lawyer. But never give up if you're told "no" the first time, especially for a large amount of money. You have too much to lose.

SUCCESS STORY

After a long day of work, on a crowded subway car in New York City, Divya Sangameshwar felt "someone sort of moving around my bag," but she didn't think much of it. *These things happen,* she thought. *It was probably nothing.* After she boarded a commuter train home to New Jersey, her perspective changed. Bank of America sent her several text messages about just-made charges on her debit card and credit card, including $500 on subway cards, $200 for New Jersey commuter train tickets, and even $150 at a McDonald's. Her wallet had been stolen.

Sangameshwar immediately called the bank, terrified and unsure what to do because it was her first card fraud experience. A 10-day investigation followed, and the bank replaced her money and removed all the fraudulent charges. It wasn't easy—especially while she waited for them to replenish the $400 stolen from her debit card—but it worked out, thanks in no small part to her own diligence.

"What I found through the whole process is how important it is to overcommunicate," she says. "Don't assume that they're going to take care of it for you." In that 10-day period, she estimates that she called the bank 15 times. "I was very polite. You don't yell at people who are trying to help you. I was like, 'I'm sorry if I come across as anxious. I'm not angry at you. I'm just upset about my money, and I really hope you can help.'" Bank of America did just that, in the process making Sangameshwar and her husband loyal customers to this day.

SKIPPING A PAYMENT DURING A DIFFICULT TIME

POSSIBLE IMPACT   **CHANCE OF SUCCESS**   **SIMPLICITY**

1 2 3 **4** 5   1 2 **3** 4 5   1 2 3 **4** 5

Q *What are you asking?*
A You're requesting to miss a payment or two during a difficult financial period.

Q *How big a deal is it?*
A Big. It will allow you to pause payment on that bill for the agreed period. It doesn't mean that you won't ever have to pay, though, and interest could continue to accrue. But if you succeed, you can skip those payments without worrying about wrecking your credit, getting hit with late fees, or dealing with angry demands for past-due payments.

Going through a difficult time consumes your whole life. Something as simple as being able to skip a payment can help on so many levels. It can give you breathing room financially, potentially allowing you to make other payments that you wouldn't have been able to make otherwise. It also can

Starting credit score	600	800
Possible decrease after one payment more than 30 days late	-30 points	-80 points
Possible resulting credit score	570	720

Numerous variables determine how much a late payment can harm your credit score, but according to FICO, the better your score, the more delinquency can damage it. (MyFICO.com)

protect your credit, which is huge because just one payment that's 30 days late or more can knock 50 points or more off your credit score. Breathing room can boost your mental health, giving you one fewer thing to worry about for a while, which is a big deal when feeling overwhelmed by life's challenges, financial or otherwise.

Q *How likely is it that you will succeed?*

A If you're legitimately in need, very likely. In April 2020, as the COVID-19 pandemic spread across America, *The Wall Street Journal* reported that nearly 15 million credit card accounts were in so-called hardship programs.[25] These programs, which most lenders have, help customers through short-term financial difficulty by allowing them to skip a payment, temporarily reducing their interest rate, waiving various fees, and providing other breaks. It wasn't just a pandemic phenomenon, either. These programs can help in cases of natural disaster, medical emergency, job loss, and other scenarios. Mileage will vary based on the lender and your specific situation, but you can't get a break unless you ask for it.

"It's not a very big ask at all if it's your first time asking for some of these protections, like the opportunity to skip a payment without penalty," says Bruce McClary, spokesperson for the National Foundation for Credit Counseling.[26] If you ask for help repeatedly over a relatively short period, your chances may shrink, but if you do it rarely and, again, have legitimate need, your chances of success look relatively high. On the other hand, if you're asking to skip a payment just because you don't want to pay it, don't expect to get your way.

Q *Does asking pose any risks?*

A The bigger risk lies in not asking. But if the changes are permanent, the lender may do a hard credit check, which may ding your credit. A lender also could note on your credit report that your account is in a hardship program. "It's not a requirement and isn't common," McClary says. "It would be up to each creditor to monitor and remove the flag when the temporary hardship expires, which is probably why most creditors don't make the notation."

Q   *Does not succeeding pose any risks?*

A   Not getting what you ask probably for won't make matters worse financially, but it could take a toll emotionally. When times are tough, it can be easy to put a lot of hope into that phone call or email, which could feel like a lifeline. Asking also can make you feel vulnerable, perhaps uncomfortably so. With emotions on edge, a "no" might hit harder than you'd expect. So it's a good idea to have your support system on standby.

Q   *How do you do it?*

A   Tell your story. Perhaps you've lost your job, experienced a medical emergency, or lost a close family member. Every person's struggle looks different, but don't be afraid to share yours. Thinking through exactly what you want to say and practicing with a friend or family member before you call can help.

The easiest way to tell your story is to pick up the phone and call the lender. They aren't going to judge you. More likely, they'll sympathize and try to find a way to help. As part of that process, they may ask for proof of your struggles, including paperwork regarding your job loss, copies of medical bills, or other documentation. They also may require you to take other steps, such as speaking with a credit counselor to create a budget or detailing your situation in writing. They could offer alternative solutions, such as temporarily reduced interest rates or waived fees. You may need to do some significant preparation before you pick up the phone, but in the long run that effort will be worth it.

Lastly, remember that you don't always have to say yes or no right away. If they give you a counteroffer but you're not sure what to do, thank them politely for their flexibility, explain that you need a little time to think about it, and ask if you can reply tomorrow. Chances are they'll say yes.

SCRIPTS

"Hello, I'd like to request to defer payment on my bill. [Explain the situation:

_____

_____]

> I'm happy to provide whatever documentation you need. Given all that, who can I speak with about arranging to defer my next payment?"

Though it isn't necessary, you can add the following . . .

> "I understand that interest will continue to accrue, and I understand that I have to pay the full amount I owe. But I'm asking to skip my next payment without being hit with any late fees or being reported late to the credit bureaus."

If they agree . . .

> "Thank you very much. Please send a confirmation email to me at [your email address]."

If they refuse the first request . . .

> "That's disappointing. I know that banks offer hardship programs for people in situations like mine, so I believe my request is reasonable. Who else can I speak with for help with this?"

If they make a counteroffer . . .

> "Thank you. That's helpful, and I accept that offer. Please send a confirmation email to me at [your email address]."
>
> OR
>
> "Thank you for the offer. I appreciate your flexibility, but what I really need is being able to defer payment for a short time. What do you need from me to make that happen?"
>
> OR
>
> "Thank you. That offer is an interesting option. But it's different from what I requested, so I'd like some time to consider it. How long will this offer be valid?"

If you escalate the situation to a manager, repeat the initial script, including the story of your situation. It may feel frustrating to repeat yourself, but the person on the other end of the line needs to understand your circumstances fully. If you succeed, it will have been worth your time to repeat yourself.

Q *What if they deny your request?*

A Ask again in a couple of days. If multiple requests fail, consider contacting an accredited not-for-profit credit counselor. The National Foundation for Credit Counseling (NFCC.org) is a good place to start. Credit counselors can help you negotiate with lenders and may be able to make arrangements that you wouldn't be able to make for yourself. In the meantime, if that bill comes due, try to make the minimum payment on it. It may mean paying less on other bills, but covering the minimum payment will protect your credit as you continue to negotiate your situation with the lender.

SUCCESS STORY

Moriah Chace didn't want to do it, but she knew she had to. "I made a really uncomfortable phone call," she said. In 2021, she told her credit card issuer about why she couldn't make the minimum payment on her bill. "I was like, 'I'm so sorry. I got a divorce. I'm having trouble paying this because I don't have two incomes anymore. What can we do so that you get your money?'"

That last sentence made a real difference. It shifted focus from the issuer giving her a break to helping the bank get what ultimately it wanted: her money. "It seems like I'm doing them a favor," she says, and it worked. With no pushback, the card issuer lowered the minimum payment from about $200 to about $160 and kept it there for the remainder of the payoff period, giving Chace a little wiggle room in her budget and a much-needed win during a chaotic time in her life.

REMOVING AN INACCURATE ITEM FROM YOUR CREDIT REPORT

POSSIBLE IMPACT	CHANCE OF SUCCESS	SIMPLICITY
1 2 3 **4** 5	1 2 **3** 4 5	1 **2** 3 4 5

Q *What are you asking?*
A You want one of the big three credit bureaus—Equifax, Experian, TransUnion—to remove incorrect information from your credit report, which could include misspelling your name, a late payment when you paid on time, or worse.

Q *How big a deal is it?*
A A 2021 Consumer Reports investigation showed that more than 1 in 3 people who reviewed their credit reports found at least one error in them.[27] Millions of people could have lower credit scores than they should because of other people's mistakes, sometimes even 100 points or more.[28] That sort of damage can cost you major money because a lower credit score means paying more fees and interest on mortgages, credit cards, auto loans, and so on. It can lead to higher insurance premiums and even keep you from landing that apartment you applied to rent or buy. But many people never know their report contains inaccurate info because they don't pay (close enough) attention to their reports. Others may discover inaccuracies but never report them because they don't know how important it is, don't know how to report the error, don't want the hassle, or don't think it will make a difference.

34 percent

of adults who reviewed their credit report found at least one error. (Consumer Reports)

Q   *How likely is it that you will succeed?*

A   Credit bureaus aren't always super-forthcoming about this type of information, but they have a vested interest in the accuracy of their reports. Remember: Lenders, not consumers, are the credit bureaus' primary customers. Credit reports help lenders understand which borrowers are most likely to pay them back. If too many reports have mistakes, banks won't have a true picture of borrowers' creditworthiness. In other words: garbage in, garbage out, which doesn't sit well with the big banks. That doesn't mean you can fix every inaccuracy easily, but you shouldn't think the deck is stacked against you when you ask.

Q   *Does asking pose any risks?*

A   Aside from the possible frustration and time on the phone or online fixing a mess that you didn't make, there's really no risk.

Q   *Does not succeeding pose any risks?*

A   If your efforts don't succeed—which happens sometimes, even when the information is inaccurate—the bad information stays on your report. You won't face penalization for making an unsuccessful dispute, but you'll be stuck with the consequences of someone else's mistake, which no one wants to face.

Q   *How do you do it?*

A   First, go to AnnualCreditReport.com, the federal government's no-strings website for free credit reports, and get your free credit report from the three major credit bureaus: Equifax, Experian, and TransUnion. You need all three because their content can differ quite a bit, and that's because each of them collects, maintains, and reports your data in different ways. A mistake on an Equifax report, for example, may not appear on those from TransUnion or Experian.

Review them carefully to see whether anything looks amiss. Some errors may be no big deal—a misspelled middle name or address—while others can prove significant. For example:

- an account in your name that you don't recognize
- a record of a late payment that you made on time
- the same debt appearing twice on the report

Any mistake is worth reporting and correcting, but the three above and some others are serious issues that you need to resolve immediately because their presence can do real damage to your credit score. Earning a good credit score is hard enough. The last thing you need is demerits that you didn't cause. An account in your name that you didn't open could indicate identity theft, also something you need to report immediately.

Once you've identified the errors, gather the documentation necessary to prove the inaccuracies. For example, if the report includes a record of a late payment on a loan that you paid on time, dig through your payment records or contact your bank for proof of payment. That process could be as simple as logging into your bank's website or app. If the transaction is older, you may need to call the customer service line or visit your branch to acquire the right paperwork.

With the documentation in hand, go to the website of the credit bureau responsible for the report with the error to begin your dispute.[29] If the mistake appears on all three reports, you have to dispute it with all three bureaus. The fastest option is to dispute the claim online, but the bureaus also offer options to dispute over the phone and by mail.

You can dispute the error(s) with the lender, but the most efficient and effective way is to go through the bureau. Let them deal with the lender instead of doing it yourself. By law, the bureau generally has 30 days to review the mistake and make a judgment.[30]

SCRIPTS

This is one of the few instances in this book in which calling *isn't* the best way to get the job done. The credit bureaus' online tools aren't perfect, but they are more efficient than doing it over the phone. If you still want to handle the matter over the phone, the following script will get you started.

> "Hello, I recently reviewed my _____ [credit bureau name] credit report at AnnualCreditReport.com, and some info on my report is [inaccurate/possibly fraudulent]. I [have gathered/am gathering] documentation to prove it, but I want to start the process of having it [corrected/removed]. Who can I speak with about doing that?"

The representative may suggest filing the dispute online. If you still prefer to handle it over the phone, politely say so, and the person will continue the process with you. Even if you make the report on the phone, you likely will have to provide the supporting documentation online, so it really may make more sense to report the dispute online.

Q *What if they deny your request?*

A It happens. Not all disputes succeed, and sometimes an error is just a misunderstanding. For example, the report might list a store credit card as coming from a bank that you've never heard of, which can look like a fraudulent account but really isn't. Other situations aren't as clear-cut, and the bureau and lender remain at odds. If you find yourself in that situation, Rod Griffin, senior director of public education and advocacy with Experian,

---

DISPUTE CONTACT INFORMATION FOR THE BUREAUS

Equifax
(866) 349-5191
Equifax.com/personal/credit-report-services/credit-dispute/
P.O. Box 740256
Atlanta, GA 30348

Experian
(888) 397-3742
Experian.com/disputes/main.html
P.O. Box 4500
Allen, TX 75013

TransUnion
(800) 916-8800
Transunion.com/credit-disputes/dispute-your-credit
P.O. Box 2000
Chester, PA 19016

recommends filing a statement of dispute with the bureau.[31] That statement, which goes into your credit report, allows you to state publicly that you disagree with the results of the dispute and why. You even can provide documentation of your reason for disagreeing. Every time a lender requests that report, the lender will see that statement of dispute.

You have other options as well, including calling the bureaus individually and asking to speak with someone about your case, filing a complaint with the Consumer Financial Protection Bureau, or even retaining a lawyer. In the case of a denied request, your best move may be to pick up the phone and speak to a person rather than following an online process. The customer service representative may offer more help than a nameless, faceless website ever could.

REMOVING AN ACCURATE BUT NEGATIVE ITEM FROM YOUR CREDIT REPORT

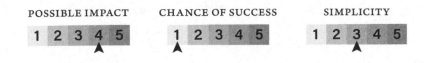

POSSIBLE IMPACT   CHANCE OF SUCCESS   SIMPLICITY

1 2 3 **4** 5   **1** 2 3 4 5   1 2 **3** 4 5

Q   *What are you asking?*
A   You're requesting that one of the credit bureaus scrub from your credit history a legitimate mistake that *you* made, such as a late payment. The item doesn't appear on your report by mistake or as a result of fraud.

Q   *How big a deal is it?*
A   A single late payment can knock 50 points or more off your credit score and stay on your credit report for seven years. Those points can make all the difference between a rejected application and an approved one. They also can impact an interest rate significantly. Eliminating that negative item and restoring those points to your score can save you thousands in the long run.

Q   *How likely is it that you will succeed?*
A   Lenders and credit bureaus don't want you to ask for this because lenders pay the bureaus to provide accurate information, warts and all. Lenders use those details to determine whether it's safe or risky to lend to you. If accurate-but-negative items disappear, those reports no longer present the most accurate picture of borrowers' creditworthiness. If lenders can't trust credit bureau data, banks can't make good lending decisions. Then fewer people receive loans, which no one wants.

Rod Griffin, senior director of public education and advocacy with Experian says, "When I've seen it [asking successfully] is if you have an otherwise pristine credit history and life happens and you miss a payment with a lender. You've never missed a payment before. Call them because they understand that, and, if you catch up on that payment and bring your account current, they'll often say, 'That's fine. We'll take it off.' " That result absolutely makes the call worth it, but even in that situation, success is far from guaranteed. Even with decades of spotless history and a tearjerker story, you still may not succeed. Also, if it sounds too good to be true, it probably is. "Generally, if they say, 'We'll fix your credit tomorrow,' you probably need to look somewhere else," Griffin says.

Q *Does asking pose any risks?*
A No, aside from the time spent making the call, there's really no risk. No lender will hold asking against you or seek retribution because you asked.

Q *Does not succeeding pose any risks?*
A Only that you'll have to continue living with the mistake that you made. No part of asking will make that worse.

Q *How do you do it?*
A Call the lender, tell them your story, and ask for a break. If you have a compelling reason— medical emergency, natural disaster, major family issue—share it. That information humanizes you to the person on the line. But as Griffin says, you don't necessarily need to say anything more than: "My credit history is perfect except for this one mistake I made. I take full responsibility for it, have paid off the debt, and haven't been late with a payment before or since." Whatever the details of your story, practicing telling it before you call, including role-playing with a trusted friend or relative, will help you share it more effectively when the time comes.

This is one of the rare requests in this book that may be accomplished better in writing. In that case, share your story in a "goodwill deletion" letter to the lender. Again, acknowledge responsibility for the item, *then* make your case for removing it from your report. There's no guarantee you'll succeed, but it's certainly worth asking.

SCRIPTS

"Hello, I'd like to request removing the record of _____ [my late payment/other item] from my credit report. The record is accurate, and

> I understand that you have no obligation to remove it. But I paid the debt in full and have made no other credit mistakes in _____ [number] years before this one and none since. Given that history, I think it's fair to have it removed."

At this point, consider providing more details about your circumstances . . .

> "The circumstances around this late payment were very unusual." [Provide rehearsed details.]

If they refuse your request . . .

> "That's disappointing. Who else on your team can I speak with about getting this removed?"

If they agree to your request . . .

> "Thank you so much for your flexibility. Please send a confirmation email to me at [your email address]."

Ask them to confirm that the change will register with all three bureaus and ask how long the change will take to appear on the reports.

Q *What if they deny your request?*

A If they deny your request over the phone, try sending a goodwill deletion letter. You can find a good template here: www.lendingtree.com /content/uploads/2019/10/Goodwill-Letter-Template.pdf. If you made the request in writing, consider picking up the phone. It can't hurt to ask a second time, but your chances probably don't look great. As a last resort, you could consider contacting a credit repair firm, but, again, you typically shouldn't trust any company that makes big promises to quickly remove accurate items from your credit history.

WAIVING OR LOWERING THE ANNUAL FEE ON A CREDIT CARD

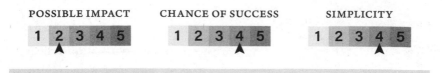

POSSIBLE IMPACT   CHANCE OF SUCCESS   SIMPLICITY

1 2 3 4 5   1 2 3 4 5   1 2 3 4 5
   ▲   ▲   ▲

Q *What are you asking?*
A You're requesting that your credit card company cancel or reduce your card's annual fee.

Q *How big a deal is it?*
A Moderate, depending on the fee. Even if it's just $50, you can put it to better use elsewhere.

Q *How likely is it that you will succeed?*
A Shockingly likely. A 2023 LendingTree survey showed that 93 percent of people who asked to have their annual fee waived saw a positive result: 61 percent had it waived in full, and another 32 percent had it reduced. With success rates that high, it likely isn't just folks with low-fee cards, long track records, and near-perfect credit scores who are winning at this request. Those three points definitely will help your chances, but lacking them doesn't seem to be a dealbreaker.

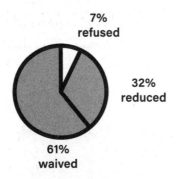

7%
refused

32%
reduced

61%
waived

93%
success rate

Proportion of people whose credit card issuers waived or reduced the annual fee when, in the past year, they asked. (LendingTree)

Q *Does asking pose any risks?*

A Not really. The card issuer isn't likely to do a hard pull on your credit to decide whether to waive the fee.

Q *Does not succeeding pose any risks?*

A Also not really. Worst-case scenario: You waste a few minutes on the phone and pay the fee as before.

Q *How do you do it?*

A Call the customer service number on the back of your card and ask nicely. If you have compelling or meaningful context—"I've been a customer for many years," "I've never missed a payment," "I have a 750 credit score"—give it. It may not be necessary, but it can't hurt. Anything that helps establish a positive connection with the person on the other end of the phone is worth trying. Also consider whether you'd accept a counteroffer. Card issuers sometimes reduce the fee rather than waive it altogether. They might offer bonus reward points or miles, a temporarily reduced interest rate, or other alternatives. Keep that possibility in mind before calling to help you make a more informed decision if the situation arises.

SCRIPTS

> "Hello, I'd like to have the annual fee on my card waived. [Provide positive context.] Given that, I think this is a reasonable request. Who on your team can I speak with about this?"

If they reject your initial request . . .

> "That's disappointing. As I said, given my track record, I think it's a reasonable request. Who else on your team can I speak with about this?"

If they make a counteroffer . . .

> "Thank you for that. I wanted the fee waived entirely, but this offer is appealing, too. I'll take it. Please send a confirmation email to me at [your email address]."
>
> **OR**
>
> "Thank you for that. I appreciate the counteroffer, but I'm interested only in having the fee waived, which I think is a reasonable request, given my track record. Who else on your team can I speak with about this request?"
>
> **OR**
>
> "Thank you. I'd like to take some time to consider that counteroffer. How long will it be valid?"

If you eventually agree on a waived fee, a reduction, or some other concession . . .

> "Thank you for working with me. I appreciate it. Please send a confirmation email to me at [your email address]."

Q   *What if they deny your request?*
A   Call back in a day or two. The next person could be more sympathetic to your story. If all else fails, you could threaten to cancel the card. That can be an effective tactic, but make sure that you understand the ramifications of cancelling your card before you decide to do it.

Alternately, you could downgrade your card to a version with no annual fee. That's not always an option, but many card issuers do offer no-annual-fee versions of their most popular annual-fee cards. Don't take this step lightly, though. No-annual-fee cards tend to come with far less lucrative rewards than their annual-fee counterparts. If you're set against paying an annual fee and the issuer won't waive the one on your card, it may be worth considering a downgrade.

Note: Downgrading won't impact your credit the way canceling a card would. Even though you'll get a new physical card and even a new account number, the issuer doesn't see the downgraded card as a new account or application. It's an adjustment to a current account, so it won't ding your credit the way a new account can.

SUCCESS STORY

Twice a year, Shannah Game blocks time to negotiate her cable bill, cell phone bill, and more. Why? Because it works.

"I have a couple credit cards that have annual fees, and I always call to get the annual fee waived," says Game, host of the *Everyone's Talkin' Money* podcast (formerly *Millennial Money*). "Probably seven of ten times, I've gotten that annual fee waived." When the issuer doesn't waive the fee, that doesn't mean that she's been unsuccessful. "A couple of times, there's been a flat-out no, but that's been rare." Issuers who pushed back offered her bonus miles and points instead, and she accepted those offers.

How does she approach the calls? "It's the simple question of 'I've been a loyal customer for X years. I would love to keep this card, but I don't enjoy the annual fee. It's making me contemplate whether I want to keep this card. Is there a possibility of getting the fee waived?' Most of the time, they say, 'We want to keep you as a customer.'"

A HIGHER CREDIT LIMIT

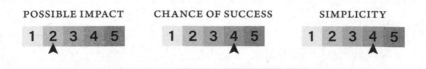

POSSIBLE IMPACT   CHANCE OF SUCCESS   SIMPLICITY

1 2 3 4 5   1 2 3 4 5   1 2 3 4 5

Q *What are you asking?*

A You want a higher debt ceiling on your card.

Q *How big a deal is it?*

A It's not a huge deal, but it can have a meaningful impact. A higher credit limit can give you more financial wiggle room during difficult times, and it can allow you to finance bigger projects, such as remodeling your home or starting a small business. It also can improve your credit score by lowering your credit utilization rate, or your ratio of debt to available credit, which is the second most important factor in FICO credit scoring formulas (after payment history). If you have a balance of $2,000 against $5,000 in available credit, your utilization rate is 40 percent, which could be a drag on your score. Increase the limit to $8,000, and your utilization rate falls to just 25 percent—still not ideal but better for your credit score. However, this strategy works only if you leave all that newly available credit unused. If you take it as an invitation to spend more, you've defeated the purpose of achieving the new limit to help your credit score. A higher credit limit also means more opportunity to overspend, so proceed with caution.

Q *How likely is it that you will succeed?*

A A 2023 LendingTree survey found that 86 percent of people who asked for a higher limit in the past year received one. The increase averaged to about $950. That success rate means that not just folks with six-figure incomes and perfect credit scores are succeeding at this request. If you ask for too many increases in a small window of time, your chances of success likely will dip.

Q *Does asking pose any risks?*

A Yes, the credit card issuer could do a hard pull on your credit when deciding whether to increase your credit limit. Hard pulls typically lead to a small, temporary decrease in your credit score, which no one ever wants. But the positive impact of the new limit often can outweigh any temporary dip in your score. For that to happen, though, you need to leave that newly available credit unused. If you increase your balance, your utilization rate will grow too high.

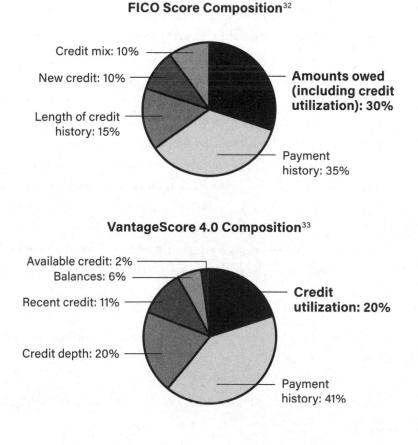

FICO Score Composition[32]

Credit mix: 10%

New credit: 10%

Length of credit history: 15%

Amounts owed (including credit utilization): 30%

Payment history: 35%

VantageScore 4.0 Composition[33]

Available credit: 2%

Balances: 6%

Recent credit: 11%

Credit depth: 20%

Credit utilization: 20%

Payment history: 41%

Q   *Does not succeeding pose any risks?*

A   Just a minor one: If they do a hard pull and don't approve you for a higher limit, you won't benefit from the new ceiling. But don't let that keep you from asking.

Q   *How do you do it?*

A   It's typically not a difficult negotiation, but it can run more smoothly with some self-reflection and homework. For example, has your income changed since you received the card? Your income doesn't impact your credit score directly, but it makes a compelling argument for raising your limit, which matters to credit card issuers. If your income has increased, tell them. Also, if you've paid off a lot of debt, seen a sharp increase in your credit score, or had other significant improvements to your financial status that you haven't shared with the issuer, tell them that, too. Feel free to tell them that you want a limit increase solely to help improve your credit score. The more truthful, accurate details that make your case more compelling, the better.

By the way, you're not limited to just personal income for that income number you share with the issuer. The Credit CARD Act of 2009 says that people age 21 or older can include spouses' or partners' income with their own applications if they have a "reasonable expectation of access" to that money. If your own income hasn't increased in a while but your spouse's has, you still might be able to bump up the number that you share with the issuer.

SCRIPTS

> "Hello, I'd like to increase my credit limit. I've been a good customer for _____ [number] years, and I've had some positive changes to my financial situation that I'm sharing to help you make this decision."

From here, you can elaborate on any relevant reasons or information, including:

> "My credit score has improved since I received this card. According to _____ [source], it's _____ [score]."

"My income has grown because of _____ [reasons]. It's now _____ [amount] per year."

"I'm older than 21, and the Credit CARD Act of 2009 says that I can include my spouse's or partner's income with credit card applications if I have a 'reasonable expectation of access' to that money. With that in mind, I'd like my income noted as _____ [amount]."

"I'm working to improve my credit score by increasing my limit in order to decrease my credit utilization rate, which I know is an important part of credit scoring formulas. I plan on using the new credit rarely, if at all, in order to get the biggest improvement possible for my utilization rate."

The customer service representative likely will ask if you approve of them doing a hard pull on your credit. If you do, let them know. If not, that's probably going to bring your call to an end.

If the first representative says they can't approve your request . . .

"Thank you for letting me know. Who else on your team can I speak with about this request?"

If they come back with a smaller increase than you were expecting . . .

"Thank you for this. I was hoping for a larger increase. How can I go about getting a higher limit than that?"

If, at any point in the process, they offer a limit that meets your satisfaction . . .

"Thank you so much. I'd like to lock in that new limit. Please send a confirmation email to me at [your email address]."

Q *What if they deny your request?*
A If they rejected you either because of your credit score or information

on your credit report, the lender should send you an "adverse action letter" detailing the reasons that they declined your request.[34] When you receive that letter, review it carefully and make sure that you understand what it says. Once you do, get a free copy of your credit report from the three major bureaus at AnnualCreditReport.com (the no-strings website run by the federal government), review it, and make sure that it doesn't contain any erroneous information. If it doesn't, begin taking steps to improve the issues noted in the adverse action letter.

You also could contact the card issuer again to ask them to reconsider. Most major credit card issuers have reconsideration lines specifically intended for these conversations. They typically are for discussing declined applications for new credit cards, but you can use it for a rejected credit limit application, too.

If you have multiple credit cards, you could request a higher limit on a card from a different issuer. That move doesn't guarantee success, but just because one issuer won't give you a higher limit doesn't necessarily mean that another won't. Just remember that any new request for more credit may lead to another hard pull, adding another small, temporary ding to your credit score. Given that result, it's probably not wise to ask a third issuer if the first two reject you.

WAIVING A LATE FEE ON A CREDIT CARD

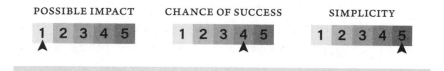

POSSIBLE IMPACT CHANCE OF SUCCESS SIMPLICITY

1 2 3 4 5   1 2 3 4 5   1 2 3 4 5

Q *What are you asking?*
A You're requesting your credit card company not to charge you a fee for paying your bill late. You also can ask them to waive any interest accrued before you made your payment.

Q *How big a deal is it?*
A The first time you miss a payment, the fee can't run more than $30. If it happens again during the next six billing cycles, it can cost you about $40. That's not a huge amount of money, but every little bit matters. When it comes to accrued interest—depending on your balance, your interest rate, and how late you paid—you could be talking about a couple of dollars or significantly more.

Q *How likely is it that you will succeed?*
A A 2023 LendingTree survey found that 81 percent of cardholders who asked to waive a late fee got their way.[35] Some card issuers have policies, written or otherwise, that they'll wipe any cardholder's first late fee but only if it is requested in a timely manner. (If your payment comes 30 days late or more, the issuer might not be so eager.) Granting this request gives

81% of people succeeded the last time that, in the past year, they asked a credit card company to waive a late fee. (LendingTree)

the credit card issuer a quick, relatively inexpensive way to create good-will. "I got hit with a late fee because I forgot to pay, and I called them and said, 'I'm so sorry. I usually pay on time,' and they were like, 'No problem, we'll get rid of the late fee,'" says Lindsay Goldwert, author of *Bow Down: Lessons from Dominatrixes on How to Get Everything You Want.* "I was so grateful that I didn't have to pay this stupid late fee. But that's the other thing, too. You get this sense of gratitude when they aren't screwing you over in some way." Beyond that first instance, your chance of success likely will shrink, though it doesn't disappear. Caitlin Meredith, a mediator and divorce coach, reports having multiple late fees waived, including multiple instances in a year.[36]

LendingTree's survey didn't ask whether folks asked to waive interest accrued after a late payment. Your chances for success there likely will vary, based on how much interest accrued.

Q   *Does asking pose any risks?*
A   Not really. The card issuer likely won't hard-pull your credit for this ask. Often, the issuer won't do more than check your payment history to confirm that you're not a repeat offender.

Q   *Does not succeeding pose any risks?*
A   Worst-case scenario: You pay the late fee and extra interest.

Q   *How do you do it?*
A   Your first time usually requires only a polite phone call. "You win more flies with honey than vinegar," says Kara Pérez of financial education company Bravely Go.[37] Make the payment first, the most important step, then call them to say you've made it and to ask to remove the late fee. If you're not a repeat offender, chances are that they'll say yes. To improve your odds, consider setting up autopay for the card and tell them so, which shows that you're serious about not paying late again. Even if you don't do that, they probably will waive the fee the first time, as long as you ask nicely.

Don't forget to ask to waive the accrued interest, too. You can do that at the same time that you ask to remove the fee. They may not waive it, but there's no reason not to ask.

SCRIPTS

> "Hello, I was a few [days/weeks] late paying my credit card bill and received a late fee. I just paid the bill [today OR date]. Can you waive that late fee and any interest accrued since the due date?"

If applicable, add:

> "It's my first time paying late, and I've set up automatic payments to make sure this doesn't happen again. Would you be able to do that for me?"

If they say no to the fee and the interest . . .

> "That's disappointing. Given my history with this card, I think this is a reasonable request. Who else on your team can I speak with about this?"

If they waive the fee but not the interest . . .

> "Thank you for being flexible with me. I appreciate you waiving the fee, but I'd like to have the interest waived, too. It's not a ton of money for a big bank, but for my tight budget, every dollar counts."

If applicable, add:

> "This is the first time I've paid late, so I think this is a reasonable request. Who else on your team can I speak with about this?"

If they agree to waive either or both . . .

> "Thank you so much. I appreciate this. Please send a confirmation email to me at [your email address]."

Q   *What if they deny your request?*

A   It can't hurt to ask again. It's worth seeing whether the next person will work with you. Depending on how badly you want the fee and interest waived, you could consider threatening to close the card if they don't help you. If you feel that they treated you unfairly, you also can consider filing a complaint with the Consumer Financial Protection Bureau at Consumer Finance.gov/complaint.

———

LATE-FEE CAP?

As this book was going to press, the Consumer Financial Protection Bureau, the federal government's watchdog agency, was considering a cap on credit card late fees of $8, with some exceptions.[38] That drop would mean significant savings for people stuck paying late fees, but it also could lead to fewer late-payers calling to waive that fee. The $8 might not be worth their time. It's also unclear how a fee reduction might impact your chances of getting the fee waived. Banks may prove more likely to waive it, given how small the amount is. But that reduction also means less money in their coffers overall, so they may become more reluctant to waive it. Either way, the scripts in this section can help if you choose to make that call.

SUCCESS STORY

I have more experience asking credit card companies to waive late fees than I'd like to admit, and almost every attempt has succeeded. Here's how it goes.

1. Apply for and receive a brand-new credit card to take advantage of awesome signup bonus.
2. Use the card to hit the minimum-spend threshold needed for the signup bonus.
3. Forget to set up automatic payments.
4. Realize a day or two late that I've missed the payment deadline on the new card.
5. Feel dumb that I allowed this to happen—again.
6. Go online, pay the bill, and set up autopay to avoid a repeat situation in a month.
7. Call the 800-number on the back of the card and apologize for paying late.
8. Tell the customer service rep that I just submitted full payment and set up autopay.
9. Ask them to waive the late fee and any interest accrued.
10. Rep: "Sure, we can waive that for you."
11. Thank the rep profusely, wish them a great day, and hang up, relieved at saving $30.
12. Promise myself that I won't do it again—knowing full well that I will.

I've lost count of how many times the above has happened. I've made that call to most of the biggest card issuers in the country. It always feels embarrassing, but it's important not to let that feeling keep you from making the same call. After all, that $30—or $40 for repeat offenders—isn't life-changing money, but that doesn't mean the bank should get it, either.

WAIVING A MINIMUM-BALANCE FEE ON A BANK ACCOUNT

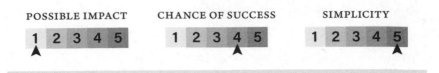

POSSIBLE IMPACT
1 2 3 4 5

CHANCE OF SUCCESS
1 2 3 4 5

SIMPLICITY
1 2 3 4 5

Q *What are you asking?*
A You want your bank to waive a fee levied for your account balance dropping below a set amount.

Q *How big a deal is it?*
A It's not a huge deal. The fee could range from a few dollars to more than $25. Still, if you have a tight budget, every dollar counts, so it's worth your time.

Q *How likely is it that you will succeed?*
A Highly likely. "Once I found out that was a thing you could do, I've done it two or three times," says Maribel Francisco, a financial coach with Our Wealth Matters. The less you do it, though, the more likely you are to succeed.

Q *Does asking pose any risks?*
A Not likely. The bank won't hard-check your credit or slap your wrist for asking.

Q *Does not succeeding pose any risks?*
A Only paying a fee that you don't want to pay. Even if you get stuck paying it, the fee usually isn't big enough to cause major financial issues for most people.

Q *How do you do it?*

A Just call the bank's customer service number and ask. But it's never a bad idea to prepare a little more detail if necessary. Why did it happen? Was it a one-time occurrence, or do you anticipate it happening again in the near future? Are you taking steps to prevent it from happening again? You don't need to tell them your life story, but providing a little meaningful detail can help.

If you anticipate your balance remaining below the required minimum for more than just the current month, tell them. They may be willing to work with you, especially if you have a legitimate reason, such as a big move or a new job, as was the case for Jeff Kreisler, head of behavioral science for JP Morgan Chase and coauthor of *Dollars and Sense: How We Misthink Money and How to Spend Smarter.*[39] "I got moved to a new bank account status, and they had a minimum amount-in-balance or a monthly fee," Kreisler says. "I knew that in about five months I'd be able to meet that balance, but I wouldn't for the next five months. I just asked if we could waive it for six months, and then, if I didn't make it, then they could start charging. They said yes."

SCRIPTS

"Hello, I recently was charged a fee because my account fell below the required minimum balance. I would like to have that fee waived. Who on your team can I speak with about that?"

Consider mentioning the following in the conversation . . .

"This is the first time I've incurred this fee. It happened because _____ [reason]. I don't anticipate it happening again, so I think it's a reasonable request."

OR

"This is the first time that this happened to me, but because of _____ [reason], I expect that it might happen again in the next ____ [number]

> months. I'd appreciate if you could waive the fee for that period. After that, I don't anticipate it being an issue anymore."

If accepted . . .

> "Thank you very much. Please send a confirmation email to me at [your email address]."

Q   *What if they deny your request?*

A   Call and ask again in a few days. Sometimes a rejection simply depends on catching someone on the wrong day, so it's worth trying at least once more. If they still say no, consider asking if there are other ways to avoid the fees, such as setting up a regular direct deposit into the account, which they might bring up as a condition of removing the fee. Finally, you may want to consider whether an account with no minimums to meet might serve you better.

2. HEALTHCARE

Improve Your Financial Fitness

How to ask for:

A REDUCED MEDICAL BILL

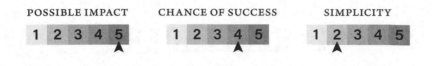

POSSIBLE IMPACT	CHANCE OF SUCCESS	SIMPLICITY
1 2 3 4 **5**	1 2 3 **4** 5	1 **2** 3 4 5

Q *What are you asking?*
A You're requesting that a medical provider reduce a fee.

Q *How big a deal is it?*
A According to Marshall Allen, author of *Never Pay the First Bill*, "you can save hundreds or thousands of dollars per healthcare interaction."[40] Impact will vary based on cost and complexity of the product or service, whether you use insurance or pay cash, and the network status of the vendor or provider. Some people can save a significant amount. In many ways, this is a uniquely American problem, given the infuriating state of healthcare in the USA. However, for those in other countries who have private insurance or use private providers in addition to public options, making sure you're being charged only for services actually rendered and trying to negotiate lower medical costs overall still matters.

Q *How likely is it that you will succeed?*
A People "throw their hands up because they assume there's nothing they can do, and the system seems so complicated. It seems like such a battle between David and Goliath, and they just don't realize that David can win," Allen says. It's not just that you *can* win, though. Your chances of success look far better than you realize. "If the bills are inaccurate or overpriced and people can make an evidence-based argument, they are usually successful in getting it reduced."

Q *Does asking pose any risks?*
A In a small, one-person private practice, you may risk alienating the doctor by pushing against the price. That's unlikely, though, and if a doctor

takes offense, that response may signal that you should look for another doctor. In medium to larger practices, there's really no risk because the business side and the medical side remain separate. That division of labor means you probably don't have to worry about your doctor getting upset because you played hardball over your bill.

Q *Does not succeeding pose any risks?*
A You could end up paying the full bill, which, given the cost of health-care, could mean a lot of money. Not getting your way won't add more to the bill, so why not ask? "Never, ever think that it's not OK to negotiate a medical bill in the United States," says Virgie Bright Ellington, MD, author of *What Your Doctor Wants You to Know to Crush Medical Debt.*

Q *How do you do it?*
A How you pay can play a huge role in how much you pay. Will you use insurance? Does the provider belong to your insurance company's net-work? The answers to those questions can affect the billed amount. When sick or suffering, no one wants to think about insurance. In those situations, people often just assume that insurance offers the best option and use it without examination. But that's likely not the case for a routine service with a high-deductible plan or if using a non-network provider. In those cases, consider asking for the "cash price" of the product or service, meaning how much it will cost without insurance. You have no guarantee that it'll be cheaper, but it doesn't hurt to ask.

Regardless of how you pay, you need an accurate bill. When you receive a bill, make sure it includes current procedural terminology (CPT) codes, which precisely identify medical services and procedures, or look for an explanation-of-benefits document, which should list the codes. "CPT codes are to medical services what bar codes are to products in a store," says Dr. Ellington. They define a procedure or item. Without those standardized codes, you can't know precisely what work took place, so call your provider and ask for an itemized bill that includes them.

If they push back on providing an itemized bill, remind them that fed-eral law—specifically the Health Insurance Portability and Accountability

80% of all medical bills contain errors, according to study estimates. (BeckersHospitalReview.com)

Act, better known as HIPAA—gives you the right to that information. This important law created national standards for protecting consumers' medical records and private health information, but it did more than that. "It also gives patients access to their records," Allen says. "Under HIPAA, we have a right to get an itemized bill from a hospital and an insurance company with every billing code and every charge listed on it. If they give you a hard time, you can cite HIPAA." If they still drag their feet, tell them that you'll file a HIPAA violation complaint with the Office of Civil Rights Complaint Portal at OCRPortal.hhs.gov. That move will get their attention, because no medical provider wants a HIPAA violation, which can lead to civil and even criminal penalties. For more on HIPAA, visit hhs.gov/hipaa.

Once you have the CPT codes, research what each of those codes means to confirm that what took place during your visit matches the codes on your bill. "We assume that whatever bill we get is accurate, and nothing could be further from the truth," Dr. Ellington says. Some 80 to 90 percent of medical bills generated in America have invoicing errors. "They're not going to be in your favor," she adds.

If the CPT codes don't represent your experience accurately, contact the provider and have them fix it. When you're satisfied that the codes on the bill are accurate, the next step is to research the prices of the line items. The most important number to know, Allen and Ellington agree, is what Medicare pays, information that you can find at Medicare.gov and the Centers for Medicare and Medicaid Services.[41] That's the rate that the federal government pays, so experts suggest that as the best place to start your negotiation. If your bill costs $5,000 but you have three codes and Medicare pays a total of $2,500 for those items, start your negotiation at $2,500. For more on the prices that Medicare pays, visit

Medicare.gov/procedure-price-lookup/ and www.CMS.gov/medicare/
physician-fee-schedule. When you've collected all that information, call
your provider, ask for the billing department, and begin the negotiation.

Depending on how you pay, urgency of negotiation and likelihood of
success can vary. If you used Medicare, you're already paying the lowest rate
that you likely will get. If you used a provider in network, haggling probably
isn't worth your time. The insurance company and provider already agreed
on pricing for the service. Why would they accept less from you? The opportunity for negotiation arises when paying out of pocket—because you don't
have insurance or choose not to use it—or using a non-network provider.
In those instances, you're dealing with just the provider's pricing, which is
when negotiating can make a real difference.

SCRIPTS
Scenario 1: Ask for the cash price.

> "Hello, I'm [here for/calling about] my _____ (procedure or service).
> What would the cash price for that be?"

If applicable, consider mentioning that you have insurance but are deciding
whether to use insurance for the payment.

If they push back, saying that you need to use your insurance…

> "I don't have to use insurance just because I have it. Who can I speak with
> about the cash price?"

If you want to negotiate the cash price …

> "Thank you for that. My research has shown that _____ [negotiation amount]
> is a reasonable price. Who can I speak with about reducing the price?"

You may not need to push more at that point. You will have the opportunity to negotiate that rate after the bill comes. (Keep reading for scripts for
that situation.)

Scenario 2: Request an itemized bill with CPT codes.

> "Hello, I recently received a bill from your office for _____ [procedure, service, or treatment]. I'd like an itemized version of the bill that includes CPT codes for each item."

If the person on the phone pushes back on your request . . .

> "HIPAA gives me the right to an itemized bill with CPT codes on it, so, again, I'd like you to send that to me at your earliest convenience."

If the person on the phone continues to push back . . .

> "Who else on your team can I speak with about this?"

If they transfer you, begin the conversation with the next person with the initial script. If they won't transfer you, thank them for their time, hang up, and plan to call back in a day or two.

If, after multiple requests, they continue refusing to send you an itemized list . . .

> "This is disappointing. I have a legal right to this information, and you repeatedly have told me that you won't provide it, so I'll be filing a HIPAA violation complaint with the OCR Complaint Portal."

It's highly unlikely that they'll continue dragging their feet after that. If they do, consider finding a new medical provider.

Scenario 3: Negotiate the charges on your bill.

> "Hello, I recently had _____ [procedure, service, treatment] and [if appropriate] I don't have insurance. The bill was for _____ [billed amount]. Using the CPT codes, I researched what Medicare pays for each of the services that I received. Based on what I found, _____ [negotiation amount] is a more appropriate price, and I'd like to speak with some-

one about creating an interest-free payment plan for that amount that fits my budget."

You likely will get pushback. When that happens . . .

"I hear you, but my research has shown that _____ [negotiation amount] is a reasonable price. Who can I speak with about arranging an interest-free payment plan?"

If you receive further pushback, still likely, say the following . . .

"Again, I hear you, but the number I mentioned is a reasonable price based on the CPT codes. I'm happy to pay that amount with an interest-free payment plan that fits my budget. Who can I speak with about putting that in place?"

If you continue to receive pushback, stand your ground and ask to speak with someone else.

"Who else on your team can I speak with about this?"

When you're connected with another team member, return to the beginning of the script, state your case, and expect to receive more pushback. Give the billing representative more detail about your research, including what Medicare pays for each CPT code.

If negotiations reach an impasse, thank them for their time, hang up, and call back in a few days.

OR

Consider increasing the amount that you're willing to pay. Determine the maximum amount that you can pay *before* you begin the conversation, though. That way, you won't feel pressure to come up with a number on the fly.

"OK, I hear you. _____ [new negotiation amount] is the most I can pay. It will be difficult for my budget, but I can make it work with the right payment plan. Who can I speak with about setting that up?"

If there's still no movement, thank them for their time, hang up, and call back in a few days.

Q   *What if they deny your request?*

A   Ask at least two or three times total. You have too much money to lose to give up after just one unsuccessful round of negotiation. Plus, the person on the phone could be having a bad day. Another polite call a few days later could yield different results.

If multiple calls and negotiations don't work, consider outside help. If you have insurance, you can contact your provider. You also can reach out to a consumer assistance program (www.cms.gov/cciio/resources/consumer -assistance-grants) or use the the Patient Advocate Foundation to contact a patient advocate near you.[42] Those services may be able to help you deal with the billing issues that you're facing. If all else fails, consider contacting a lawyer about the situation. If you can't or don't want to do that, you may have no other choice but to pay the bill. If that's the case, consider whether it makes sense to shop around for another provider who might prove more willing to negotiate.

BALANCE BILLING AND NO SURPRISES

A medical provider belonging to an insurance company network means that the insurer has agreed to pay the provider an arranged amount when patients use that insurer to pay for services or products. Depending on the details of your plan, you may have to meet a deductible, pay a co-pay, or pay a percentage of the overall bill, but at least you won't receive an extra bill from the provider. Using an in-network provider and paying with insurance defeat the point of negotiating an accurate bill. If your provider knows that she'll receive, say, $100 from the your insurance company for performing a test, she has no incentive to accept a lower amount from you.

Going out of network changes the rules, though. Generally speaking, a non-network provider doesn't have to charge only what the insurance company will pay. So if your insurance company says they'll pay $100 for that test, the provider can charge $150, which leaves the difference in your lap. That's called "balance billing," and that's why staying in network matters so much. So why would anyone knowingly go out of network? Not everyone knows that this situation happens. Plus, not every provider hikes rates sky-high. Sometimes insurance changes, and a favorite provider falls outside the network. Some people would rather pay more than switch. In small towns or rural areas, people might not have other options.

Also, sometimes people don't have a choice. A woman who gives birth in a network hospital with the help of a network ob-gyn may receive treatment from a non-network anesthesiologist through no choice of her own, for example. The No Surprises Act, which went into effect in January 2022, means that patients no longer can be charged more than network costs for those types of services, though certain exceptions apply. The act eliminated so-called surprise medical bills that countless people receive when dealing with the American healthcare system. It also gives consumers more power to contest those bills. If you think that you've been balance-billed unfairly, visit https://www.cms.gov/medical-bill-rights for more information on this important law. The act can't help if you visit an non-network provider by choice. But if you do and you receive balance billing, you can negotiate those costs with the provider. Given the high costs of healthcare, that absolutely can be worth your time.

SUCCESS STORIES

When Winnie Sun, a financial adviser in Los Angeles, lost two family members in a short period, a parade of medical bills followed. Her father had decent insurance, so the costs for his end-of-life care weren't too daunting. But for her mother-in-law, the family faced a stack of bills from a variety of places, and, Sun says, "everybody's demanding that you pay them." But Sun remembered that Jack Phan, a friend and CEO of AirDeck, had told her that she could reduce medical bills by calling and explaining the situation. So that's what she did. "I had my husband try. He reached out to the different medical professionals. He explained that she passed and that she didn't have a lot of means," she says. "One by one, the bills started to disappear, and he didn't have to pay most of them."

Often it took only a phone call. "It was, 'Well, we'll get back to you,' and then eventually a new bill would come showing a zero balance," Sun says. Not all the bills were waived entirely, but Sun estimates that her family never had to pay more than $500 for a single medical bill. Her mother-in-law's credit card issuer even wiped out her balance. It wasn't a huge amount, but when you're wrestling with myriad bills, every one matters.

Kathryn Tuggle, an award-winning journalist and cofounder and chief content officer of HerMoney Media, has danced for most of her life, resulting in chronic plantar fasciitis, which can cause excruciating pain. In 2019, she carefully selected a podiatrist in-network with her health insurance, meaning that the visit shouldn't have cost more than a small co-pay. But she received a bill for $1,680. "So of course, I freak out," she says, "thinking that maybe I got it wrong." She reviewed the bill, which indicated an out-of-network visit but no other specifics. She called the doctor's office to request an itemized bill. "Everything the doctor had done was accurate on the itemized bill, so I'm sitting there thinking, *Maybe I am going to have to pay this*."

Then she spotted the problem. The very bottom of the bill listed a different doctor than the one Tuggle had seen. Some podiatrists in that group accepted Tuggle's insurance, but others didn't, making them out-of-network—a common and often costly problem in hospitals and medical practices. She quickly contacted the practice to inform them of the clerical error, and after about two weeks of pushback the practice finally corrected the bill, leaving her owing nothing.

Tuggle understands why people sometimes hesitate to push back when they suspect billing mistakes. Correcting them can take a lot of time and prove frustrating. Ultimately, however, it's well worth your time. "I probably spent four hours dealing with this problem to save close to $1,700. That's a darn good hourly rate."

AN EXPLANATION OF THE COST AND IMPORTANCE OF A PROCEDURE BEFORE YOU AGREE TO IT

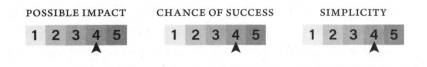

POSSIBLE IMPACT
1 2 3 **4** 5

CHANCE OF SUCCESS
1 2 3 **4** 5

SIMPLICITY
1 2 3 **4** 5

Q *What are you asking?*
A You're seeking details of the significance and price of a procedure, service, or treatment recommended by a doctor or other medical professional.

Q *How big a deal is it?*
A Medical treatment can prove incredibly expensive, regardless of whether you have insurance. Refusing or delaying unnecessary prescriptions, procedures, or services could save you hundreds or even thousands. This request has to do with more than just money, though. Feeling empowered to ask questions of your medical provider fundamentally changes the relationship in a way that can lead to better understanding and treatment for you. But many people don't question their doctors for the same reason that they don't feel comfortable asking detailed questions of mechanics. They feel like they don't know enough to ask.

Q *How likely is it that you will succeed?*
A When it comes to the importance and urgency of the treatment, "any professional doctor would be comfortable having that conversation with you, would be comfortable telling you to get a second opinion, would be happy to talk through the options," says Marshall Allen, author of *Never Pay the First Bill*. "Doctors aren't usually steering the conversation that way, so patients might need to be aware that they need to ask."

When it comes to knowing the cost of a treatment in advance, the law may require a doctor to give you an estimate. Under the No Surprises Act, doctors must provide good-faith estimates of costs for treatment if patients don't have insurance or don't use it. In those cases, you don't even have to ask for an estimate. But doctors don't have to do the same for patients planning to pay with insurance. In that case, any reputable doctor should provide detail about potential costs.

If your measure for success is saving money or reducing costs, the prognosis looks less clear. Sometimes a treatment is essential and urgent, meaning that skipping or postponing it could be a bad or even dangerous idea—even if it could save you some money. In less urgent instances, you could save money by shopping around for a lower-cost provider. The cash price and insurance price among different labs or imaging facilities can vary wildly, so consider asking your doctor whether it's OK for you to go somewhere else for those services.

Q *Does asking pose any risks?*
A Questioning could put off your doctor, but that risk is minimal, Allen says. "Good doctors won't be threatened at all by that." If yours is, consider looking for a replacement.

Q *Does not succeeding pose any risks?*
A If you can't get a proper explanation of the importance or costs of treatment, you can't make a properly informed decision about what to do. That's a big deal. Few choices in life require as much clarity and understanding as the decision to undergo or forgo medical treatment. What you don't know can cost you, and not just financially.

Q *How do you do it?*
A "The number-one question I always tell people to ask their doctor or clinician who's recommending an elective treatment, test, or drug is: 'What happens if we wait?'" Allen says. "'If we don't do it right now, am I going to walk out of here and die? Am I going to go blind? Be crippled? Am I going to be harmed somehow if we don't act right now?' A lot of times, when they're recommending these treatments, they're assuming that you're going to do it, so they kind of push you in that direction. By asking what happens if we wait,

it reframes the conversation so you can take a step back, hear the options, hear the worst-case scenario if you don't do anything." From there, if you choose, do some research, get a second opinion, or even seek alternative treatments.

You may have several options. If you have insurance, ask the provider to give you a cost estimate for the service if you use your coverage, but don't dismiss the possibility of not using that coverage. Ask for the cash price as well. (You don't pay literal cash for it; it just means that you pay it all yourself rather than using insurance.) If you have a high-deductible policy and know that you likely won't reach the deductible threshold, it could make sense to pay the cash price. You might even be able to negotiate it a bit. Obviously, if you're having a baby or undergoing heart surgery, the cash rate won't make sense, but in other circumstances it might.

It also doesn't have to be a now-or-never situation. If you prefer to delay a non-urgent treatment until a more financially convenient time, tell the doctor. According to Virgie Bright Ellington, MD, it's perfectly OK to say, " 'I'm paying for healthcare out of my pocket, or my budget's really tight. What happens if I don't do this now, or if I wait until I'll have more resources in a few weeks or months?'" Just be polite when asking. Your relationship with your doctor matters because you likely want to maintain it for a long time. That relationship works best when both parties treat each other with sincere respect.

SCRIPTS

"I'd like to know more about what you're recommending. What would happen if we waited? I don't want to put my health at risk, but I have a tight budget, and [if appropriate] I'd be paying for this out of my own pocket. I want to understand as much as I can before we move forward."

At this point, you can ask additional questions, such as

"Will my insurance cover all, most, or part of the treatment?" "Are effective lower-cost treatments available?" "What's the cash price for the service you're recommending?" and "May I have a good-faith estimate of the costs involved in what you're recommending?"

If the doctor says the treatment can wait and you feel comfortable waiting…

> "Thank you. That's great to know. I'd like to delay the treatment for a little while and possibly get a second opinion. Do you have any recommendations for other people or resources for me to consult?"

If you're willing to do the treatment but the cost concerns you …

> "Thank you for the explanation. I'm willing to have the treatment, but the cost concerns me. Who can I speak with about the cash price of this service and any payment plans or financing options?"

At this point, consider sharing more about your financial situation, including if you think you might qualify for financial assistance based on your income.

Q *What if they deny your request?*

A Unfortunately, you may need to find a new doctor. Consider reaching out again a few days after your appointment to see whether the doctor is willing to talk more. Everyone has bad days, after all. But answering these types of questions is good doctor 101. In some cases, the law might even require it. "The patient has the right, always, to ask questions," Allen says. You shouldn't have to beg for answers. If you do, it might be time for a change.

SUCCESS STORY

While eating lunch one Friday afternoon, Lisa Rowan noticed that her dental crown felt loose. The following Monday morning, she arranged a same-day appointment with the closest dentist who accepted her insurance. In the dentist chair, the crown fell out, and the dentist told her it was time for a new one, which didn't surprise her. She was prepared financially to handle it—or so she thought.

She received a bill for about $9,000, which included the cost of replacing the now-missing crown for a few hundred dollars, X-rays, and a proposal for replacing all her still-intact fillings with crowns. She asked why all the fillings needed replacing with crowns and was told that crowns would be more efficient and last longer than the old fillings. Stunned, she instructed them to replace only the missing crown and leave the rest of the work for another time.

With the new crown in place, Rowan sought a second opinion on the remaining work. Another dentist asked whether any of the teeth were bothering her or hurt, which they weren't. "Then you don't need any of this replaced," the dentist said. "Unless you have a tooth with a filling that's cracked or you get a cavity somewhere else on the same tooth, everything you have can stay as it is."

The second dentist didn't even charge her for the office visit. As a result, she stayed loyal to that practice until she moved out of state four years later. "I never saw the first dentist again, even though I could see their office building from my apartment. It wasn't worth it for me."

A LOWER PRICE FOR PRESCRIPTION MEDICATION

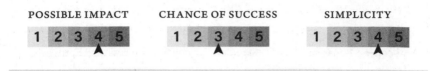

POSSIBLE IMPACT   CHANCE OF SUCCESS   SIMPLICITY

1 2 3 **4** 5   1 2 **3** 4 5   1 2 3 **4** 5

Q *What are you asking?*
A You're requesting a reduced cost for a prescription.

Q *How big a deal is it?*
A It's no secret that the cost of prescription drugs in America has spun wildly out of control. Asking a pharmacist how much a medication would cost if you paid out of pocket, direct, rather than through insurance can save hundreds or thousands over time. This strategy often goes by the name "cash option," but you don't have to pay with hard currency to use it. Credit and debit cards likely will work just fine, too. Paying direct streamlines the transaction for the pharmacy—removing insurance companies, various middlemen, and their sometimes outrageous markups—saving the pharmacy time and money and essentially making the deal no different from buying a bottle of aspirin. Beth Waldron, a patient advocate from Chapel Hill, North Carolina, says that she spoke with a patient who paid $28 cash for a prescription for oseltamivir (generic Tamiflu) for his daughter that would have cost $200 through insurance. "I see that all the time," she says. Saving $172 on one set of medication is definitely a big deal!

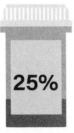

25% In 2018, people overpaid for generic prescriptions with insurance a quarter of the time, compared to paying cash, direct. (University of Southern California's Leonard D. Schaeffer Center for Health Policy & Economics)

Q *How likely is it that you will succeed?*

A If you ask, pharmacists generally will tell you the cash price of a medication. Until recently, many pharmacists contractually couldn't disclose that information because of gag clauses in contracts among pharmacies, benefit managers (middlemen), and insurance companies. New federal laws in 2018—the Patient Right to Know Drug Prices Act and the Know the Lowest Price Act—outlawed those gag clauses.[43] If you don't ask, pharmacists might not volunteer the information, though.

Once you do ask, the cash price could cost less than with insurance. Your experience will vary based on your insurance, the medication, the pharmacy, and other factors, but according to a 2018 report from the University of Southern California's Leonard D. Schaeffer Center for Health Policy & Economics, people who paid for generic prescriptions with insurance *overpaid* 25 percent of the time, compared with paying cash direct.[44] Robert Popovian, PharmD, chief science policy officer with the Global Healthy Living Foundation, believes that number has increased in subsequent years.[45] Now "it's probably more like 40 or 50 percent of the time."

Q *Does asking pose any risks?*

A For you, no. The folks behind the scenes no doubt would prefer that you didn't ask. "That's something that most insurance companies don't want patients to do," says Monique Whitney, executive director at Pharmacists United for Truth & Transparency.[46] "It basically cuts them out of the equation, and they don't get to make a profit." But experts agree that you won't face any repercussions for asking. Remember, though, that, if you don't use insurance to buy the medications, the amount you pay out of pocket won't go toward meeting any deductible.

Q *Does not succeeding pose any risks?*

A These savings could mean the difference between life and death. Every day, many people must decide between financial health and physical health because prescription costs have risen so outrageously high.

Q *How do you do it?*

A It's as simple as it sounds: "What's the cash price of this medication?" Again, you have no guarantees that the cash price will be lower than the insurance price, but it can't hurt to ask. Also, an independent pharmacy—not a chain store, such as CVS, Rite-Aid, or Walgreens—often makes for the best place to ask. When working with an independent pharmacy, you more likely are dealing directly with the store owner, Waldron says. "They're very aware of 'Here's how much I paid for the drug, here's my acquisition cost, and here's what I can afford to do,' and they can negotiate with you." Corporate policies and vendor agreements often bind the hands of chain-store pharmacists, making them less able to negotiate.

SCRIPTS

"What's the cash price of this medication?"

OR

"What would this medication cost if I paid direct, instead of using my insurance?"

If the cash price is the same as or higher than the insurance price . . .

"Oh, that's too bad, but thank you for letting me know. Do you know of other discounts available for this medication, such as a manufacturer's rebate?"

If they tell you that they can't share that information with you . . .

"That's not true anymore. The Patient Right to Know Drug Prices Act made it illegal for companies to keep pharmacists from sharing that information. Can you tell me what the cash price is? If not, I'll take my prescription to another pharmacy."

Q   *What if they deny your request?*

A   They might, and you can't do much about it, though you can file a complaint with the pharmacy board in your state or province. For a list with contact information, visit nabp.pharmacy/about/boards-of-pharmacy.

In some cases, insurance will offer the best price—particularly with newer, name-brand medications rather than generics—but it's always worth asking. If you think that you've been treated poorly or that the pharmacy could've done more to mitigate the price, consider taking your business elsewhere. Other pharmacies, especially independently owned ones, may have more wiggle room with price. It may not sound fun when you're feeling bad, but the savings can make it worthwhile. A tool such as GoodRx can help you search for lower prices on specific medication from pharmacies in your area. Doctors interviewed for this book also recommended investigating Cost Plus Drug Company and Costco as other potential ways to save on medications.

You also can seek help with costs. Numerous organizations advocate for people with various diseases or conditions and help them manage their situations, financially and otherwise. Your doctor's office can put you in touch with relevant groups in your area.

REDUCING OR WAIVING THE FEE FOR SENDING YOUR RECORDS TO ANOTHER DOCTOR

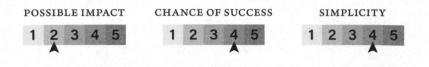

POSSIBLE IMPACT   CHANCE OF SUCCESS   SIMPLICITY

1 2 3 4 5   1 2 3 4 5   1 2 3 4 5

Q *What are you asking?*
A You're requesting that a medical provider cancel or lower the charge for sending your records to another provider.

Q *How big a deal is it?*
A Your experience may vary, but the savings could prove significant. Elizabeth Broden, an attorney in Los Angeles, saved $100 charged by an emergency-visit dentist to send the record of that visit to her regular dentist.

Q *How likely is it that you will succeed?*
A If you know how to ask, very likely. Overcharging people for copying and sending medical records can violate the Health Insurance Portability and Accountability Act (HIPAA), a federal law that protects consumers' private medical records. It's one thing for doctors to charge a small fee for mailing a USB drive to you. They can pass on the basic costs of doing that. But charging someone $100 to email an existing electronic file counts as a HIPAA violation. Few phrases will grab a billing administrator's attention as quickly as "HIPAA violation."

Q *Does asking pose any risks?*
A It could leave a bad taste in the collective mouth of the doctor's office, but a place that charges egregious fees and then balks when people object probably doesn't deserve your business.

WHAT CONSTITUTES A REASONABLE FEE

The HIPAA Privacy Rule "permits a covered entity to impose a reasonable, cost-based fee if the individual requests a copy of the PHI [protected health information] (or agrees to receive a summary or explanation of the information).[47] The fee may include only the cost of:

1. **labor** for copying the PHI requested by the individual, whether in paper or electronic form;
2. **supplies** for creating the paper copy or electronic media (e.g., CD or USB drive) **if the individual requests** that the electronic copy be provided on portable media;
3. **postage, when the individual requests** that the copy, or the summary or explanation, be mailed; and
4. preparation of **an explanation or summary** of the PHI, **if agreed** to by the individual.

The fee may *not* include costs associated with verification; documentation; searching for and retrieving the PHI; maintaining systems; recouping capital for data access, storage, or infrastructure; or other costs not listed above even if such costs are authorized by State law."

Q *Does not succeeding pose any risks?*
A Just that ill will and having to pay an unnecessary fee.

Q *How do you do it?*
A If you're in a rush, play the HIPAA card. Otherwise, ask nicely and drop the hammer later if necessary. You may need to see these folks again in the future, so use the kinder, gentler approach until it's clear that it isn't working. Also, they might counteroffer, for example, by saying that they can lower the fee from $100 to $50. If the counteroffer still sounds too high,

stand your ground and remind them of HIPAA. That approach worked for Elizabeth Broden. After flexing her HIPAA knowledge, she received a call almost immediately. She said that they told her, "'You know what? We just decided it wasn't worth it. It wasn't worth the trouble. We're going to send you the file.' Of course you are, because otherwise it's a HIPAA violation, and you know that *I* know my rights."

SCRIPTS

If you're in a hurry, call the office and ask to speak with the billing administrator.

> "Hello, I'd like you to waive the fee for sending my records to my other doctor. HIPAA allows you to charge a fee for the basic costs of sending the information, such as supplies and postage if I request them [if appropriate], which I didn't. The charge you're billing is excessive. Who can I speak with about removing that?"

If they counter with a lower fee, determine whether you think their counter sounds fair. Depending on the amount, it might not be worth all the back and forth, and that's your choice. If you're OK with the counteroffer, take it. If not, continue.

If they refuse to waive it or give you an unsatisfactory counteroffer . . .

> "That's disappointing. My request was reasonable, so I'll be filing a HIPAA violation complaint with the OCR Complaint Portal."

The kinder, gentler approach

> "Hello, I'd like you to waive the fee for sending my records to my other doctor. I'm on a tight budget, and that fee sounds high for sending records. You need to cover the cost of supplies and postage [if applicable], which I requested, but I was hoping you could waive the fee for me."

If you've been a long-time patient or have another special connection to the office, consider sharing that information as well.

If they lower the fee and it seems fair, take it. If not, hold steady and continue. If they refuse to waive or make an unacceptable counteroffer . . .

> "That's disappointing. I know that HIPAA allows you to charge a nominal fee, again, to cover supplies and postage that I requested, but the existing charge looks excessive. Who else can I speak with about waiving the charge?"

If they refuse to waive it or don't budge from an unsatisfactory counteroffer . . .

> "I'm sorry to hear that. My request was reasonable, so I'll be filing a HIPAA violation complaint with the OCR Complaint Portal."

Q   *What if they deny your request?*
A   You probably should find a new medical provider. Depending on the urgency of the medical issue, you may be stuck paying the fee just to keep everything moving, but you should file the HIPAA violation complaint either way. You also can contact your credit card issuer, if paying the fee by credit card, to see whether they'd waive the fee, but you have no guarantee that they will. If you tell them your story and mention the HIPAA issue, the card issuer might work with you.

WAIVING A LATE OR CANCELLATION FEE FROM YOUR DOCTOR'S OFFICE

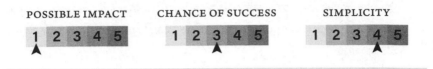

POSSIBLE IMPACT	CHANCE OF SUCCESS	SIMPLICITY
1 **2** 3 4 **5**	1 **2** 3 **4** 5	1 **2** 3 4 **5**
▲	▲	▲

Q *What are you asking?*
A You're requesting that a medical provider cancel the charge for showing up late or not giving sufficient notice to cancel an appointment.

Q *How big a deal is it?*
A Probably not huge—most likely tens of dollars rather than hundreds—but on a tight budget, every dollar counts. Plus, healthcare is expensive enough; the last thing you need is to pay for an appointment that didn't happen. For medical providers, however, these fees can be a big deal. A 2020 report from the National Institutes of Health's National Library of Medicine said that, depending on the type of doctor, no-show rates can range from 12 percent to a stunning 80 percent.[48] A report from the Medical Group Management Association (MGMA) pegged that number at 7 percent in 2019, prior to the start of the COVID-19 pandemic.[49] Either way, those statistics mean that millions of people miss appointments, which means lost revenue for providers. The good news is that a separate MGMA report said that fewer than 20 percent of "single-specialty practices" charged fees to patients who failed to show for appointments in 2019.[50]

7% The 2019 median no-show rate for patients who had appointments at medical practices. (MGMA)

Q *How likely is it that you will succeed?*

A Not as likely as you might think. From a customer-service standpoint, it seems reasonable for medical providers to exercise some flexibility in waiving these fees to keep patients from seeking service elsewhere. The healthcare space is insanely competitive, after all. On the other hand, sometimes patients don't want to change doctors, and in some areas people may not have any other options. In other words, your doctor's office knows that they probably won't face meaningful consequences for refusing to waive the fee.

Q *Does asking pose any risks?*

A In the majority of cases, your doctor won't know that you asked. It'll be between you and the billing department. Worst-case scenario: They say no.

Q *Does not succeeding pose any risks?*

A Beyond paying a fee that you don't want to pay, the only real risk is frustration with your provider for not being flexible. If you're treated harshly or rudely, that experience could color your view of the office and make you consider switching, though that's pretty unlikely. Assuming that you have a good relationship with the doctor, having to pay one fee probably wouldn't spur you to make that change.

Q *How do you do it?*

A It shouldn't take much more than a polite call. Call the office, ask to speak with someone in the billing department, and then ask them to waive the fee. Don't be afraid to share meaningful details about what happened. Maybe it was your first time missing an appointment with a doctor you've been seeing for years. Maybe your kid is sick and spent all night and morning throwing up. Maybe you recently lost your job. Maybe your car wouldn't start. Whatever happened, share it. It may feel awkward or embarrassing, but that vulnerability helps create connections that can encourage people to help you when they otherwise might not bother. Also, let them know whether you already rescheduled or want to reschedule the missed appointment. Knowing that they'll make money on that next appointment may make them more likely to waive the fee for the one you missed.

SCRIPTS

> "Hi there, I had an appointment with _____ [provider's name] on _____ [time and date] that I [wasn't able to make/was late for] because _____ [reason]. I should have called [sooner] to let you know, but that was such a crazy day that it slipped my mind. I've been a patient for _____ [number] years, and [if appropriate] this is the first time that this has happened. My budget is tight these days, so who can I speak with about waiving the fee for [missing/arriving late to] the appointment?"

If they initially refuse to waive the fee . . .

> "I hear you. I know that your office loses money when people don't show. But [if appropriate] I've been a patient for a long time, and [if appropriate] this is the first time I've missed an appointment. I think asking you to waive it is a reasonable request. Who else can I speak with about this?"

Q   *What if they deny your request?*

A   As with any negotiation, threatening to walk away can give you power. It's unlikely that a medical provider will want to lose a patient over a $40 late fee, so don't be afraid to make that threat. You don't even have to be willing to follow through with it. Just the threat of leaving may sway the other person on the phone. If it doesn't, try again in a few days. You could end up speaking with someone more willing to help. If none of that works and you feel poorly treated, it might be time to look for a new provider.

3. HOUSING

Shrink Your Biggest Monthly Bill

How to ask for:

REDUCING THE INTEREST RATE ON A MORTGAGE

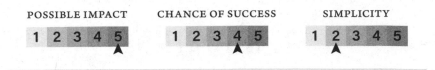

POSSIBLE IMPACT   CHANCE OF SUCCESS   SIMPLICITY

1 2 3 4 **5**   1 2 3 **4** 5   1 **2** 3 4 5

Q *What are you asking?*
A You're requesting a lower interest rate for your home loan.

Q *How big a deal is it?*
A "We're talking about the most expensive purchase of someone's life here," says Lauren Bowling, an Atlanta-based realtor and blogger at FinancialBestLife.com.[51] "It's not like, 'Oh, I'll save $20 at Nordstrom.' No, you could save *$20,000* by shopping your rates, asking for discounts, and comparing closing costs."

For a $400,000 home with a $40,000 down payment, a 30-year mortgage, and a 7 percent interest rate, a buyer will pay an average of $502,000 in interest over the life of the loan. Drop that rate to 6 percent, leaving everything else the same, and total interest drops to $417,000, a whopping difference of $85,000. Even if you drop the interest rate by just a fraction of a percentage point, from 7 to 6.95 percent, that tiny difference will save you about $4,000. Over the life of a 30-year mortgage, $4,000 might not equal much savings per month, but it's still significant money.

For a $400,000 home, with 10 percent down and a 30-year mortgage	
Interest Rate	**Total Interest Paid**
7 percent	$502,000
6 percent	$417,000

Q *How likely is it that you will succeed?*

A Very, depending on what you're willing to do to get that lower rate. Austin-based realtor Cheri Martz says that, if lenders really want your business, they'll work with you. Of course, you have no guarantee that a lender will work with you just because you ask. Jacob Channel, senior economist at LendingTree, says, "How much a lender will be willing to move their original offer to accommodate you will depend on factors such as your credit score and how much money you earn. The stronger your overall financial profile, the more flexible a lender is likely to be when working with you." Even if they don't work with you, you have options. You just need to understand the risks that go along with them.

Option 1: Points

You can buy points—paying more up front for a lower rate—but it'll cost you. A point on a mortgage typically costs 1 percent of the total loan price and lowers the rate by 0.25 percent. Using the same example as above, 1 point would cost $3,600 (1 percent of the loan price = $400,000 total cost - $40,000 down payment = $360,000 / 100) and drop the rate from 7 percent to 6.75 percent, saving you more than $20,000 in interest over the life of the loan. That's a lot of money. But Greg McBride, chief financial analyst at rate-comparison site Bankrate, says it can take 5 to 6 years to break even when you factor up-front costs against monthly savings, so points might not make sense if you're not planning to own the home for a long time.

Option 2: Shorter Term

You can lower your rate by agreeing to a 15-year mortgage rather than the more standard term of 30 years. But a shorter term means a higher monthly payment because you'll be paying the mortgage off in half the time. On that same $400,000 home with the same interest rate, you'll pay about $850 more per month for a 15-year mortgage versus a 30-year term, but you would save more than $260,000 in interest. Push the rate lower, and the savings grow, but significantly higher monthly payments don't work for many people.

Option 3: Adjustable Rate

You also can pursue an adjustable-rate mortgage. With fixed-rate mortgages, the rate remains the same for the life of the loan—unless you refinance later. Adjustable-rate mortgages also amortize for 30 years but start with a lower rate for a set period, anywhere from 3 to 10 years, after which the rate increases, typically adjusting every six months for the remainder of the loan's life. These loans can work well if you're not planning to own the home for long, if you know you'll make more money by the time the rate adjusts, if you plan on refinancing, or if you make good money now but have difficulty securing a more traditional loan for various reasons that could include inconsistent or unpredictable income. But those higher rates can make monthly payments untenable for homeowners down the line, which can spell significant trouble, so proceed with caution. That caution should include working with a lender that has calculated your ability to repay if the loan adjusts to the maximum allowable rate, which sometimes can increase five points or more above the initial rate. Taking that situation into consideration can help ensure that you can afford to stay in the home regardless of rate fluctuations.

Q   *Does asking pose any risks?*
A   It could slow closing on the home.

Q   *Does not succeeding pose any risks?*
A   In that case, you'd pay the higher rate, which can be a big deal—especially if you've fallen in love with a home beyond your price range and hoped that a lower rate might make it more affordable. That's another reason that it's important to secure preapproval before you start shopping. That way you can focus only on homes in the range that you know you can afford.

Q   *How do you do it?*
A   Start by comparing rates from multiple lenders, which sites such as Bankrate, LendingTree, and NerdWallet make it easy to do. With initial quotes in hand, apply to three to five lenders on the same day, so you get an estimate of the complete costs from each lender. (There's more to mort-

gages than just interest rates. Fees play a huge part, too.) Having all those estimates at the same time enables you to play the lenders off one another. "You can ask the lender, 'Will you give me the same rate that this other guy gave me in order to win my business?'" Bowling says. You don't have a guarantee of success, but you'll never know if you don't ask. But compare apples to apples. Make sure that both rates apply to the same type of loan rather than comparing, say, a 30-year fixed-rate mortgage with one for 15 years.

From there, you can talk with each lender's loan officer about other ways to lower your rate, including buying points, shorter terms, adjustable rates, and other fees and closing costs that may be negotiable. (The next section of this chapter looks at closing costs in more detail.) If you're considering any of those alternatives, you *must* do your homework before speaking with the loan officer so you thoroughly understand how each option works. When rushed, people tend to make bad decisions about matters they don't understand. With any financial transaction, anxiety or panic can cause trouble. With a home, they can lead to disaster, so, again, tread carefully.

SCRIPTS

"Hi there, I've received rates from a few other lenders, including ___ [number] lower than what you offered. Would you be able to match the [lower/lowest] rate or go even lower to win my business?"

If they say they can't, escalate the conversation to a manager or see what other cards they're holding.

"That's disappointing. [Who else can I speak with about a competitive rate?/What else can you do to reduce the costs for this mortgage?]"

At this point, you can bring up points or other options that you're willing to pursue, or you can wait for the loan officer to mention them.

Q   *What if they deny your request?*

A   You still have options. You could accept the offered rate. You could wait to see whether mortgage rates dip in coming weeks or months, which can happen. Even in stable economic times, rates can fluctuate significantly. You could approach other lenders to find one more flexible with rates. Otherwise, you may have to adjust to the situation. For example, you might need to lower the price range that you're considering or shelve the home hunt altogether until you can save more money or until housing prices or interest rates fall. Those options may sound drastic, but they're better than locking yourself into a mortgage that you can't afford.

LOWER CLOSING COSTS ON A MORTGAGE

POSSIBLE IMPACT
1 2 3 **4 5**
▲

CHANCE OF SUCCESS
1 2 **3 4** 5
▲

SIMPLICITY
1 **2 3 4 5**
▲

Q *What are you asking?*
A You're requesting reduced costs and possibly fewer fees for a home loan.

Q *How big a deal is it?*
A It's not as impactful as reducing the interest rate, but it's not insignificant. On average, closing costs equal 3 to 6 percent of the sticker price. If you buy a $400,000 home, closing costs will range from $12,000 to $24,000. Don't expect to negotiate away all or even most of those costs, but asking could shave a decent amount off that total. Kimberly Wasielewski, a real estate investor from Indianapolis, advised a friend to shop around for lenders, and her friend saved about $9,000 in closing fees.

On a $400,000 house, closing costs will run 3 to 6 percent of the sale price, or **$12,000 to $24,000.**

Q *How likely is it that you will succeed?*
A Success depends on what you're trying to reduce or waive. Some fees are negotiable, such as application fees, origination fees, and underwriting fees. Others—for appraisals, credit checks, and some government-mandated fees—aren't. "The lender needs to be compensated for providing the loan, but you want to avoid paying through the nose or getting hit with

a bunch of ancillary junk fees," says Greg McBride, chief financial analyst at Bankrate. "Being a more informed consumer can help you avoid that."

Q   *Does asking pose any risks?*
A   Negotiating some of the fees could delay the closing.

Q   *Does not succeeding pose any risks?*
A   You could end up paying more fees than you want to pay.

Q   *How do you do it?*
A   As with negotiating a lower interest rate, start by obtaining offers from multiple lenders. First, use a comparison site such as Bankrate, Lending-Tree, or NerdWallet to see lender rates. Submit applications to three to five lenders on the same day. The same day matters because individual lenders' rates can move, albeit slightly, each day. Same-day applications will give you the most accurate comparison. Within three business days, each lender will provide a detailed estimate of the loan's total costs. "Then you get a true side-by-side comparison of the different fees being charged, and that's where your negotiating power comes in," McBride says. Those fee differences can be substantial. Lauren Bowling, a realtor from Atlanta, says that one lender gave her a quote showing closing costs *three times* more than what other lenders were charging.

Some lenders will give detailed explanations of closing costs, while others will give a simple grand total. LendingTree chief economist Jacob Channel says, "If you can ask for discounts on specific aspects of your closing costs, then it might be easier for a lender or seller to help you, as opposed to if you just ask for a blanket discount on the total cost of the fees." McBride suggests starting with title insurance, which he says should be your biggest single closing cost. Home buyers typically must purchase title insurance for the lender, which protects against property-title problems, including someone else making a claim to the property. You usually need to purchase it to secure a mortgage, but you don't have to buy it from the lender. Shopping around for title insurance can save you real money. Some states regulate the insurance industry so heavily that you won't find much price difference among companies, but the rates and fees in other states can vary significantly, making shopping around a must. "On the title insurance, the juice is definitely worth the squeeze because there's a lot of juice there," McBride says. "There's a lot of potential savings."

Some of that juice might not require squeezing around. You could qualify for a reissue rate, meaning a discount rate, on title insurance. If you're buying a property last sold in the past seven to ten years and the previous owner had title insurance on the home and can provide a full copy of the policy, the discount on your title insurance could run to 40 percent or more.[52] If the property falls within that window, request a copy of the current owner's policy so you can prove that the last transaction took place within the specified timeframe. Take that step early in the process to avoid delays, and it shouldn't require much more effort than that.

When refinancing your home, you also can get a reissue rate, sometimes called a substitution rate specifically for a refinance. If you refinance within that window and you can provide proof of title insurance, you have a good chance of receiving that discount. Whether you're buying or refinancing, you may not hear about the possibility of a reissue rate unless you ask—so ask!

SCRIPTS

Depending on the level of detail provided by the lender and how granular your request, your approach can vary.

Focus on reducing total closing costs.

> "Hi there, I recently applied for a mortgage with you, and I've been comparing closing costs among _____ [number] other lenders. Your rates are competitive, but your closing costs are running higher than the others. How can we lower those costs to match or beat what the others are charging?"

If they refuse to lower the costs . . .

> "That's disappointing. I know you need to make money off this loan, but given the estimates from other lenders with similar rates, I think my request is reasonable. Who else on your team can I speak with about this?"

If they counteroffer with a smaller reduction of closing costs . . .

> "I appreciate your flexibility, thank you. Your competitors are offering lower fees with a similar interest rate, though, so I'd like you to reduce them to match or beat the other offers. Otherwise, my business has to go elsewhere."

Target specific fees.

> "Hi there, I recently applied for a mortgage with you, and I've been comparing closing costs among _____ [number] other lenders. Your rates are competitive, but your closing costs include several fees that the others don't, including _____ [details]. Who can I speak with about waiving those fees?"

If they refuse to lower the costs . . .

> "That's disappointing. I know you need to make money off this loan, but given the estimates from other lenders with similar rates, I think my request is reasonable. Who else on your team can I speak with about this?"

If they counteroffer with waiving some but not all the fees . . .

> "Thank you for working with me on this. I appreciate it. None of the other lenders who provided estimates charges [this fee/these fees], so I'd rather not have to pay [it/them]. What can we do to remove them?"

Q *What if they deny your request?*

A You should apply to multiple lenders because, if one isn't willing to work with you, you can take your business elsewhere immediately. Don't get too emotional or impulsive if you don't get your way, though. Fees constitute a major part of mortgage costs, but there's more to it. Review *all* the math carefully before kicking a lender to the curb. For example, if that lender has the lowest rate and no one else will match or beat it, it might be worth paying a few hundred extra now to save thousands more later.

SUCCESS STORY

You can save money when buying a house in other ways. A J Smith and her family saved themselves thousands with a simple question about furniture. In July 2021, Smith and her husband bought a house in upstate New York, a couple hours north of their previous home in New York City. The house had less square footage than their old apartment, but it came with a dining room and two more bedrooms. They knew that they'd need additional furniture to fill the extra rooms. They also knew that the house had been the sellers' summer home rather than their primary residence. Smith sensed an opportunity.

"We asked, 'Does this come furnished?' and they said, 'Just tell us what you want.' That was really as easy as it was." For no extra cost, they basically got the house "70 percent furnished," including a dining room table and matching chairs, a couch, a bed, dressers, a toy chest, and more, much of which they still have today. "They were relieved," she adds. "It was a relief for us. We got the house mostly furnished, and they didn't have to pay to have things moved, so it worked out for both parties." Not all housing negotiations go quite so smoothly, but creating a win-win situation for all involved can improve your chances of success.

A REDUCED RATE FOR A CONTRACTOR OR HANDYMAN

POSSIBLE IMPACT   CHANCE OF SUCCESS   SIMPLICITY

1 2 3 **4** 5   1 **2 3 4** 5   1 2 **3** 4 5

Q *What are you asking?*
A You're seeking a better deal from hired help.

Q *How big a deal is it?*
A Depending on the project, it can be significant. Repairs, remodeling, or renovation can cost insane amounts of money. But with multiple bids and the right questions, it doesn't have to break your bank account.

Q *How likely is it that you will succeed?*
A It depends on the type and scope of the project, whether you already have a relationship with the contractor, how busy (or not) the company is, and other factors. A company with a fully booked calendar may charge more and not negotiate pricing because they don't need to. "They're like, 'I don't need this job, so I'm going to price it up. If I get it, I'll make it happen because the margin will be worth it. If I don't, it's totally fine,'" says Barbara Sloan, author, real estate investor, and owner of Manhattan Renovations in New York City.

That exact situation happened in 2022, when my wife and I had a door that needed fixing. We told the contractor that we'd be soliciting other bids, and they told us that they weren't interested in working with folks who got multiple bids. That response surprised us, but we knew that haggling wouldn't accomplish anything, so we dropped them from our list and continued collecting other estimates.

Q *Does asking pose any risks?*
A Yes, says Tom Brickman, real estate investor and creator of the *Frugal Gay* blog. "You don't want to overplay your hand, screw yourself, and

get a reputation that 'Hey, this guy's cheap.'" That's a big deal because a good relationship with a reliable, skilled contractor or handyman can prove extraordinarily valuable whether you're a real estate investor with a dozen properties or a first-time homebuyer. The luxury of trusting someone to get the job done right when something goes wrong—and something usually goes wrong—can save you countless headaches. But a good contractor will be in high demand. Being pushy about price can push a contractor away before that relationship even starts. That doesn't mean you can't negotiate, though. It just means not being so aggressive that a contractor or handyman won't want to work with you.

Q *Does not succeeding pose any risks?*

A You might wind up paying more than you want or working with someone who wasn't your first choice.

Q *How do you do it?*

A Do your homework to understand at a high level what the job might cost. "There're lots of resources where you can put in 'How much should it cost to install a window?'" Brickman says. "Then you have an understanding that in Dallas, Texas, it should cost $300 to $500 to install a window. When they come out and say, 'It's going to be $1,600 to do this,' you can say, 'Hmm, that sounds off.'" The research process can be as simple as Googling. A search for "How much should it cost to install a window in Dallas, Texas?" brings up lots of results. They'll vary widely, but reviewing a number of the sites can give you a feel for what to expect and can help you frame future conversations.

When you know the lay of the land, contact at least three different contractors for bids. Ideally, you'll have word-of-mouth references from family or friends, but online resources and reviews can point you in the right direction, too. The bigger and more complex a project, the more important a detailed estimate becomes, which can empower you to deal with more nitty-gritty details in your negotiations. For example, contractors might include high-end items in the estimate, but you may want standard-issue pieces.

When you have all bids in hand, negotiations can begin. This book is all about how to save money, but the lowest bid isn't always the right choice. If reviews or recommendations point to a clear favorite that isn't the cheapest, consider whether the extra skill or quality is worth the extra cost. Kristin McGrath, a homeowner in Austin, Texas, opted for a slightly more expensive electrician, recommended by a friend, instead of choosing the lowest bid. She was glad she did. In the process of making the repair, workers caused some minor damage. "We were able to call and say, 'Hey, they damaged this. Can you make this right?' and they did," she says. "I'm glad in that case that I hadn't gone to the bare-bones price because they might have been less likely to work with us. But the one we chose was a reputable company, really cared about their reputation, and fixed the damage."

"Get everything in writing," Sloan says. "Start with a written proposal that has a detailed description of the scope of the work and the materials. If they send just a few lines, create your own description to make sure they're on the same page and have that included with the contract documents." Project paperwork also should include project timelines, payment schedules, and any warranties or insurance. This level of detail may not sound as crucial for a small, simple project as for a big, complex one, but it's always a good idea to have everything in writing.

SCRIPTS

Ask for a lower overall price.

> "Hi there, I'm calling about _____ [short description of job]. You have a great reputation, and I know you'd do great work, but other companies gave me estimates lower than yours. I'd like your team to do the work, but I'm on a tight budget. What can we do to reduce the price on your estimate?"

If they won't negotiate, you need to know for certain that their work will have significantly higher quality than the other bidders'. If not, thank them for their time and move on to the other companies. If they'll match or beat another offer . . .

> "Thanks so much for your flexibility. I really appreciate it. Please email me an updated estimate at [your email address]."

If they'll match only part of it . . .

> "I appreciate you working with me on this, but my budget is tight. What can we do to match or beat your competitor's overall price?"

At this point, they might pitch a superior reputation or service, suggest that you reduce the scope of the project, float using lower-quality materials or supplies, or say that they can't do anything more. At that point, you must choose whether to accept the higher price or move on.

Ask about a specific item on a detailed estimate.

> "Thanks for providing this level of detail, which really helps because my budget is tight. I have a question or two about it."

Mention your specific concern(s), whether that's the price of a specific item or something else. But before you ask, thoroughly research the average cost of the item *in your area* in order to make a more informed request.

Q *What if they deny your request?*
A The answer to this question depends on your opinion of the contractor or handyman. If the company's reputation still inspires you to work with them, then their not bending on price may not matter much. But if, based on your research, all the companies more or less align in reputation and quality, inflexibility on price may help make the decision easier. That's especially true if the person responds rudely or unprofessionally to your request. If that happens, move on to another option.

LOWERING YOUR RENT

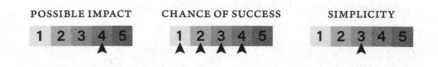

POSSIBLE IMPACT	CHANCE OF SUCCESS	SIMPLICITY
1 2 3 **4** 5	1 **2** **3** **4** 5	1 2 **3** 4 5

Q   *What are you asking?*
A   You're requesting a reduced monthly rent payment.

Q   *How big a deal is it?*
A   It's not always a big deal, but it can be. Paying less rent can keep you from having to move if the landlord hikes the rent again. It can allow you to afford a bigger apartment for a growing family. It can free up income for an emergency fund, retirement savings, or a down payment for buying a home. Whether you've knocked it down $10 or $100-plus, that money adds up over time.

Q   *How likely is it that you will succeed?*
A   Success depends on lots of factors. How's the rental market in your area? Are you renting from an individual or a large company? Do you have a good relationship with the landlord? How long do you want to stay? Do you consistently pay on time? Do you have good credit? Do you have pets? Have your neighbors ever filed complaints about you? Do you smoke? The list is endless.

Sometimes your chance of negotiating a lower rent payment is zero, and the property manager or landlord could laugh at your request. But keep in mind that it's more expensive to sign a new tenant than to hold onto an existing one, says Daryl Fairweather, chief economist at real estate comparison site Redfin. That's especially true if the space needs major repairs or goes unrented for an extended period. In many cases—not all, but many—the owner would rather keep you around, especially if you've been a good tenant. "You want to be somebody easy to work with and who's likable," says Indianapolis-based real estate investor Kimberly Wasielewski, "because if somebody likes you and they want to work with you, they'll bend the rules a little bit if they can."

Q *Does asking pose any risks?*
A The main risk lies in irritating the landlord or property manager and setting a bad tone for your future relationship or, in a highly competitive market, running the risk of them deciding not to rent to you at all. But that doesn't mean that you shouldn't ask. Focus on being polite and not over-playing your hand.

Q *Does not succeeding pose any risks?*
A When you're talking about your home, the stakes can run high. If your negotiations don't succeed, you may have to move, give up the idea of that new apartment that you love, or even take on a roommate.

Q *How do you do it?*
A Research. Arm yourself with knowledge of the current rental market in your area to frame the conversation. Are many similar-sized properties available nearby, and how do their prices compare? That information can help you read the room. If there's not much availability, adjust your expectations. The manager or owner may not have an incentive to negotiate because lots of others will want to rent the property. If you find plenty of places nearby to rent, you may have wiggle room to ask for a break. Either way, asking does no harm, as long as your request is reasonable.

For a new place, you can ask the landlord or manager to match the price of a similar property nearby, to lower your security deposit, or to waive a pet fee. In a complex with multiple units, you can ask to rent a slightly bigger place for the rate of a slightly smaller one. To boost your chances of success, Wasielewski recommends asking for a lower rate by signing a longer lease. "I would always ask that as a renter," she says. You can mention your great credit score or provide references from previous landlords who vouch for you. You even can promise to refer friends in the future. All those strategies can make you a more appealing renter.

If you're trying to reduce or eliminate a rate increase on your current rental, remind them what a stellar tenant you've been. Remind them that you always pay on time, have never received a noise complaint, and have maintained the property well. Remind them that it costs more money to find a new tenant, and a new one might not prove as reliable as you. There's no guarantee that saying any of that will help, but it might. Different land-lords have different perspectives on what matters. "Figuring out what your landlord values can help you negotiate," Fairweather says, "because then you can offer something of value that might not be money."

SCRIPTS

Negotiate a new rental.

> "It's a great place, but there's a lot of availability in the area. I'm looking at a similar place nearby that's cheaper. Can you match or beat that price? It really would help my budget to bring the price down. I have great credit and always pay on time." If you like, offer to send references from previous landlords to help make your case.

If they refuse to budge . . .

> "That's disappointing. Would you consider lowering the rent if I sign a longer lease?"
>
> **OR, if a longer lease isn't realistic for you . . .**
>
> "That's disappointing. If reducing the rent isn't possible, how about lower-ing the security deposit or [if appropriate] waiving the pet fee?"

If they counteroffer . . .

> "Thank you for working with me. I appreciate it. That's an interesting offer, but I was hoping to match or beat the other place's price. Can you go a little lower?"

OR

"Thank you for working with me. I appreciate it. That's an interesting offer, but I was hoping to match or beat the other place's price. Can you go lower if I sign a longer lease? Like I said, I've been a great tenant, and I can provide references."

OR

"Thank you for working with me. I appreciate it. That's an interesting offer, but I was hoping to match or beat the other place's price. If reducing the rent isn't possible, how about lowering the security deposit or waiving the pet fee?"

Negotiate a rent increase.

If the increase is relatively small, you could ask to waive it altogether. Otherwise, asking for a reduction may be the best way to go.

"I like living here, and I've been a good tenant. I always pay on time. There haven't been any noise complaints or big maintenance requests. I even refer other people to live here. But this increase is going to hit my budget hard. Can you reduce the amount of the increase?"

If they offer a sufficient reduction . . .

"Thank you for working with me on this. I really appreciate it. Please email me confirmation of this new rate at [your email address]."

If you don't like their offer or counteroffer . . .

"That's disappointing. Can you be flexible on this? Would extending my lease make a difference?"

Q *What if they deny your request?*
A Unless you think that you've been treated unfairly, you may not have many options. If you're negotiating for a new place, you likely will have to find another place to live. If you're negotiating a rent increase, you politely

can remind the owner or manager, again, that you've been a good tenant, and good tenants are hard to find. Also remind them how expensive replacing someone can be. If none of that works, you probably have run out of luck. You'll have to pay the increase or find a new place to live.

SUCCESS STORY

Niccole Caan, a former consumer reporter from KENS 5 TV in San Antonio, Texas, negotiated down multiple rent increases. After living in their apartment for a year, she and her husband received a notification that their rent was going up. "I went to them, and I said, 'Would you consider dropping the price on the increase somewhat?'"

Caan didn't just ask cold, though. She took the time to build her case. "It's really important to come with some sort of evidence," she says. She reminded the landlord of their good record as tenants. They always paid on time. They never had any noise complaints or police called to their apartment. They maintained the property well. "I brought all of that to their attention," she says, and it worked on two separate occasions. "Each time, they dropped it [the increase] by half, so the first time it saved us $50 a month, and then $100 a month."

She didn't get her way quickly either time, however. The first time she asked, it took several weeks to receive a final answer. "I kept checking back and saying, 'Where are we on this?'" she says. "It's always up to you. They're not going to contact you and say yes. I had to keep going in." Her persistence paid off the second time, too, and it took only two weeks to get an answer that time. Caan's journalism skills certainly didn't hurt her negotiations—she talks for a living, after all—but before she became a consumer reporter, she didn't know people could negotiate rate increases.

Her approach didn't differ from what anyone else could do. Make the request. Tell your story. Build your case. Do that, and your chances of success look better than zero.

REDUCING YOUR REAL ESTATE AGENT'S COMMISSION

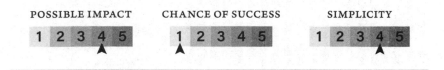

POSSIBLE IMPACT 1 2 3 **4** 5   **CHANCE OF SUCCESS** **1** 2 3 4 5   **SIMPLICITY** 1 2 3 **4** 5

Q *What are you asking?*
A You're requesting to pay a lower percentage of the sale of your home to your real estate agent.

Q *How big a deal is it?*
A It can be significant. Sellers traditionally pay about 6 percent of the final sale amount to listing agents, split equally between the buyer's and their own. For a $400,000 house, that amount equals $24,000. You never will be able to waive that entire amount, but even just a small reduction can mean big savings. On that $400,000, if you can knock off even just half a percentage point, to 5.5 percent, you can save $2,000. That's real money.

Q *How likely is it that you will succeed?*
A A 2019 Consumer Federation of America report said that 73 percent of real estate agents refused to negotiate down their commission.[53] But the report also said that those with the highest rates are the most likely to negotiate. If your agent is charging 7 percent, rather than the standard 3, he or she probably work with you; if 4 or 5 percent, probably not.

LendingTree chief economist Jacob Channel says that your location and the condition of your home can affect your odds. "It may make more sense to negotiate if you have an up-to-date home that's reasonably priced and likely to sell relatively quickly without much effort on the part of a real estate agent. Similarly, if you're living in a hot seller's market, it may be easier to negotiate an agent's commission. On the other hand, if your home is going to require a lot of work to sell, then negotiation probably isn't worth your time."

In October 2023, a federal jury found that the National Association of

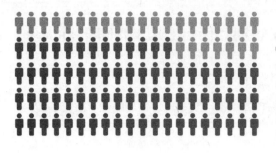

73%
of real estate agents won't negotiate their commission. (Consumer Federation of America)

Realtors and others had conspired to keep commissions high. That ruling could make real estate agents more open to negotiating commissions in America, potentially a big deal for many consumers.

Q *Does asking pose any risks?*
A You risk alienating the agent, who then may push you down the priority list or not work with you at all. For example, a listing agent might show a house less frequently if there's less money in doing so. Also, accepting a lower commission could signal that the agent lacks a key skill. "An agent who readily will give up commission probably isn't a very good negotiator," says Austin-based realtor Cheri Martz. "They probably don't understand their own value. They probably don't have a lot of value to add yet. They're just hustling for the business. The amount that can cost you as a buyer in overpaying for that home, that's real money as well." But again, that doesn't mean that you shouldn't ask. Just know that a good negotiator could make you more money on the sale price and closing costs than a commission discount.

Q *Does not succeeding pose any risks?*
A Beyond a damaged relationship with the agent, the biggest risk is having to pay more in closing fees than you wanted.

Q *How do you do it?*
A Shop around. "Talk to multiple agents and find out exactly how they're paid and what they're offering," says Daryl Fairweather, chief economist for

real estate comparison website Redfin. "Then you can use that to show a different agent to get them to start negotiating." Ideally, you'd speak with at least three agents.

More than just the commission rate should come into play when choosing an agent, though. You should feel comfortable with and trust that person, so take the time to learn a little about his or her personality. Otherwise, you risk making an already exhausting, stressful process worse.

SCRIPTS

> "Would you consider reducing your commission on this sale? I understand that you work hard for that commission and not all the money goes into your pocket. But I'm on a tight budget and trying to control my costs. How can we work together to make that happen?"

If they refuse to negotiate, read the room. If you like the agent and the reduced commission falls under "nice to have" rather than "must have," you may not want to proceed. If the agent becomes angry or reacts badly to your request, consider ending the conversation and moving to another agent. Anger at this point in the process is a red flag that the agent probably will be difficult to work with.

If you want to continue the conversation . . .

> "I hear you. I've reached out to a few different agents, and [number] of them [has/have] a lower commission than yours. With that in mind, I think my request is reasonable. Would you be willing to match that rate?"

Q *What if they deny your request?*

A Don't be surprised because your chances aren't great. In this case, it's perfectly OK not to get your way. A great real estate agent delivers value in lots of ways, most importantly by negotiating a better deal on the home that you're selling. Don't give up on the relationship just because the agent won't work with you on that one cost.

4. SHOPPING

Haggle for It

How to ask for:

A LOWER PRICE OR CHEAPER FINANCING FOR A VEHICLE

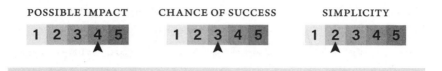

POSSIBLE IMPACT   CHANCE OF SUCCESS   SIMPLICITY

1 2 3 **4** 5   1 2 **3** 4 5   1 **2** 3 4 5

Q *What are you asking?*
A You're requesting a better deal when buying a vehicle from a dealership. This could mean a lower sticker price or a reduced interest rate on the auto loan. You can negotiate fees, add-ons, and trade-in value, too.

Q *How big a deal is it?*
A For those of us in car country, few expenses cost more than a vehicle. Not shopping around or negotiating can mean paying thousands more for that car, motorcycle, RV, SUV, or truck than necessary.

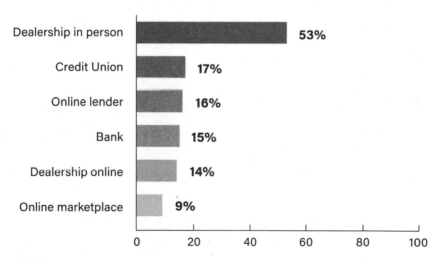

Where Drivers Get Auto Loans

Dealership in person	53%
Credit Union	17%
Online lender	16%
Bank	15%
Dealership online	14%
Online marketplace	9%

0   20   40   60   80   100

Roughly two-thirds of vehicle buyers secure a loan from the dealer, but dealerships traditionally offer higher interest rates than outside lenders. (Guides Auto Team, MarketWatch Guides)

Q *How likely is it that you will succeed?*

A Some vehicles are in such high demand that dealers have no incentive to negotiate. You probably can't haggle for a new Tesla. Also, the seller's policy matters. Some have strict no-haggling rules, meaning no negotiating sticker price. But that shouldn't stop you from negotiating fees, trade-in value, and financing. With other sellers, everything is negotiable. They might even expect you to haggle a bit, so your chances of some success look fairly good. When you buy matters, too. If you're shopping at the end of the month or quarter, a salesperson might prove more willing to negotiate in order to meet a quota.

Q *Does asking pose any risks?*

A The biggest risk, particularly for women and people of color, is facing unfair treatment. Vehicle salesmen have a longstanding reputation for dismissing or even disrespecting women, and some women still have to deal with that sexism. "A woman takes a man with her to a car dealership not because he's more knowledgeable about the car, haggling, or hammering out a deal," says Scotty Reiss, founder of the Girl's Guide to Cars. "It's because she feels like she won't be victimized." It's absurd that women still encounter this type of conduct, but many do, as do many people of color. A 2018 report from the National Fair Housing Alliance said that non-white car buyers "who were more qualified than their White counterparts received higher-cost offers 62.5 percent of the time."[54] If you think that you've been treated unfairly, take your business elsewhere. That said, don't let the specter of discrimination keep you from asking important questions and trying to secure a lower price.

Q *Does not succeeding pose any risks?*

A You could end up paying more than you want or should. You also might not be able to afford that vehicle that you love on the dealership floor. But good news: vehicles aren't snowflakes. Another seller probably has that same swoon-worthy vehicle, maybe at a price you can afford.

Q *How do you do it?*

A Determine what you want, prioritize, then shop around to see what's available at what prices. The process can take a while, but it's never been easier to comparison-shop for automobiles. Take advantage of all the information out there and extend your search beyond your town or city. If a two-hour drive can save you $1,000 or more, consider it.

"I'm not buying a pizza; I'm buying a car," says Elaine Rubin, a Las Vegas–based educational services spokesperson and daughter of a car mechanic. "Put in some time, effort, and research. See what else is competitively on the market." That research should include financing. When you've found a vehicle that you like, contact lenders—either directly or through comparison sites such NerdWallet, LendingTree, and Bankrate—to get pre-approved for an auto loan. You need to shop around with financing because you most likely will find better rates from third-party lenders than the dealership.

After you've done your homework, use your newfound knowledge to frame the conversations. If you want a specific vehicle from a local dealer but a dealer in a neighboring city offers it at a lower price, tell the local dealership. But make sure that you're comparing apples to apples. For an SUV with all the bells and whistles, asking to pay the same price as one with only the basics won't get you far.

If you can, leverage your trade-in and your financing options, too. The dealer makes money off both those items, so it's in their best interest to include those in the deal. Ask them if they'll lower the sticker price if you finance with them, but don't cut off your nose to spite your face. Paying more in interest to lower the sticker price a little doesn't make financial sense. Also, consider telling them that you'll sell your old vehicle yourself rather than trading it in. That possibility could entice them to increase their trade-in offer. Consider selling your old vehicle in pretty much any circumstance. Yes, it requires more time and effort, but you likely will make more money in the sale than you would save by trading it in. Just make sure the extra money is worth the effort.

SCRIPTS

A competing dealer doesn't have to be in a different town. Even one in the same city will work for the purposes of this ask.

"Hi, I love this _____ [maker and model of vehicle] that I saw on your [website/lot], but another dealer in _____ [location] has the same vehicle for _____ [amount]. Can you match or beat that price?"

If they say no . . .

"That's too bad. I was hoping to save myself the drive, but that's a lot of money on your sticker. I'm on a budget, so I guess I'll be on my way. Thank you for your time."

If they say no but indicate willingness to work with you in another way . . .

"Well, price matters most to me, so if we can knock costs down in other ways, I'm willing to have the discussion."

At this point, you can provide alternative ways to save.

Scenario 1: Financing

"I'm preapproved for financing. If you can match the rate and knock a bit off their price, I'd be willing to finance through you instead. I know you make money when that happens, so let's make it a win for everyone."

Scenario 2: Your Trade-In

"Let's talk about my trade-in. I probably can make more money by selling it myself rather than trading it to you, but you guys make money off it after you get it. If you increase the amount you'll give me for my old _____ [maker and model of old vehicle], I'll do the trade here, and everyone wins."

Scenario 3: Fees

"I see a lot of fees here. Some of them have to stay, I know, but can we lose some of them? Which fees can you waive or reduce for me?"

Scenario 4: Add-Ons

> "This vehicle has a lot of add-ons that I don't want. What can we do to get rid of them and lower the price at the same time?"

If you receive an offer or counter but don't know immediately what you want to do . . .

> "Thank you. You've given me a lot to think about. How long will this offer be valid?"

The salesperson likely will pressure you to decide then and there because the salesperson knows that, if you walk out the door, you might never return. Don't succumb to the pressure, though. When rushed, people usually make bad decisions. If you need time, take it. Chances are probably good that, if you return the next day, you still can get the same deal. If you do head for the exit, they may throw their "last, best" offer at you before you leave to see whether they can convince you to sign on the dotted line.

Q *What if they deny your request?*

A You have options. You could settle for the initial offer and call it a day. You could threaten to walk in hopes that they suddenly decide to work with you. You also could try another dealership for a salesperson more willing to bargain with you. When it comes to auto shopping, there're lots of fish in the sea. Don't settle for a bad deal just because you don't like the process. There's too much money at stake.

SUCCESS STORY

The last time he bought a car, Luís Rosa, a certified financial planner in Los Angeles, landed a better deal for financing by shopping around. His credit union preapproved him for financing, and then he went to the dealership. After test-driving a used car at a dealership in Henderson, Nevada—where he lived before moving to Southern California—he offered $24,000 for the vehicle. The dealership rejected his offer. They also discussed financing, but the dealer rate didn't beat the credit union. "I said, 'I'm willing to do the financing through you guys but still get the car for $24,000,'" Rosa says. "They went for that because they make money on the financing." Rosa took the slightly higher rate because he was willing to refinance later, if necessary. His primary aim was getting a lower price overall, which worked.

REDUCED PRICES FOR AUTO REPAIRS

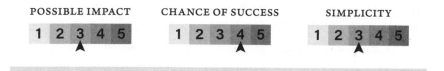

POSSIBLE IMPACT	CHANCE OF SUCCESS	SIMPLICITY
1 2 **3** 4 5	1 2 3 **4** 5	1 2 **3** 4 5

Q *What are you asking?*
A You're requesting a break, along with a detailed explanation of the importance or urgency of repairs recommended by a mechanic.

Q *How big a deal is it?*
A Even a small repair can cost hundreds, and bigger ones can run into the thousands. That can wreck a budget in a hurry. Asking the right questions, including whether you safely could delay a fix until a more financially convenient time, can make these unexpected expenses more manageable. Don't think, just because a charge runs $100 or less, that it isn't worth contesting or negotiating, either. "Some people don't realize, if they're like me, that the little things add up," Luís Rosa says. "They may let a $15 charge here and there slide, and then it adds up to a lot."

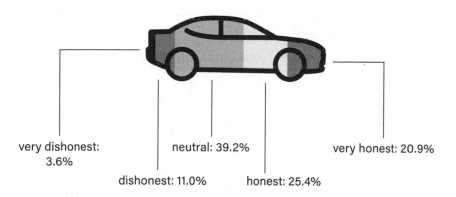

very dishonest: 3.6%

neutral: 39.2%

very honest: 20.9%

dishonest: 11.0%

honest: 25.4%

Among people surveyed, almost half rate auto-service providers as honest. (Numbers don't total 100 due to rounding, AutoNetTV)

Q *How likely is it that you will succeed?*

A Fairly likely. Every profession has bad apples, including mechanics. If you discover one, take your business elsewhere without hesitation. But a reputable mechanic will answer your questions, including whether you can delay a repair safely. Good mechanics understand that candor builds trust with customers, and trust underpins long-term relationships that can prove far more lucrative than any one-time fix. But far too few people ask. Scotty Reiss, founder of the Girls' Guide to Cars, says people are "intimidated and afraid" to speak frankly with mechanics. "It's a shame because people spend money that they shouldn't."

Q *Does asking pose any risks?*

A Deferring a repair could endanger your safety. If a mechanic says it's dangerous to drive your vehicle in its current condition or it could become unsafe quickly, have it fixed immediately. Your safety is worth more than any savings from shopping around. A much less significant risk: The mechanic could react poorly and talk down to you or worse. That situation can make for a few uncomfortable minutes that could be a blessing in disguise. If a mechanic reacts that way after a simple question or two, you probably don't want to trust your vehicle to that person.

Q *Does not succeeding pose any risks?*

A You could spend more money than you want or more time searching for a second opinion from a mechanic whom you trust. But don't let these risks deter you from asking questions and becoming a more informed customer.

Q *How do you do it?*

A The process starts well before you set foot in the mechanic's garage. Consult your owner's manual or search online to determine what maintenance the manufacturer recommends for your vehicle, based on its age and mileage. "Being aware of what you need to do to take care of your car is probably the first step to avoiding an expensive surprise," Reiss says. "That expensive surprise could be just the maintenance that the manufacturer says you need to do." That maintenance could include changing the oil, replacing belts or pumps, rotating or replacing tires, and so on. As all vehicles age, they need this kind of attention, so it's reasonable for a mechanic to recommend doing them. You can delay some repairs safely, so it's also reasonable for you to ask questions.

When dropping the vehicle off, Reiss recommends requesting an itemized estimate. Mechanics often rattle off a few words and a price over the phone, but you should ask for more. The mechanic should provide a detailed summary, including costs of labor, parts, fees, and taxes. Use that to frame your discussion. For example, you could tell them not to do a specific service, ask for a lower cost on a specific part, or request that they waive a particular fee. "I had a bill once where they charged me $200 for a diagnosis, and I already knew what the problem was," Reiss says. "So I said, 'Do you really need to charge me for that? Because that's why I brought it in,' and he took it off the bill." Even if they don't cooperate to that degree, the detailed estimate still has value because you can use it to compare pricing for a second or third opinion, and you can use it to track what needs fixing when.

SCRIPTS

When leaving your vehicle with the mechanic, describe the problem, then...

> "When you've identified the problem, please send an itemized estimate, including costs for parts, labor, fees, and taxes to [your email address]. Also indicate how long the estimate will remain valid."

If the mechanic recommends multiple repairs beyond what will fix the immediate problem...

> "Thank you for these recommendations. Which of these repairs are absolutely necessary now? I'm on a tight budget and would prefer to delay any nonessential fixes." If you recognize some of the repairs as manufacturer-recommended maintenance, say so. You can be specific with your ask.

If they say that all the repairs are necessary . . .

> "As I said, my budget's tight, and I'd like to put off some of these repairs until I have more flexibility. Will I be putting my safety at risk if we do any of these later?"

If you're trying to negotiate costs on an itemized estimate . . .

> "Thank you for the detailed estimate, which was very helpful. I have a few questions about what you sent." Dive into specifics about what you want to negotiate. For example:

> "I'm happy to pay the labor costs for your team's hard work, but do you have any wiggle room on the price of parts? You listed _____ [name of part] for _____ [amount]. Would you be willing to take _____ [negotiation amount] instead? My research shows that's a more reasonable price."

> "Could alternative parts work for this repair? Would a rebuilt part cost less but work as well?"

> "Would you be willing to waive the _____ [name of] fee?"

If you're certain that the vehicle is safe to drive and want another opinion on the repairs . . .

> "Thank you so much for your help with this. Don't do any of these repairs yet, though. I want to get a second opinion on what needs to be done. When will my vehicle be available to pick up?"

Q *What if they deny your request?*

A If a mechanic remains unwilling to answer questions or provide an itemized estimate, take your business elsewhere. That step can prove problematic if your vehicle isn't drivable, however. You could need to call a tow truck to move the vehicle from one garage to the next. Still, in that case, the extra effort and cost are worth knowing that you're working with a mechanic who has your best interests in mind.

If a communicative mechanic won't budge on price, seek a second or even third opinion. Before you do, decide whether the time and inconvenience of that step seem worth it. If you're haggling over $25, it might not be; if you're trying to knock a thousand or more off the bill, it might.

A relationship with a mechanic is just that: a relationship, and it can last for years. Vehicle problems can cause considerable chaos quickly, so trusting a professional is a big deal. As with any relationship, trust takes time, openness, and honesty to grow, and it all starts with a few basic questions.

SUCCESS STORY

Jenn Jones used to work in the finance office for a car dealership. Since then, she's written numerous articles to help people avoid getting ripped off by dealers and mechanics. She says that "90 percent of the salespeople you find at car dealerships" want to help, but she's had run-ins with bad apples, just like everyone else, including a time when she took her car in for an oil change and the representative tried to upsell her. "They told me, 'Hey, your oil was like sludge. It had really bad consistency. You need to do a $500 engine flush.'"

Jones knew she didn't need that flush, but instead of saying no, she offered the excuse that her budget was tight. Instead of backing down, the representative said she could consider one of the personal loans that the company offered. According to Jones, using those loans can turn into an "egregious mistake" because of the high interest rates and fees. She stuck to her guns, however, refusing the flush. "The next time I went to get my oil changed, the next guy complimented me on my vehicle maintenance," Jones says with a laugh. "I was like, 'Oh, this other person said my oil was sludge.' He said, 'Really? Interesting. He tried to pull a fast one on you.'"

JENN JONES'S FIVE TIPS FOR DEALING WITH VEHICLE MAINTENANCE AND REPAIR

- **Solicit recommendations.** This tip may seem super-obvious, but it's important. Good mechanics are worth their weight in gold, and people love to talk about their favorites. Ask family and friends and/or post a call for recommendations on social media.
- **Ask for an itemized list.** Details matter. A list can give you time to review, consider, and research the recommended repairs or services. A detailed list allows you to comparison-shop each item and ask another mechanic for a second opinion and a second quote.
- **When in doubt, Google it.** The Internet can offer lots of help to those of us who don't know a lot about cars. A quick search of routine maintenance schedules by maker and model can go a long way toward helping you call foul on an upsell.
- **Stick to your guns.** Salespeople often learn to find a reason behind a no and give solutions until you say yes. If you know you don't need something, don't let them talk you into it. If pressed, say "The maintenance schedule doesn't call for that yet" or "No, I'm not doing that now."
- **Refuse offers for personal loans.** If an "amazing" finance deal could help you afford to have work done, say thanks but no thanks. Technicians often receive financial rewards for originating such loans and have no incentive to help you pay less in interest or fees. If you legitimately need financing help, you likely can find better deals elsewhere.

LOWER FUNERAL COSTS

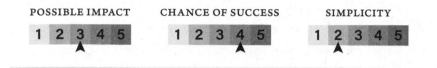

POSSIBLE IMPACT

| 1 | 2 | **3** | 4 | 5 |

CHANCE OF SUCCESS

| 1 | 2 | 3 | **4** | 5 |

SIMPLICITY

| 1 | **2** | 3 | 4 | 5 |

Q *What are you asking?*
A You're requesting a lower rate for funerary services.

Q *How big a deal is it?*
A The average cost of a funeral today runs between $7,000 and $8,000.[55] That big expense comes at an intensely emotional and often chaotic time.

Average cost of line items	
funeral service fee	$2,300
vault	$1,572
cremation casket	$1,310
embalming	$775
funeral home staff for ceremony	$515
funeral home rental	$450
funeral home staff for viewing	$450
hearse	$350
transportation of remains	$350
urn	$295
cosmetic services	$275
pamphlets and materials	$183
transportation for the family	$150

Average costs for funeral service line items, according to 2021 data from the National Funeral Directors Association.

Add financial challenges to the mix, and any savings that you can secure make sense.

Q   *How likely is it that you will succeed?*
A   Greg Johnson, a former funeral home director in Indiana, says family-owned funeral homes may have more flexibility than larger, corporate-owned facilities. "I worked in smaller funeral homes, which was good because we sometimes could negotiate with people who needed help," he says. "My boss was right there. It wasn't corporate, so we had a little more leeway in how we could help people out as far as pricing." Still, even with larger companies, it's worth asking whether lower rates are possible. Even if the funeral home isn't willing to move on the price of specific items on their price list, they likely will present you with lower-cost alternatives or even suggest some costs that you might be able to eliminate if you're willing to do some things yourself. "There are lots of ways that you can save money and still have a personalized, beautiful goodbye," says Brittany DeMarco-Furman, a licensed funeral director and the marketing manager at Glenville Funeral Home in Glenville, New York.[56]

Either way, your chances look better if you plan and comparison-shop rather than scrambling to find a place after your loved one has died.

Q   *Does asking pose any risks?*
A   No, and if you do receive a lot of pushback from asking a few simple questions, take your business elsewhere. If you're talking with a loved one about planning a funeral, you could encounter some awkwardness or even anger. Not many people want to talk about their own mortality, even if planning makes good sense.

Q   *Does not succeeding pose any risks?*
A   Other than potentially upsetting a loved one, the only real risk is paying full price for the services in question.

Q *How do you do it?*

A Consider the services that you or your loved one wants. Burial or cremation? Formal service in the funeral home or small gathering at a home or place of worship? Military or civilian? Thinking through these and other questions ahead of time, even just on the way to the meeting, will help you make more informed decisions.

If you're planning, shop around at a few different funeral homes, including at least one family-owned, independent facility. If you're not sure whether they're corporate or family-owned, ask them directly. You also can ask whether the owners work at the facility and if it's possible to speak with them. Regulations require funeral homes to provide detailed price lists to consumers who contact them in person or over the phone. They don't have to post prices online (at time of publication), though the Federal Trade Commission is considering amending the law to mandate that disclosure as well. With that in mind, it should be easy to compare prices among facilities.[57] When you have those price lists, negotiations can begin. If your loved one has passed already, shopping around still makes sense. It might not be realistic, though, given other demands on your time. If that's the case, consider deputizing a trusted friend or family member to collect the information from the various companies for you.

Cremation may be the biggest way to save on funeral costs. That action alone can save thousands, but it might not make for an easy decision.[58] Religious implications and other considerations could apply. The good news, however, is that you have plenty of other options for saving. If a funeral home isn't willing to work with you to operate in or close to your price range, consider that a major red flag.

DeMarco-Furman advises that using the funeral home's in-stock inventory can help people save. In that instance, you'd buy a casket already in the building rather than having them ship one in. "Here's a little secret from funeral homes," she adds. "We want to get rid of the merchandise."

You can save by opting for a concrete grave liner instead of a burial vault, she also suggests. State and federal law typically don't mandate using one of these products, but cemeteries often require them because they support the weight of the soil above the casket, keeping the site from collapsing, which could damage the casket and create dangerous sinkholes at ground level.[59] Burial vaults typically run much fancier and pricier than concrete grave liners, so the latter option can be a smart, lower-cost alternative.

"A funeral director is an important role," DeMarco-Furman says, "but that doesn't mean that you need us for everything if money is an issue." Her cost-saving suggestions also include:

- Save on flowers by going to a local market or a backyard garden instead of a florist.
- Assemble your own slideshow instead of paying hundreds for a funeral home's memorial montage package.
- Skip the limo and use your own vehicle.
- Post a full-length obituary to the funeral home's website rather than paying to run it in the newspaper.

Whether you're planning or scrambling, it's OK to tell the funeral director your or your loved one's story. Depending on circumstances, they may be willing to work with you on price or they may recommend organizations that could help. For example, veterans may qualify for financial assistance from the Department of Veterans Affairs and could be eligible for free burial in a state or national cemetery.[60] Others may qualify for other benefits. Various charities and religious organizations could help as well. Any reputable funeral director can point you toward institutions that might be able to help.

Note: Some funeral homes often pitch the idea of paying in advance to lock in costs and save loved ones the headache and expense when the time comes. But the not-for-profit Funeral Consumers Alliance says, "It is usually not wise to pay ahead. No matter how attractive the business makes it sound, there are serious drawbacks to prepaying," including losing that money if the company goes out of business or you want to move the service to another facility.[61] Planning can save you money, but don't prepay.

SCRIPTS

When comparing prices at various facilities

> "You have a beautiful space, and I know your team would do a great job, but the prices are a little higher than I budgeted. In researching options, I saw that _____ [other facility] has better rates on a few line items. Can you beat or match your competitors' prices?"

If they present a counteroffer that's still too high . . .

> "I appreciate you working with me on this, but I was hoping you at least could match the other place's price on this. What can we do to make that happen?"

If they say they don't match prices . . .

> "That's disappointing. What else can we do to lower prices to a level that fits my budget? Otherwise, I may have to go elsewhere." At this point, consider telling them more about your story and your financial situation. You don't need to go into minute detail, but briefly mentioning the financial bind caused by your loved one's death or end-of-life medical care can make your point and establish a more personal connection.

When trying to negotiate without price matching . . .

> "You have a beautiful space, and I know your team would do a great job, but the prices are a little higher than I budgeted. What sort of flexibility do you have on pricing?"

If they present a counteroffer that's still too high . . .

> "I appreciate you working with me on this, but that's still a stretch for my budget. What can we do to get that down a little bit more?"

If they won't negotiate at all . . .

> "That's disappointing. What else can we do to lower prices to a level that fits my budget? Otherwise, I may have to go elsewhere." Again, consider telling your story and sharing details about your loved one.

Q *What if they deny your request?*

A If your loved one has died already and you're scrambling to arrange the service, you may be stuck paying full price because you might not have time to shop around. If you're planning, however, that puts you ahead of the game, so walking out might be your best decision, especially if you didn't feel a personal connection with the folks with whom you spoke. If you have the time, another company might treat you better.

REDUCED PRICES FROM RETAILERS

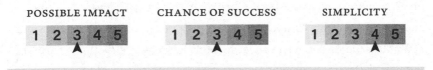

POSSIBLE IMPACT   CHANCE OF SUCCESS   SIMPLICITY

1 2 **3** 4 **5**   1 2 **3** 4 **5**   1 2 **3** **4** **5**

Q *What are you asking?*
A You're requesting lower costs when buying something from a store.

Q *How big a deal is it?*
A You could save hundreds, primarily on big-ticket items such as appliances and furniture.

Q *How likely is it that you will succeed?*
A If you try to haggle over jeans and a shirt at a chain store in the mall, you probably won't get anywhere. You'll have a better chance at negotiating a lower price on a sofa and mattress from a family-owned furniture store. Appliances and furniture tend to have more wiggle room on price, says Kristin McGrath, an Austin-based shopping expert with RetailMeNot. Also, locally owned stores may prove more likely to work with you. "You're increas-

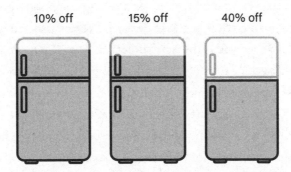

10% off   15% off   40% off

Floor models don't have standard discounts, but most sell for between 10 and 15 percent off, and some, depending on condition or age, can receive a 40 percent discount. (HomeServe.com)

ing your ability to negotiate, the smaller you shop," she says. Timing also can play a role. HouseLogic recommends buying a snow blower, for example, in March or April, after the weather warms.[62] It's like buying Halloween candy on November 1 or an artificial Christmas tree on December 26. You also could land discounts without even asking. For example, some retailers automatically send discounts if you leave items in an online shopping cart without completing the purchase, though there's no guarantee that will happen.

Measure success not just by the final sticker price, says shopping expert Andrea Woroch. "If they can't offer you as big a discount in terms of money off, that's when you probe further," she says. "Can you get free delivery, free installation, or a discount on those services?" Eliminating any of those costs can make just as much difference as a lower sticker price. So can learning about an upcoming sale or freebies, such as pillows when buying a box spring and mattress. But none of that will happen unless you ask.

Q *Does asking pose any risks?*
A Other than a few moments of possible awkwardness, no one is going to boot you from the store or not sell you the item if you ask for a deal.

Q *Does not succeeding pose any risks?*
A Worst case, you pay full price.

Q *How do you do it?*
A Shopping expert Trae Bodge suggests asking about sales or other discounts. It's easy to miss those types of deals, but a sales associate at the store should be able to steer you in the right direction. "It's good for consumers to ask a sales associate at a store, 'Hey, are there any offers that I could apply to this product if I decide to buy it?'" That's a good, low-pressure way to start a conversation with the associate. If deals are available, you might not need to negotiate further. If not, continue the conversation by asking whether they ever accept a lower amount for the item, such as confirmation of a competitor's price.

From there, you may need to get creative. If they turn you down, consider asking about a display model, free delivery and/or installation, or some other relevant perk. If, after a few minutes, the conversation clearly is going nowhere, let it go. Badgering a sales associate who either can't or won't help creates only unnecessary tension.

As with most negotiations, proper preparation pays. Do your homework, understand the typical price for the item, and find out what else, if anything, often comes with it, such as delivery and installation. Role-play the conversation with a friend or relative. Look at reviews of the store to see whether other customers talk about having negotiated there successfully. All these strategies will give you confidence when the time comes, and confidence can make all the difference.

Picking the right person also helps, says Bodge. "Read the room. If you see someone rushing, that's not the person to ask. You want to ask the one moving slowly, stocking shelves, maybe dusting, someone who seems calm—especially if you're shy. If someone's dashing by, don't expect them to stop and look in their computer for an extra sale."

SCRIPTS

"Hi there, can you tell me if you have any sales or discounts on the _____ [item] right now or coming soon?"

If there's a sale coming up . . .

"Oh, that's interesting. Thanks for letting me know. Could I get that discount now, or do I need to wait and come back?"

If there aren't any sales or deals . . .

"Got it. While I have you, does store policy ever allow you to accept a lower amount?—like matching a competitor's price."

Again, this tactic works primarily for big-ticket items, though there's no harm in asking anywhere.

If they say they don't accept lower amounts, you can try one of several responses, depending on the item . . .

"Understood. One last question for you . . .

What about a display model? Do you sell those at a lower price?"

What about delivery and installation? Do you ever include those for free?"

What about that _____ [ancillary item(s)]? Could you throw [that/ those] in as well?"

Q *What if they deny your request?*
A You have plenty of options. You can come back a few days later and see whether another associate might be more willing to work with you. You could try another store. You could search online for a better deal, though, for bigger items including appliances and furniture, buying online can mean waiting far longer than buying in person. Worst-case scenario: You're stuck paying the sticker price at the store, which likely isn't the end of the world.

SUCCESS STORY

Kristin McGrath and her husband wanted a sofa and two loveseats for their living room. "We went to a local furniture store and told the salesperson what materials and color we wanted," McGrath says. "She didn't have what we wanted as a matching set but made some suggestions similar to the color we wanted in the material we wanted. We really liked a set that wasn't the exact color we wanted but figured we could use throw pillows and blankets to make it work in our space. We told the sales rep that we probably were going to look at some other places to see if we could get a closer color match but might be back later. The rep told us some more about the set, how well made it was and that we could have it delivered that week, which other places might have trouble doing. We already knew from shopping around that quick delivery was going to be rare.

"We calculated the grand total for the three pieces (sofa + loveseats). It was a few hundred more than we wanted to spend. I didn't feel comfortable asking for a few hundred dollars off, so we rounded down, essentially asking for a little more than a $100 discount. I just said, 'We like it, but it's more than we were planning to spend. Could you do it for $X,XXX?' We got a pretty quick 'Yeah, we can do that,' so maybe I should have asked for a bigger discount. But we really did like the set, we knew from our previous shopping that it was comparatively a good deal for the quality, and $100 is nothing to sniff at when you're furnishing an entire home.

"A small $100 to $200 discount or free small-ticket item thrown in gets someone to hand over the credit card and gets the store $1,000+ in business that they otherwise might lose to a competitor if the shopper decides to 'shop around a bit.'"

A LOWER FEE FOR A KIDS' ACTIVITY

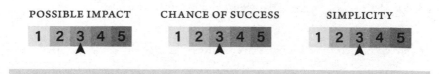

POSSIBLE IMPACT   CHANCE OF SUCCESS   SIMPLICITY

1 2 **3** 4 5   1 2 **3** 4 5   1 2 **3** 4 5

Q *What are you asking?*

A You're asking for reduced sign-up or participation costs for an extracurricular activity for your little one, such as sports, scouting, or arts programs.

Q *How big a deal is it?*

A These activities can cost crazy money, sometimes thousands per year, so a break on costs can offer significant breathing room for a tight budget. The bigger deal consists of the discount making it possible for your kiddo to participate in activities otherwise financially beyond reach. These activities can have an incredibly positive impact on kids' lives—physically, mentally, emotionally—so being able to open that door literally can change their lives for the better.

Q *How likely is it that you will succeed?*

A With some activities, you can swing a discount, but not with all. Mark Eby, CEO of the Oklahoma City Police Athletic League, says that not-for-

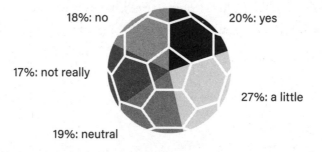

18%: no   20%: yes

17%: not really

27%: a little

19%: neutral

Do your kids' activities strain your finances? *Numbers don't total 100 due to rounding.* (LendingTree)

profit sports leagues around the nation work with families all the time to make it possible for kids to play. "If the coaches and the people involved in the leagues really want to help kids, they're going to figure out a way to get them involved," he says. The opportunity for savings goes beyond just sports, too. The Girl Scouts of America website says, "We don't want fees to be a barrier, so don't hesitate to ask your local Girl Scout council about financial assistance."[63] Other youth-focused not-for-profit organizations may include similar language on their websites, but even if they don't, it's worth asking.

Not all organizations are quite so philanthropic, however. Anton Marchand—of the Greater Brooklyn Youth Sports Club, a scout for the NBA's Cleveland Cavaliers, and cofounder of the Conrad McRae Youth League and Rose Classic basketball tournaments in New York City—says that higher-end youth sports leagues that require travel and often serve as gateways to college scholarships or even professional playing prove far less likely to work with families struggling with sky-high costs.[64] "I don't see that very often, honestly," he says. "It's become such a lucrative business." Other types of activities—culinary schools, high-end language or music lessons, robotics camps—have similar problems with too many businesses trying to separate parents from their money. But that doesn't mean that you still shouldn't ask for a break. Just make sure to adjust your expectations when you do.

Q *Does asking pose any risks?*
A You may feel uncomfortable with the vulnerability of asking for help. That feeling's OK, though. We grow most when we push beyond our comfort zone. Plus, you're doing it for your kids to help them pursue a passion. Keeping that in mind should help you power through any nerves that you might feel.

Q *Does not succeeding pose any risks?*
A Your kid might not get to participate. Worse things in life happen, but these extracurricular activities matter. They can boost kids' confidence and self-esteem. They can help them learn to solve problems and work coopera-

tively with others. They can teach them discipline. The list goes on. All that makes it worth asking, even if you might not succeed.

Q   *How do you do it?*

A   Tell your story. Don't be afraid of your own vulnerability. You don't have to share every last detail, but divulging some information about your financial situation and your kids' passion for the activity can create a connection with the people who can help. When it comes to sports leagues, "Narrow it down to why you want your son or daughter to be involved in the sport, why it's important to you," Eby says. "Explain that part of it first, then say, 'I'd love to do this, but I just don't have the means right now.' A lot of people will help you." That strategy holds true for other activities, too. To get the help, you may need to provide some documentation, but help can come in the form of scholarships, grants, or even just waived fees. Help also could come with requirements, including volunteering, perhaps coaching or chaperoning, working a concession stand, helping clean up after events, fundraising, or even contributing professional skills that you might have, such as accounting, social media expertise, or web design. A family struggling with a budget might not have more free time than income, but consider those options.

SCRIPTS

> "Hi there, my child _____ [name] absolutely loves _____ [activity]. [S/he] has a real passion for it, and I love that [s/he] loves it. It has helped [him/her] in so many ways. [if appropriate] [S/he] has friends who participate, and they say it's amazing. We really want [him/her] to be part of it, but we don't have the extra money right now to cover it. Is there anything we can do to enable [him/her] to join in?"

If they agree to waive the fees . . .

> "Thank you so much. This means the world to us. Please let us know if there's anything you ever need from us."

Not all will, but a representative from the organization may ask questions about your financial situation, perhaps requesting a pay stub or other documentation of the hardship. Some simply will waive any relevant fees or offer some other form of assistance. If not, consider volunteering.

> "My family would be more than happy to volunteer our time to the organization if that would make a difference. [Consider mentioning options such as coaching, chaperoning, working concessions, fundraising, helping with clean-up, etc.] Whatever we could do to help. We just appreciate the opportunity."

Q *What if they deny your request?*

A You can ask a second time. Consider contacting someone with higher ranking in the organization than the first person. You don't have any guarantee of better luck, but it's worth asking. If they won't budge and your kiddo's heart is set on participating, consider other ways to raise money or lower costs. Second-hand equipment costs a lot less than brand new. Sacrificing some nice-to-haves, such as streaming services and eating out, can help, too. A crowdsourced fundraiser among family and close friends can help—particularly when timed with a birthday or gift-giving holiday—as can a side hustle done by the parent(s) or the kid.

Ultimately, though, you may need to shop around. Many areas have lots of options for kids interested in coding, cooking, dance, government, sports, theater, and most any activity you can imagine. If your first option isn't willing to work with you, another might be. Different organizations could have downsides—more travel, lower-quality facilities, fewer friends involved—but if the goal is your kid participating at an affordable price, those inconveniences shouldn't matter much.

REDUCING THE RATE ON YOUR CABLE, INTERNET, PHONE, OR STREAMING BILL

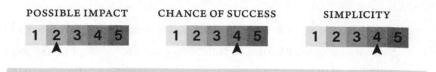

POSSIBLE IMPACT   CHANCE OF SUCCESS   SIMPLICITY

1 **2** 3 4 5   1 2 3 **4** 5   1 2 3 **4** 5

Q *What are you asking?*
A You're requesting to pay less for staying connected to the rest of the world.

Q *How big a deal is it?*
A Not a huge deal monthly, but, unlike many other asks in this book, this one doesn't lead to just a one-time win. Small savings every month add up to significant money in a year or more. If you knock $10 off one of these monthly bills, that keeps $120 in your pocket over the course of one year and $240 over two years.

Annual Cell Phone Bill Costs

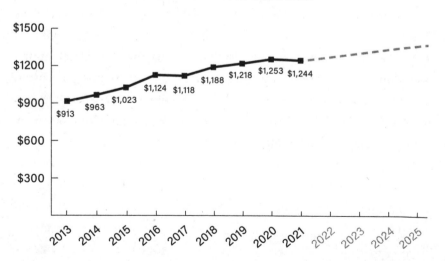

(US Bureau of Labor Statistics)

Q *How likely is it that you will succeed?*

A Telecom businesses compete fiercely with one another, and they know you have options. They likely won't want to lose you over a few dollars per month. Shannah Game, host of the *Everyone's Talkin' Money* podcast, said that she calls her Internet and cell phone providers at least once a year in search of better deals and succeeds more often than not. "Probably eight of ten times, I save at least $10 or more," she says "That's real money." Your experience may vary, but the bottom line is that these companies will work with many customers who take the time to ask.

Q *Does asking pose any risks?*

A Nothing major. They receive these kinds of calls all the time, and their representatives know how to handle them. The only real risk is that you may have to sit through a few minutes of the representative trying to upsell you on pricier products before eventually agreeing to cut you a deal. That situation can prove frustrating, but it could be worth it if the savings are big enough.

Q *Does not succeeding pose any risks?*

A Only that you keep paying the same price or you have to find a new service provider. Neither possibility should deter you from asking.

Q *How do you do it?*

A A little advance legwork can make the call easier. Visit the provider's website to see whether they're offering any promotions to new or current customers. Depending on what you find, you might not even need to pick up your phone. Also check their competitors' sites for offers. That intel should frame your conversation with them. You may not need to use it to secure a better deal, but preparation instills confidence when the time comes, and that's important, too.

The company may counteroffer. Rather than lowering the cost of your current plan, they could offer a higher-tier plan at roughly the same price. They could offer a free subscription to one of their parent company's services, such as a cell phone provider offering a free year of a streaming service. It's impossible to anticipate all possible counteroffers, but you can prepare by deciding, in advance, what matters most to you in the deal. Are you looking only to pay less, or do you want more bang for your buck, even if your overall costs don't change? Answering that question ahead of time can guide your decision if a counteroffer comes.

SCRIPTS

> "Hi, I've been a customer for _____ [number] years, and I'm looking to reduce some of my monthly expenses. I'm calling to see whether you might have a better plan for me. Who on your team can I speak with about this?"

If you prefer playing hardball right off the bat . . .

> "Hi, I've been a customer for _____ [number] years, and I'm looking to reduce some of my monthly expenses. Your competitors have some offers that are a better deal than the one I have. [Give the name of the provider(s) and a few meaningful details of the offer(s).] Before I jump ship, what can you do to help me lower my costs?"

If they agree to lower your rate . . .

> "Thank you. I appreciate you working with me. Please send a confirmation email to me at [your email address]."

If they make an acceptable counteroffer . . .

> "Thank you for your flexibility. I appreciate it, and that offer sounds good to me. I'll take it. Please send a confirmation email to me at [your email address]."

If you're unsure about whether to accept the counteroffer . . .

> "Thank you for the offer. It sounds good, but I need to think about it. How long will it be valid?"

If they're unwilling to work with you at all . . .

> "That's disappointing. I've been a customer for ____ [number] years. My research shows that you're offering new customers a better deal than my plan. If you're not willing to work with me on this, I'm sure that one of your competitors will be. Who else on your team can I speak with about this?"

Q *What if they deny your request?*
A You have three options:

- Try again in a few days and see whether you have better luck the second time.
- Accept that you have to keep paying the same rate.
- Change companies.

None of those choices is right or wrong, nor is any of them final. If you change companies, your previous provider likely will contact you with a better offer. Exactly that happened to shopping expert Andrea Woroch at the end of a fruitless negotiation with an Internet provider. "Finally, I did get an email from Comcast that said, 'OK, we don't want to let you go. Would you consider this?' and I did get a better discount." It wasn't as big a discount as she initially wanted, but it was worth accepting to avoid the headache of changing providers—an important point, too. Ultimately, these decisions aren't about money. They're about *value*. If making a change requires too much time and effort, it may not be worth it, even if it could save you a few bucks.

SUCCESS STORY

Just like phone bills, insurance bills tend to creep steadily upward. Marcus Garrett, author of *Debt Free or Die Trying*, spotted that his monthly insurance bill had increased by $6. It wasn't a hardship, but he wanted to know why he had to pay more. After six months, he decided to act. "I called, and they didn't have a reason" for the increase. "They were like, 'Oh yeah, you're right.'" They credited the $36 back to his account and, going forward, reduced the bill by $6.

For many folks, $6 a month might not be worth their time, but there's always value in asking why a bill increased without an obvious reason. "A lot of times, people assume they raised it for a reason," Garrett says. "'I might not understand the reason, but there's a reason behind it.' That's optimistic because the reason may just be that they can." Also, remember that small increases add up. That one call saved Garrett $72 that year. For a tight budget, that's a meaningful chunk of money. You probably have at least five to ten monthly bills: house, electricity, car or transit, insurance, phone, Internet, gym, and more. Now we're talking serious money for anyone. If a couple of three-minute phone calls can stop increases on just a couple of those bills, that's definitely worth your time.

A LOWER FITNESS MEMBERSHIP RATE

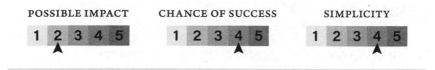

POSSIBLE IMPACT	CHANCE OF SUCCESS	SIMPLICITY
1 **2** 3 4 5	1 2 3 **4** 5	1 2 3 **4** 5

Q *What are you asking?*
A You're requesting to pay less for your gym, yoga studio, or other fitness center dues, including lower monthly payments and fewer fees.

Q *How big a deal is it?*
A The amount you save each month or at sign-up probably won't change your life, but, as with your phone or streaming bill, those savings can add up to real money over time. So it's worth doing.

Q *How likely is it that you will succeed?*
A If you're trying to haggle with the hottest new gym in town, don't hold your breath. In many other cases, competition runs so fierce among fitness facilities that that they'll listen when you ask for a better deal. Even if they don't give you a lower monthly rate, they might waive an initiation fee or an annual fee or throw in some free merch, such as a branded T-shirt or water bottle, for your trouble. Ask at the end of the month or quarter because that's when sales reps need to hit their quotas, making them more willing to haggle.

Q *Does asking pose any risks?*
A Nope.

Q *Does not succeeding pose any risks?*
A With a small gym or a personal trainer, pushing too hard or lowballing too low could start the relationship on the wrong foot. You might not want to keep pressing if they say no the first time, but that doesn't mean that you shouldn't ask at all.

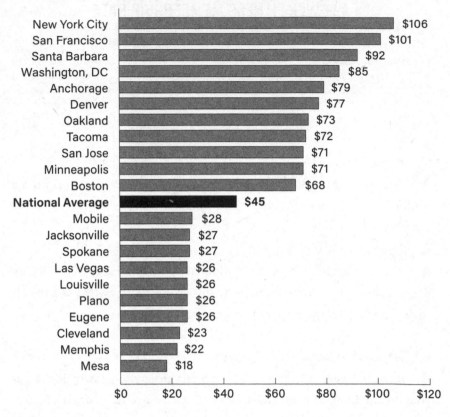

Monthly Gym Memberships in 2022

New York City	$106
San Francisco	$101
Santa Barbara	$92
Washington, DC	$85
Anchorage	$79
Denver	$77
Oakland	$73
Tacoma	$72
San Jose	$71
Minneapolis	$71
Boston	$68
National Average	**$45**
Mobile	$28
Jacksonville	$27
Spokane	$27
Las Vegas	$26
Louisville	$26
Plano	$26
Eugene	$26
Cleveland	$23
Memphis	$22
Mesa	$18

Average costs vary widely. (TotalShape.com with data from Numbeo)

Q *How do you do it?*

A For waiving initiation fees, just ask nicely. If you get pushback, don't be afraid to tell your story. Perhaps your budget allows for the monthly membership fees but not the initiation fee. Maybe money's tight because your kid just started daycare. Perhaps you just landed a new job after having reduced income for a while. Stories create connections, and connections can lead to better deals. Don't be afraid to try.

Monthly rates are a different story. Larger and franchised gyms probably don't have the power to tweak the rate, which the head office sets, but you can stack the odds in your favor. If you've seen ads promoting lower rates, mention them. Agreeing to a longer contract may help, too, and agreeing to pay the annual contract upfront might help even more. Timing may play a role as well. Consider waiting until the end of the month to join. Who you know also may matter, as Nicolette Amarillas, a trainer in New York, discovered. "I knew others who had memberships for a cheaper cost than the current membership price and asked to be brought on at that cheaper rate," she says. "It worked!"

SCRIPTS

> "I'd love to join your gym, but the fees are a little above what my budget will allow. Who can I speak with about getting a lower monthly rate?"

If they say they can't adjust the monthly rate and you want to play hardball, walk away. That could increase the odds that they'll work with you, but it might not work. Otherwise . . .

> "That's too bad. As I said, the cost is a little more than I can manage right now. Who else can I speak with about this?"
>
> **OR**
>
> "That's too bad. As I said, the cost is a little more than I can manage right now. If I signed a longer contract, could you lower the cost?"
>
> **OR**
>
> "That's too bad. As I said, the cost is a little more than I can manage right now. If we can't change the monthly rate, can you eliminate the initiation and/or annual fee?"

If they counteroffer . . .

> "Thank you. I appreciate you working with me on this, but that's still more than I'm looking to pay. I think my request is reasonable. What else can we do to get the price down?"
>
> **OR if they counter with merchandise rather than a discount . . .**
>
> "I appreciate the offer, but I need the lower price to fit my budget. What else can we do to get the price down?"

Q *What if they deny your request?*

A Walk away. If you do and they have your contact info, you likely will hear from them again. Gyms usually don't give up easily. Some of them aggressively pursue people who show even a little interest in joining. If you exercise patience, you may find that they're more willing to work with you the second time around.

REDUCED PRICES AT A MARKET OR GARAGE SALE

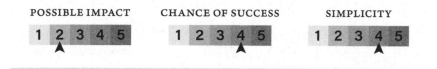

POSSIBLE IMPACT	CHANCE OF SUCCESS	SIMPLICITY
1 **2** 3 4 5	1 2 3 **4** 5	1 2 3 **4** 5

Q *What are you asking?*
A You're haggling when shopping second-hand.

Q *How big a deal is it?*
A This isn't change-your-life money, but if you shop regularly at these places, learning how to negotiate with sellers can save you plenty in the long run.

Q *How likely is it that you will succeed?*
A At a garage sale or other independent market, your chances look good, especially later in the day, when the stream of customers dwindles. "Remember that this person wants to get rid of their stuff," says Lisa Rowan, cohost of the *Pop Fashion* podcast and former owner of a vintage clothing store who sourced her merchandise at markets and sales.[65] In many cases, if the vendors can't sell the items, they'll donate them to charity or even throw them away. They probably won't turn you away if you offer a little less than the sticker price.

In an indoor facility, such as an antique mall or flea market, the likelihood doesn't look as strong. "Each merchant is going to be different because someone may be like, 'I'm moving. I need to get rid of this stuff,'" says shopping expert Trae Bodge, "and another person might be like, 'I'm here every week, and I don't care, so I'm not budging on my price.'" That uncertainty shouldn't keep you from negotiating, but it does mean that you should temper your expectations.

Q *Does asking pose any risks?*

A You could offend the seller, but at a one-off garage sale, that's no big deal. If that happens at an established market that you frequent, that's different. "If, for instance, you're a regular flea market shopper and you're lowballing people all the time, they're going to remember you," Rowan says. "They remember the people who constantly come around and offend their sensibilities."

Q *Does not succeeding pose any risks?*

A Beyond paying full price, the risks are minimal. Yes, you could offend the seller, who might refuse to deal with you, but that's not very likely.

Q *How do you do it?*

A If you're not sure whether prices are negotiable, ask. "The best way to ask someone without sounding like a jerk is: 'Are your prices firm, or do you negotiate?'" Rowan says. If there's wiggle room, jump in—strategically. Rowan suggests these tips:

- **Don't lowball too much.** It's one thing to suggest $2 for a $5 toy. Don't offer $20 for a $50 bicycle. Generally speaking, don't offer less than half the sticker price.
- **Buying more could mean saving more.** Vendors at these locations love nothing more than when someone buys a tableful of items. Their gratitude could land you extra savings. If you're buying eight items worth $50, you could say, 'Would you take $35 for the whole bunch?' There's a good chance they'll work with you.
- **If you're stuck on price, share your budget.** It's OK to tell sellers that you have a fixed amount for that purchase. That tells them that you're not haggling just to haggle. Depending on how close your limit comes to the best price, they may be willing to work with you.
- **The "best" price probably isn't.** The seller happily will sell the item at that price, but you still might have a little wiggle room to go a little lower. Again, don't start too low, but you don't have to settle for the seller's "final" counter either.

SCRIPTS

> "Hi there, you've got some great stuff here. Are your prices firm, or do you negotiate?"

If they're willing to negotiate . . .

> "I see the price for _____ [item] is _____ [sticker price]. How about _____ [negotiation price]?"

If they reject your first offer or counter higher than you want to pay . . .

> "Can you go lower? My budget for _____ [item] is _____ [budget limit], so I can't go higher than that number."

Q *What if they deny your request?*

A At markets and garage sales, you may have to pay full price. You could walk away, hoping to find something close to that item elsewhere at a lower price, but the randomness and unpredictability of these sales may reduce your options to the following: accept the price; leave and return later to see whether the item's still there *and* the seller is more willing to work with you; or walk away and forget about it.

SUCCESS STORY

Taylor Price, better known as PricelessTay to the million-plus Tik-Tokers who follow her for money tips, says she is "someone who loves a good negotiation. I always take advantage of any opportunity to haggle. Even if the answer is no, it never hurts to ask."[66]

On a recent visit to a street market in Washington, D.C., Price and her brother saved big on vintage clothing, and that savings began with some friendly banter. "It was a casual conversation about how the business got started and how she buys clothing in bulk," Price says, "so I said, 'Do you offer discounts for buyers like us? We're getting a few pieces here, and I'd love to work with you on it.'" That simple, easy approach landed her a 20 percent discount. "In my experience, 20 percent tends to be the maximum amount that can be negotiated, so I usually start there and adjust slightly based on the situation," she says.

Negotiation comes naturally to Price, but for those who struggle with it, she suggests a little preparation. Whether you're haggling in a farmer's market, a job interview, or anywhere else, Price says that "practicing what you want to say beforehand can be incredibly beneficial," so research prices and role-play with a trusted friend or relative to help make you as comfortable as possible when it comes time to negotiate for real.

LOWER PRICES AT THE GROCERY STORE

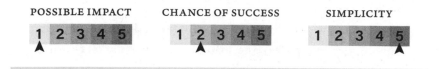

POSSIBLE IMPACT
1 **2** 3 **4** 5
▲

CHANCE OF SUCCESS
1 **2** 3 **4** 5
▲

SIMPLICITY
1 2 3 4 **5**
▲

Q *What are you asking?*
A You're requesting to pay less than sticker price when shopping at a supermarket.

Q *How big a deal is it?*
A You won't be able to negotiate significant savings, but little amounts add up.

Q *How likely is it that you will succeed?*
A Grocery stores sometimes price-match their competitors. You can try other strategies, but none of them has huge odds of success.

Q *Does asking pose any risks?*
A Other than irritating a cashier or the manager, no.

Q *Does not succeeding pose any risks?*
A No.

Q *How do you do it?*
A Just asking for a lower price, as you would at a furniture or appliance store, won't work at a grocery store. It *might* prove effective at the farmer's market, particularly at the end of market hours, but grocery stores are a different animal. With that in mind, you have a few options:

- **Ask if the store matches competitors' prices.** Grocery stores do this less than other retailers, but it can happen. You probably will need to provide proof of the lower price, such as a weekly flyer or website promotion, and even then some stores price-match only on certain items at certain times of year (turkeys before Thanksgiving or hams before Christmas).

- **Ask if a sale is coming that you could take advantage of early.** This option may prove more doable in a smaller market than a large chain store.
- **Ask for discounts on imperfect produce, soon-to-expire baked goods, or items already on clearance.**

Shopping expert Andrea Woroch suggests a totally different way to save your money at the grocery store: "Always check your receipt," which can prevent you from paying for clerical errors, such as a cashier accidentally entering the wrong code for produce, double-scanning a single item, the shelf price not matching the computer price, or the computer not applying a valid sale price. You'll never know if you don't look, and it's easier to fix the problem right away, while you're still in the store, than to go back later.

SCRIPTS

Asking for a price-match

"Hi, do you match your competitors' prices? I saw that _____ [competitor] is offering _____ [item] for a lower price than you do, and I'd like you to match that price." Then provide proof of the lower retail amount.

Asking for a future sales price

"Hi, do you know whether any of these items are going on sale soon? If so, could I get the lower price today?"

Asking for a discount on older or imperfect items

"Hi, I noticed that this _____ [item] is [nearing/at/past] its expiration date. Would you consider selling it at a lower price?"

OR

"Hi, I noticed that this _____ [item] is slightly damaged. Would you consider selling it at a lower price?"

Asking to fix an overcharge

> "Hi, I just checked out and was reviewing my receipt. It looks like I was overcharged for _____ [item]. [Provide details about whether the receipt shows an incorrect code, a double scan of a single item, or a price that doesn't match the shelf price or sale price.] Who can I speak with about fixing this?"

Q *What if they deny your request?*

A Of the above scenarios, only denial of an overcharge warrants further pushback. Do what you can to recoup that money, though, depending on the amount, it may not be worth your time. You also could shop around to see whether you have better luck at another grocery store. Most people stick to a favorite store, so it might take more than not getting a price-match to make you switch.

5. TRAVEL

Keep Trip Costs from Going Sky-High

How to ask for:

A REFUND FOR A CANCELLED FLIGHT

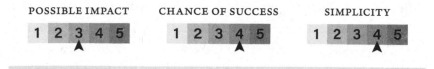

POSSIBLE IMPACT   CHANCE OF SUCCESS   SIMPLICITY

1 **2 3 4** 5   1 2 **3 4** 5   1 2 **3 4** 5
     ▲   ▲   ▲

Q *What are you asking?*
A You're requesting cash in exchange for a flight that didn't happen.

Q *How big a deal is it?*
A Fairly big, depending on the cost of the tickets and how often you fly. When an airline cancels a flight, the company typically gives you a credit for future flight rather than a refund because they want to keep your money rather than returning it. If you travel frequently with that airline, a credit might be fine. If you ask, they might throw in a food voucher or extra miles. But if you don't travel often or don't want the company to keep your money, getting that cash back matters.

Reimbursement rules for cancelled flights vary widely by country. In

ON TIME   CANCELLED

2019   79%   2%

2022   77%   3%

In 2022, flight cancellations spiked in December with the travel surge around the holidays. But even that small proportion of cancelled flights means *millions* of travelers with a legal right to a cash refund. (US Department of Transportation)[67]

Canada, the airline can offer a voucher instead of a refund, but "it must have a higher value than the monetary compensation required and cannot expire," per the Canadian Transportation Agency.[68] In Australia, the airline's responsibility for providing a refund depends, in part, on whether the cancellation lay within the airline's control, such as a mechanical issue or staffing problem, or not, such as inclement weather or a natural disaster.[69] In Britain, the airline must let you choose between a refund and an alternative flight.[70]

Q *How likely is it that you will succeed?*
A According to the US Department of Transportation's website, "Under US law, airlines and ticket agents have a legal obligation to refund consumers if the airline cancels or significantly changes a flight to, from, and within the United States and the passenger does not wish to accept the alternative offered. It is unlawful for an airline to refuse refunds and instead provide vouchers to such consumers."[71] In other words, the reason for the cancellation doesn't matter. If you want a refund, they *must* give it to you.

Q *Does asking pose any risks?*
A Beyond navigating counteroffers that you don't want, no.

Q *Does not succeeding pose any risks?*
A Getting a voucher instead of a refund isn't the worst thing in the world, but a credit won't help you pay bills or buy food.

Q *How do you do it?*
A If an airline cancels your flight and you don't want a voucher or credit, tell a ticket agent or customer service representative that you want a cash refund. You need the flight information, flight number and date, and that's about it. If they push back, remind them that federal law requires that they refund a flight canceled *for any reason* and that you don't want a voucher or credit. If the representative continues to push back, escalate the conversation to a manager. You have a right to that money by law. If you want it, don't take no for an answer.

SCRIPTS

> "Hi there, I was on flight _____ [number] from _____ [origin] to _____ [destination] on _____ [date]. You cancelled the flight and offered me a flight credit, but I want a cash refund instead. Who can I speak with to take care of this?"

If they push back . . .

> "The law requires you to refund me in cash if I don't want a credit or voucher. Who else on your team can I speak with about this?"

If they say no one can help, ask specifically to speak to their supervisor.

Q *What if they deny your request?*
A Try again in a day or two. If you don't succeed again, file a complaint with the Department of Transportation. "DOT requires airlines to acknowledge consumer complaints within 30 days of receiving them and to send consumers written responses addressing these complaints within 60 days of receiving them," according to the DOT website. The next time you plan a trip, opt for a different airline.

HOW TO FILE A COMPLAINT IN THE UNITED STATES

- **Online:** airconsumer.dot.gov/escomplaint/ConsumerForm.cfm
- **By mail:** Office of Aviation Consumer Protection, US Department of Transportation, 1200 New Jersey Avenue, SE, Washington, DC 20590. Include your full address, phone number, and details of your trip and interaction with the airline.
- **By phone:** (202) 366-2220, but from the DOT website: "for a case to be processed as a complaint, it must be submitted in writing."[72]

UPGRADING A HOTEL ROOM

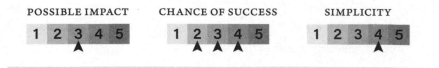

Q *What are you asking?*
A You're requesting better accommodations for the same price that you paid already.

Q *How big a deal is it?*
A This is more of a nice-to-have than a must-have. But a nicer, more comfortable hotel room can make a difference on vacation or a business trip, so it's worth asking, especially if you're looking to stretch your budget.

Q *How likely is it that you will succeed?*
A Success depends on a million variables. Do you belong to the hotel's loyalty program? Is the hotel sold out? Are you there for a special event? Has the person behind the counter had a rough day? What day of the week is it? Even time of day that you check-in matters, says Gabe Saglie, senior editor of Travelzoo. He's had some of his best luck with upgrades when checking in late in the day, after most other guests have arrived already. By that point, hotel clerks have a better feel for potential no-shows and overall availability and may feel more comfortable offering upgrades. The biggest factor is time of year, Saglie says. "Seasonality is probably the kingmaker when it comes to upgrade probability in the world of travel." The busier the time of year, the less likely you'll land an upgrade.

Q *Does asking pose any risks?*
A As long as you're not a pest about it, the desk clerk won't yell at you or banish you to the basement or a room by the elevator because you asked about an upgrade.

Q *Does not succeeding pose any risks?*

A Worst case, you end up with your original room.

Q *How do you do it?*

A "It's more social engineering," says Richard Kerr, vice president of travel at Bilt Rewards. "It's recognizing that the person at the desk at 9:00 p.m. has been there probably since 1:00 p.m. and has been yelled at seven or eight times. If you walk up with a smile and say, 'How's your day going?' chit-chat a little bit, and say, 'Hey, by the way, it'd be awesome to have a little bit more space. I'll be here for four nights. Is there anything you can do?' Then the success rate goes up significantly regardless of who you are or what you've done."

Having status with that hotel will help your chances of success, too. The easiest way to attain status is to enroll in one of that hotel's credit cards. Status level typically aligns with the annual fee associated with the card, so keep that in mind when comparing cards. If you travel regularly, card perks—such as free nights, free upgraded wi-fi, late checkout, and other benefits—can make the annual fee well worth it. Still, when looking for an upgrade, having status isn't a deal breaker. Upgrades are "an option for anyone even if you don't have status," says money-saving expert Andrea Woroch, who often asks for upgrades and other breaks from hotels when traveling. "I'm always shopping around for hotels, so I don't have a favorite. I'm not loyal to a certain brand. But if you do have that status, that definitely helps push you up on the list."

Doing your homework helps, too, Kerr says. Look at the hotel website or app to see whether rooms are available during your stay. If not, you probably can't get an upgrade even with top-level status. If there are, use that information to frame your request. Kerr also suggests making specific requests, including a specific type of room. If you saw a "grand deluxe corner king" room or a "junior suite" available on the app or website during your stay, ask for one of them specifically instead of just "an upgrade." "When the front desk hears you ask for a specific room type in their hotel," Kerr says, "they lean toward, 'Oh, he's a regular' or 'She knows what she's talking about.'"

You also can contact the hotel in advance. Saglie frequently calls a hotel before check-in to confirm his reservation or to share when he'll arrive. That conversation offers a perfect segue into a possible upgrade. Making that human connection over the phone can help. Also, if you're traveling for a special occasion or circumstance—from good, such as birthday, wedding, or retirement celebrations, to more solemn events, such as a funeral—call the hotel to let them know. They might upgrade you if that means making a special occasion even more memorable or a difficult situation a bit easier. That's exactly what happened to Alison Morris Roslyn. She took her mother to London to celebrate her mother's 70th birthday. Arriving at Claridge's, a luxury hotel in the posh Mayfair district, they learned that their room wasn't ready for check-in yet. Roslyn and her mother took it in stride, telling the clerk about the special occasion and mentioning that it was her mother's first visit to London but that Roslyn had stayed there previously. When the hotel contacted them later, they upgraded them to a suite.

SCRIPTS

Start with a smile and a warm, sincere greeting, then ask.

> "... By the way, I'd love to have a little extra space while here. Your [app/website] says that you have some availability over the next few days. Is there any chance that you could upgrade my room?" Now add some details ...

- "It's my birthday!"
- "My spouse and I are here on our honeymoon."
- "My dad is retiring."
- "We're celebrating my kid's college graduation."
- "I'm here for my mother's funeral."
- "We're scouting places to renew our wedding vows, and your place is in the running."

> **OR get specific with your request ...**
>
> "I saw that you have a corner room with two queen beds available tonight. Could you upgrade us to that room?"

> "It looks like you have a junior suite available while I'm here. Could you upgrade me to that room?"

If they turn down your initial request . . .

> "Thanks for considering it. If that's not possible, what about . . ."

- waiving the parking fee
- upgrading the wi-fi for free
- a discount at the hotel [restaurant/bar]

If you do receive an upgrade or any other break on your bill, consider tipping the person behind the counter. A $10 or $20 bill shows your appreciation and likely costs less than the face value of what they gave you. Also consider leaving a glowing review of the hotel on travel websites. You may not want to mention the upgrade, though, because then everyone who sees what you wrote might expect to receive one, too.

Q *What if they deny your request?*

A Thank them for considering your request and head to your room or on your way. Don't harass the desk clerks if there's nothing they can do. If you're staying for a while, maybe check again in a day or two with a different clerk. Your chances probably don't look great, but it can't hurt to ask politely one more time.

SUCCESS STORY

Christine Burke, a Pennsylvania-based parenting editor for *Highlights for Children* magazine, always asks for upgrades when staying at a hotel. She starts the conversation with a line from her father, Arthur McDevitt. "He'd say, 'Do you want to be a hero today?' He used to say something like, 'You can be a hero today if you help me, and then you can spend the rest of the day telling people you're a hero.'" She estimates that the line worked for her dad "about 50 percent of the time." Now she uses it herself.

If that sounds too cheesy for you, that's OK. Yes, it's a little over-the-top, but it's also a friendly, fun icebreaker. Say it to a hotel clerk with a genuine smile and you may get an eye roll from time to time, but it can kickstart a conversation. Most importantly, it playfully makes your request not all about you. People are more likely to go out of their way to help if they stand to gain something. With this tongue-in-cheek line, you're giving people something positive, which they weren't expecting, in return for helping you. It won't work every time, but even if it doesn't, you've given the person behind the desk something to smile about during a long shift.

A LOWER RATE OR FEE AT A VACATION RENTAL

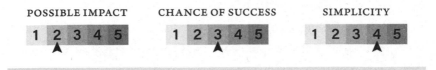

POSSIBLE IMPACT	CHANCE OF SUCCESS	SIMPLICITY
1 2 3 4 5	1 2 3 4 5	1 2 3 4 5

Q *What are you asking?*
A You're requesting a reduced price on a vacation rental property, such as Airbnb or VRBO, which could include a lower per-night rate, waived fees, or other breaks.

Q *How big a deal is it?*
A Not a huge deal. Depending on how long you stay, it could save you a few hundred, which is the kind of savings that can turn "Too expensive, we can't do it" into a reality.

Q *How likely is it that you will succeed?*
A Securing a lower rate depends on seasonality, location, and other factors—just as with hotel rates. If you're visiting Vermont when the leaves are changing, Midtown Manhattan when the Rockefeller Center Christmas tree goes up, or Tuscaloosa on a University of Alabama football gameday, you probably can't negotiate much. Buffalo in the dead of winter, Phoenix in August, or a tiny town on a random Tuesday—you might snag a deal. Another big factor? When using a rental app such as VRBO or Airbnb, you can deal directly with the property owner, who has total freedom to bend rates in a way that most hotel chains can't. Not all owners will negotiate, nor are all rental costs negotiable, but if they're flexible, you can save some money quickly. Waiting until the last minute also can pay off. "An empty home is lost revenue," says Sunitha Rao, a short-term rental owner and chief sanity officer with Afford Anything. "Hosts don't want to lose revenue," so they may yield a bit more than usual. According to a NerdWallet report,

you should book an Airbnb four weeks ahead of time for maximum savings. Year-in-advance planning and last-minute reservations will cost you more.[73]

Q *Does asking pose any risks?*
A "There's a feeling among short-term rental hosts that people who ask for discounts are going to be problems," says Lauren Keen, who owns short-term rental properties in the Tampa Bay, Florida, area. The request could raise red flags for owners, who may wonder whether other requests will follow and who may worry that a poor review could follow denying an unreasonable request. With that caveat in mind, it's still worth asking. If you're rebuffed, maybe look for another property.

Q *Does not succeeding pose any risks?*
A Beyond owner pushback, just paying full price or the hassle of having to find another place instead.

Q *How do you do it?*
A Again, do some legwork first. Are other comparable rentals available nearby? Is this property priced competitively with other area rentals? Is a big event in the area likely to bring a flood of renters? These and other questions can help you determine whether it's worth negotiating. If there's a lot of supply but not much demand, haggle away. If there's a ton of demand and not enough supply, it's probably not worth your effort.

If you do pursue a lower rate, be kind. You're not dealing with a global hotel empire, after all. You're talking to a person. If you have a compelling story behind your visit—family reunion, graduation, wedding, funeral—share that to build a connection, which could help convince the owner to work with you on a better price. If you are a current or retired member of the military or police, a nurse or EMT, or a teacher, share that, too. The owner might offer a discount as thanks for your service. You have no guarantees, but it's still worth asking.

If you're staying for an extended period, you might have more room for negotiation. "It's easier to manage versus if you're getting multiple shorter stays," says Victor Zeledon of Upland, California, who owns a short-term rental in Texas and another in Oklahoma. "It's less of a headache, too, and less wear and tear." How much you can save depends on the length of your stay, location, timing, demand, and so on, but again, it's still worth asking.

SCRIPTS

You can use this script in an email or direct message or for a phone call.

> "Hello, I'm interested in renting your _____ [kind of property], but the price is little beyond my budget. Instead of _____ [listing rate], would you be willing to accept _____ [negotiation rate] per night? My research shows several vacancies in the area, so I think that's a reasonable price."

OR

> "Hello, I'm interested in renting your _____ [kind of property] for _____ [reason for visit], but the price is a little beyond my budget. Do you offer discounts for retired or current _____ [service or frontline worker category, such as EMTs, military members, nurses, police officers, teachers, etc.]?"

If they agree to the lower rate . . .

> "Thank you very much. I really appreciate it. Please send a confirmation email to me at [your email address]. I'm excited to stay at your beautiful place, and I'll be sure to take good care of it."

If they don't agree to the lower rate . . .

> "OK, thank you for letting me know. As I said, it's a stretch for my budget. Are there other ways to reduce the costs?"

Q *What if they deny your request?*

A Accept it. There's little to no point in asking again. After all, you can't escalate the issue to a manager. Your two options are to pay the published rate or find another place to stay.

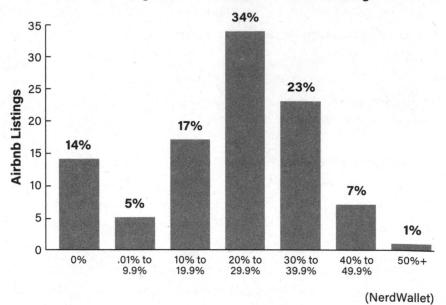

Airbnb Cleaning Fees as a Percent of Total Booking Cost

(NerdWallet)

PRO TIP: CREATIVITY AND CLEANING UP

When trying to reduce the cost of a vacation rental, there's nothing wrong with getting a little creative, but remember that it's not all about you. "Finding a way to help owners is the best way to get them to help you," says Rao. The best way to help them is to bring them more business. If you visit regularly and are considering renting the property multiple times a year or for long stretches, say so. If you can steer colleagues, friends, and relatives toward the rental in a meaningful way, mention that, too.

Don't ask to waive the cleaning fee if you clean the place yourself, though. "Offering to clean isn't a way to help," Rao says. "I get a lot of that, and that's a no-go because the cleanliness of the home is critical for the satisfaction of the next guest." That doesn't mean that you shouldn't clean up after yourself, however, which could damage your review score as a renter.

SUCCESS STORY

For about a decade, Andrew Geonetta worked in the online travel space for Expedia, HomeAway, and VRBO. He left the industry, but he still uses the knowledge he gained during that period to save money. In 2023, he booked a one-bedroom condo at a resort in Playa del Carmen, Mexico, for a family vacation. The five-day stay cost about $2,650. After booking, he remembered that his current employer, a popular job-search website, offered travel discounts via an employee program. Through that program, he could get the same condo for the same amount of time for $2,400. He called the resort and left a voicemail asking: Would the resort match the program rate if he booked through them, or would they upgrade him to a penthouse for the original $2,650 if he booked through the resort rather than the employee program?

The resort emailed, offering him the following options:

- the original booking for $2,370 if he paid the first night in advance
- the original booking for $2,220 if he paid in full
- the penthouse for $2,460, nonrefundable, if he paid in full

Leaving that voicemail allowed Geonetta to save up to $400 off the amount that he originally expected to pay. He knew, which many other travelers don't, that hotels typically pay a significant fee, anywhere from 10 to 30 percent, for the privilege of listing rooms on online travel sites *and* employee discount portals. Those percentages hold whether for a $125 room or a $500 suite. If the hotel doesn't have to pay that fee, that gives you a real advantage. They can offer you the same or even a lower rate and likely still make more money on it than by using a third party. You won't always get a deal like Geonetta did—and he went with the penthouse—but it can't hurt to ask.

UPGRADING A RENTAL VEHICLE

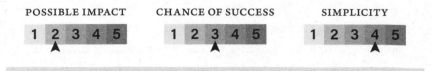

Q *What are you asking?*
A You're seeking a better class or kind of vehicle for the same price that you already paid.

Q *How big a deal is it?*
A Not financially but, depending on the use, it could be a big deal personally. A bigger vehicle with extra space can make a family vacation easier and better, while a luxury SUV or convertible sports car could elevate a romantic getaway or a girls/guys weekend a notch or two.

Q *How likely is it that you will succeed?*
A Having status in the company's loyalty program can help. With high enough status, some rental companies may upgrade you automatically, depending on availability, but you can succeed without it. "It happens," says shopping expert Andrea Woroch. "It's more a matter of what's available at that airport at that time." For example, if you reserved an economy car but they're out of that size, you could end up with a free upgrade without even having to ask. But it's generally a good idea to ask.

Q *Does asking pose any risks?*
A Pushing too hard or coming on too strong could annoy representatives behind the counter, causing blowback. For example, if you reserved an economy car, they could give you the worst one on the lot. If you ask nicely, you shouldn't have anything to worry about. Also, upgrades can come with unexpected expenses. Bigger vehicles mean more visits to the pump and bigger refueling costs.

Q *Does not succeeding pose any risks?*

A Beyond the above, the worst case is driving what you origi-
nally booked.

Q *How do you do it?*

A As with a hotel upgrade, it starts with a smile and a friendly greeting.
Assume that the person behind the counter has had a long day and that at
least one or two other customers have yelled at or talked down to them. A
simple "Hi there, how's your day been?" delivered with a kind smile could
make the person a little more willing to help. Still, you need to read the
room. If the line snakes around the corner or out the door, tensions are running high, and nerves are fraying, the rep may not feel like small talk. In that
case, a quick, friendly "Any chance that I could swing a free upgrade today?"
is still worth it, but manage your expectations.

One of the best ways to improve your odds is reserving the cheapest car
possible, says Travelzoo senior editor Gabe Saglie. That's what most people
want when they rent, so the odds of that category being out of stock usually
run relatively high. If the kind of car you reserved isn't available, the company has to give you a bigger car for free because "you shouldn't be paying
for the upgrade that comes from them not having the car that you selected
or reserved," Saglie says. Make sure that what you book will fit your needs,
though, because you can't count on an upgrade.

If they don't bump you to a higher category of rental, Saglie suggests
asking whether other types of cars are available within the category that
you reserved. For example, "instead of getting a hatchback, maybe a sedan.
It's not a fancy-schmancy sedan, but perhaps it gives you more trunk space,
maybe more seating options, or a more comfortable ride."

SCRIPTS

Start with a smile and a warm "Hello, how are you doing today?" After providing your reservation information and any other required documentation, engage in a little small talk—weather, sports, uncontentious current
events, how busy the counter is, or other easygoing chit chat that pops to
mind—then ask for an upgrade.

> "You know, I'd love to have a little extra room for the drive. Any chance you could upgrade me to something bigger for the same price?" If you like, add: "I'm not looking for the biggest, most expensive car you have, but something a little roomier would be nice, if that's possible."

If they agree to an upgrade . . .

> "Oh, that's amazing. Thank you so much. I really appreciate it. This is a great way to start the trip!"

Consider offering a small cash tip. A $10 or $20 bill shows your thanks and likely costs less than what you saved. Also consider giving the rental car company a great review online. You don't need to mention the upgrade because everyone who reads it might expect one, but a glowing writeup nicely thanks the company for great service.

If they refuse . . .

> "No problem, I understand. Figured it couldn't hurt to ask. Thank you for considering it."

Q *What if they deny your request?*
A For many asks in this book, you should keep pressing and not take no for an answer. This *isn't* one of those cases. If you really want to push the envelope, you could ask to speak to a manager. But that probably won't do much more than antagonizing the counter rep and delaying an already tedious process. You're better off saying thank you politely and moving on with your trip.

PRO TIP: FOR A BETTER DEAL, LEAVE THE AIRPORT

Experts agree that never looking beyond the airport for car rentals could cost you money. A 2022 NerdWallet report comparing rental car prices at the nation's 20 largest airports to downtown locations nearby found that renters spent 26 percent more at airport locations, to the tune of an extra $126 on a seven-day rental.[74] That's real money that still represents good savings even after you add a cab or rideshare to the other location.

Why the price difference? Airport locations often have to pay more taxes and fees than other locations. "Renting a car from an off-airport location is generally cheaper because of additional taxes levied at airport locations," confirms travel writer Lee Huffman, creator of the *Bald Thoughts* blog. "Politicians often find it easier to tax tourists than locals because tourists don't vote in local elections."

If you rent a vehicle from an airport location, on average you'll pay 26 percent more than you would elsewhere in the same city.

WAIVING A FOREIGN-TRANSACTION FEE ON A CREDIT CARD

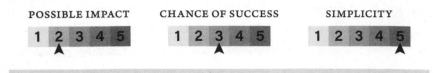

POSSIBLE IMPACT   CHANCE OF SUCCESS   SIMPLICITY

1 **2** 3 4 **5**   1 2 **3** 4 5   1 2 3 4 **5**

Q *What are you asking?*
A You're requesting that your card issuer remove foreign-transaction charges applied to your account.

Q *How big a deal is it?*
A It can be a big deal, especially for frequent travelers. These fees, which typically range from 1 to 4 percent, apply to *any* transaction done in a foreign country.[75] International travel already costs crazy money, and these fees make it worse. The average foreign-transaction fee, 3 percent, equates to an additional $30 for every $1,000 that you spend. That kind of money can add up fast. This charge doesn't impact only travelers, either. It could hit when you order your favorite Premier League club jersey from their online store or a bottle of Burgundy from the winery's website. Any transaction that takes place in a foreign currency could trigger one of these fees.

Q *How likely is it that you will succeed?*
A A 2023 LendingTree survey showed that 53 percent of cardholders who asked had their request granted.[76] So your chances don't run as high as if you ask to waive a late fee or annual fee, but they still look good. Not

In 2023, 53 percent of cardholders who asked their issuers to waive foreign-transaction fees succeeded. (LendingTree)

all cards charge foreign-transaction fees, either. They have become rarer recently, as card issuers bend over backward to entice more travelers to apply for their cards.

Q *Does asking pose any risks?*
A If the card issuer hard-pulls your credit, that would ding your credit score slightly and temporarily, but that step is highly unlikely when asking to have credit card fees of any kind removed.

Q *Does not succeeding pose any risks?*
A You could wind up paying hundreds in unnecessary fees, making an expensive vacation or special order even more costly.

Q *How do you do it?*
A Call your card issuer, remind them how long you've had the card, how much you regularly spend on it, and your (hopefully) stellar payment record. Then ask them politely to waive the fee. If you're not sure exactly how much you spend each month, check five or six of your most recent statements and average the totals. The more you spend on the card, the more likely the issuer will waive the fee. Every time you use the card, the bank or financial institution makes money from swipe fees that merchants pay to the company. No bank wants to alienate a profitable customer over $100. That's a meaningful amount of money for most people but less than a grain of sand on the beach for a megabank. Many banks will forgo that extra drop in the bucket to keep you happy because they know they'll make more money off you in the long run.

SCRIPTS

"Hi, I'm calling about some foreign-transaction fees recently charged to my account. I've had the card for _____ [number] years, spend about _____ [average amount] each month, and haven't missed a payment [in _____ (time period)]. Given all that, I think it's reasonable to waive these fees. Who can I speak with about doing that?"

If they rebuff your initial request . . .

> "That's disappointing. Who else on your team can I speak with about this request?"

If they counteroffer with extra rewards points, a higher credit limit, a temporarily lower interest rate, or something else . . .

> "I appreciate the offer, but I'm most interested in having the fees waived. Who on your team can I speak with about that?"
>
> **OR**
>
> "That's an interesting offer. Thank you for that. I'd like to think about it. How long is that offer valid?"

If they agree to waive the fee or you agree to their counteroffer . . .

> "Thank you for working with me. I accept that offer. Please send a confirmation email to me at [your email address]?"

Q   *What if they deny your request?*

A   Don't take a first no as the final answer. The credit card business is too competitive. Call back in a day or two and ask again. You don't have any greater chance of success for round two, but the money you can save makes it worth trying. You also can threaten to close the card. Fewer credit cards charge foreign-transaction fees anymore. Someone with good credit easily can find another card without foreign-transaction fees. That information, which banks know quite well, should give you real power when negotiating. Use this threat only as a last resort, however, because you shouldn't close a credit card lightly. That step requires forethought and planning; otherwise, you risk damaging your credit.

DYNAMIC CURRENCY CONVERSION

If you've traveled abroad recently, you probably have heard this question: "Would you like to complete this purchase in dollars or in [local currency]?" The correct answer is almost always the local currency. Here's why.

Your credit card's exchange rate is probably better than what a merchant can offer. The merchant also may charge additional fees for the conversion. To make matters worse, they might not tell you that the service comes with a fee, which could make for an unpleasant surprise when you get home and review the costs of your trip.

If you choose the local currency, you shouldn't receive any pushback from the merchant. They're not going to want to lose the sale. But if someone won't take no for an answer, take your business elsewhere.

6. WORK

Negotiate Your Worth

How to ask for:

PROFESSIONAL MENTORING

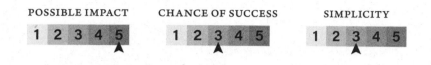

POSSIBLE IMPACT
1 2 3 4 **5**
▲

CHANCE OF SUCCESS
1 2 **3** 4 5
▲

SIMPLICITY
1 2 **3** 4 5
▲

Q *What are you asking?*
A You're requesting seasoned guidance for your career.

Q *How big a deal is it?*
A Success often comes from who you know rather than what you know. The right mentor can open doors and bolster your prospects. But it's about more than just making connections. Good mentoring means benefiting from the wisdom of someone else's experiences as you build your own career.

Q *How likely is it that you will succeed?*
A Some people will brush you off, but others happily will help. "Most people with good hearts in the business world want eager people who want to expand, grow, and learn, and very few people shut that down," says Doug Lebda, CEO and founder of LendingTree. Your chances of success look better if you approach someone with whom you already have a connection, such as a more experienced colleague. But it often doesn't take much to create that connection. Sometimes attending the same high school or college or sharing the same quirky hobby can jumpstart a conversation that leads

84% of Fortune 500 companies in America have mentoring programs. (MentorcliQ/Forbes)[77]

to a long-term professional relationship. "I've had people who got mentors from things as silly as they always like this person's LinkedIn post or, when this person has an event, they send them a thank-you email," says career coach Carlota Zimmerman.

Q *Does asking pose any risks?*
A Other than a potentially awkward conversation, not really, and even that shouldn't stop you from asking.

Q *Does not succeeding pose any risks?*
A Again, nothing that should keep you from asking. If you approach someone for guidance and get shot down, that can hurt in the moment and maybe lead to some unease in the office. But if a potential mentor says anything cruel or inappropriate to you just for asking, you obviously don't want advice from someone who does that.

Q *How do you do it?*
A If you have an established relationship or easy rapport with someone, it's as easy as: "Hey, can I ask you a few questions?" or "Can I buy you a coffee and ask you a few questions?" A mentor relationship also can evolve organically from a bond with a coworker, and you never even have to ask permission for that person's counsel.

If you don't have a relationship or rapport with someone, develop one. First, you need to pick the right person. The right match for a mentor can follow shared values, specific skills, or common experiences, according to career coach Ella Wright. For example, if you value work-life balance but the other person struggles in that area, that person's advice may not work for you. You don't have to agree with everything the person says, but you both should align on issues or concerns related to the guidance you're seeking. You can suss that out in a coffee meeting, but do a little homework *before* approaching anyone with this goal in mind.

When you know whom you'd like to contact, always respect the other person's time. If emailing, keep it brief and clear. If requesting an in-person chat, ask for 15 minutes in the next week or two—not an hour tomorrow. If you're meeting for coffee, pick someplace nearby and plan on paying. Successful people usually have a lot of demands on their time. Make it easy for them or you won't get anywhere.

Also, consider whether you could offer something in return. Could you do some research for a big upcoming meeting or presentation? Could you write a review or social-media post promoting the person's book? Could you subscribe to the person's newsletter? Could you recommend an amazing food truck? Proceed ethically, of course, but even a small gesture can go a long way. It's not always necessary, though, says Lebda. "What's in it for the other person is the psychic income to help develop you and the respect they're getting in an organization." That kind of positive action can offer a welcome break for executives who spend a lot of time wrestling with faceless problems.

Lastly, after you have that initial conversation, follow up. A handwritten note thanking the person may sound old-fashioned, but it can make a lasting impression. If you don't send a handwritten note, absolutely send a quick thank-you email, which gives you the opportunity to suggest chatting again. ("Thank you so much, Linda. I really appreciate your insight. Let's do it again later in the year. In the meantime, have a great day!")

SCRIPTS

If you already have a relationship or rapport with the person . . .

> "Hey, would you be available for a quick coffee in the next week or two? I'd love to get your [advice/thoughts] on _____ [topic]. If a call or video chat is easier, that's great, too. Just let me know some days and times that look good. I appreciate your time. Thanks!"

In this initial outreach, give a quick description of what you want to discuss but keep it succinct. Save granular details for the conversation. For example:

> "I'd love to get your advice on a presentation that I have to give to the team next month."

"I'm planning to ask my boss for a raise, and I'd like to know your thoughts about how best to do that."

"I'm still getting my feet under me, so I'd value your insights on what it takes to succeed here."

If you don't have a relationship with the person already . . .

"Hi _____ [name], would you be available for coffee in the next week or two? [If appropriate] I started here not long ago and would love to chat about your experiences and hear any insights you might have about what it takes to succeed. If it's easier, I'm happy to do a call or email you some questions instead. I appreciate your time. Let me know when you're available. Thank you!"

Depending on the person and circumstances, each email will look different, but establish a connection, make the ask clear, summarize what you want to discuss, and make it as easy as possible for the person to say yes. Some possible ways to establish a connection:

Mention that you both attended the same university.

Say that you enjoyed a recent LinkedIn post or presentation given—but only if you really did. Remember, the person might ask you about it later.

If the person displays something prominently on a desk or is vocal on social media about something that you enjoy as well, mention that. ("Boy, that [game/episode] was incredible last night.") Make sure the fandom is obvious. You don't want to seem creepy.

After your initial meeting . . .

"Thank you so much for your time and insight. I'd love to grab coffee again in a few months. In the meantime, have a great day!"

Q   *What if they deny your request?*

A   Don't be surprised or take it personally. If the person isn't a jerk about it, offer your thanks and best wishes. You never know when your paths might cross again; if they do, you'll be glad that you didn't burn a bridge. In the meantime, turn your attention to finding someone else more willing to offer guidance. Who knows, it might even happen organically without having to seek it.

SUCCESS STORY

Money coach Chloé Daniels firmly believes in the power of mentoring. Mentors helped her in her career, and she founded a networking group in Chicago for women and formed a mastermind group in which she mentors up-and-coming finance creators. Some of her tips for mentor relationships include:

- **The right match matters.** "It's just like any relationship! You have to get to know them to see if your personalities align."
- **Add value.** "No one wants a relationship where all they're doing is giving. If it's someone you work with, that's an easy way to make it mutually exclusive. You volunteer for projects, take on extra work, be the go-to person for whatever it is you're doing, and then that mentor exchange is easy."
- **Make it easy.** "If it's someone you're getting to know, finding ways to get access to their time in a way that doesn't inconvenience them is important. For example, when I thought I wanted to start a marketing firm someday, I started engaging with content creators on LinkedIn, sharing their posts. Eventually when I DM'd them and asked if they'd be interested in having a quick call with me to hear about their careers, they were happy to do so. It was only about 30 minutes of their time, but I had been engaging with their content weeks before I went in for the ask."
- **You don't have to keep in constant contact with everyone.** "A mentor can be single-serving. When I used to host FIRE [financial independence, retire early] events in Chicago, I met a woman who had owned an organizational development consulting firm and retired. After I hosted a few events where she came, I asked if she'd consider being interviewed for a blog. She was happy to do it, and I learned so much. She may not be a lifelong mentor, but she's absolutely someone I would feel comfortable reaching out to again because of our connection then."

REIMBURSEMENT FOR TUITION

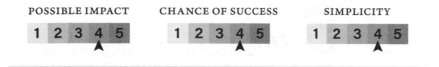

POSSIBLE IMPACT	CHANCE OF SUCCESS	SIMPLICITY
1 2 3 **4** 5	1 2 3 **4** 5	1 2 3 **4** 5

Q *What are you asking?*
A You're requesting that your employer cover some or all your expenses for continuing your education.

Q *How big a deal is it?*
A For millions of people, college lies financially beyond reach unless they take on soul-crushing debt. Tuition reimbursement can turn that academic dream into an affordable reality. Yes, in many cases, you still must make the initial payment yourself—because it's *reimbursement*, after all—but it's still a big deal.

Q *How likely is it that you will succeed?*
A A 2022 report from the Society for Human Resource Management said that 48 percent of organizations offered undergraduate or graduate tuition reimbursement.[78] So, for almost half of companies, the ask is "How?" rather than "Do we?" But even if a company doesn't have an established program, it's worth asking. You probably aren't the first person to ask.

Q *Does asking pose any risks?*
A Your supervisor could question whether the additional workload will hinder your day-job performance, so, before you ask, outline why it won't. If the economy or your company's overall performance isn't looking good, your supervisor might not want to authorize spending company money, though that's unlikely with an existing program. If you face significant resistance, consider it a red flag. Good, strong companies want their employees to grow. If your employer doesn't see it that way, think about finding a new one.

Almost half of employers surveyed by the Society of Human Resource Management offer tuition assistance, undergraduate or graduate, as an employee benefit. (SHRM)

Q *Does not succeeding pose any risks?*
A You may not be able to afford to take those classes or pursue that degree. That's a big deal, which is why it's so important to ask, even with no guarantee.

Q *How do you do it?*
A If the company has a program, it's easy. If you're interviewing, ask about details when discussing the overall benefits package. If you're looking for more information from your employer, shoot a quick chat, email, or call to HR to get the scoop. Whatever the case, you need to understand the fine print because what you don't know could cost you.

If your company doesn't have a program, you'll have to pitch why helping you will benefit the business. "Put together a proposal about how the certificate or degree will help you have a greater impact in your role," career coach Ella Wright says. "If you position how you'd like to help the company advance their operational goals and a few thousand dollars will help you achieve that, you're more likely to get support." Be specific. Drill down to exact courses you plan to take and how they can help make you a more effective employee. "The more you can demonstrate, 'Hey, I want to get this certification because it'll improve my work expertise, I'll learn cutting-edge tech and ideas in our field, and it'll make me a better employee and team member,' the better off you'll be," says career coach Carlota Zimmerman. "That's what management wants to hear, that you're going back to school because you're committed to your career and, by extension, the company."

Your pitch can include a broader perspective as well. Tell them why they should offer the perk to the whole company. Remind them, if applicable, that their primary competitor offers tuition reimbursement, as noted on Glassdoor and other websites. Let them know if you've heard other employees talking about how much they'd like this perk. (If you haven't, don't fib.) Share recent articles in which recruiters talk about this perk and how many prospective employees ask them about it. Don't forget about the tax benefits, either. Federal law allows employers to deduct up to $5,250 in tuition and other selected costs per employee per year for reimbursements made through qualified programs.[79]

WHAT TO KNOW ABOUT YOUR COMPANY'S TUITION REIMBURSEMENT PROGRAM

- **What it covers:** Some businesses may cover all tuition, fees, and even textbooks, but others have maximum reimbursement amounts and may cover only certain expenses.
- **Where you can use it:** In some cases, organizations make these benefits available only if you attend certain schools or take certain classes.
- **What you must do to keep it:** Some companies may require you to maintain a minimum grade-point average to qualify.
- **Who is eligible:** Some businesses make these benefits available to everyone, regardless of position on the org chart; others reserve it for higher ranks in the company. Some organizations may require you to have worked for the company for a specified period before becoming eligible.
- **How long you're committing to the company by accepting it:** Some businesses may require you to stay with them for a defined period after you receive the benefit.
- **Who pays the school:** Some organizations pay for tuition and other costs up front, while others require you to pay out of pocket and reimburse you afterward.

SCRIPTS

In a job interview with a company that has a program . . .

> "Your website says that you offer tuition reimbursement to employees. What more can you tell me about that program?"

Asking via chat, email, text, or call about your company's program . . .

> "I know that our company has a tuition reimbursement program, but I don't know much about it. Where can I find more information, or who can tell me more about it?"

If your company doesn't have a program . . .

> "I'm considering enrolling in classes to help increase my performance and make me a stronger asset for the company. Tuition is expensive, though, so I'd love to discuss the possibility of the company offering some help. Lots of businesses offer tuition reimbursement, including some of our competitors, and I'd like to make the case that offering this benefit to all employees could be a big win for the company. When would you be available to talk about this?"

Q *What if they deny your request?*

A If your supervisor doesn't support your request, consider taking your case to HR or another high-ranking person in the company. If you do that, though, tread lightly. Even when done openly and carefully, going over your boss's head can look bad and engender ill will. The possibility of a brighter future may warrant that risk, but only you can decide whether it's worth it. If your company outright dismisses your request or even reacts harshly to it, you could be looking at a red flag. Good companies invest in their employees and understand that people who feel appreciated and engaged tend to stick around. If your company is falling short in that department, you may want to look elsewhere.

LOWER COLLEGE TUITION

POSSIBLE IMPACT   CHANCE OF SUCCESS   SIMPLICITY

1 2 3 4 5   1 2 3 4 5   1 2 3 4 5

Q *What are you asking?*
A You're requesting to pay less for college courses.

Q *How big a deal is it?*
A College costs a lot of money, sometimes prohibitively so. But you could save thousands per year on it by asking the right questions. That savings can turn a dream of higher education into a reality.

Q *How likely is it that you will succeed?*
A Probably more than you'd expect. Mark Salisbury founded TuitionFit to increase transparency around the price of college and says that, while schools such as Harvard and Stanford don't have to negotiate because of the enormous demand to go there, most others aren't as fortunate. He says about 10 to 15 percent of schools are in the same boat as Harvard and Stanford, but the rest are "basically in the same place: They're not getting enough students to fill their classes or not getting enough students paying enough money to meet their ideal budget goals. So in that context, they are—to varying degrees, for different reasons—willing to haggle," he says.

Q *Does asking pose any risks?*
A "If you've done everything right, the worst thing that can happen is the school says, 'Sorry, that's the aid package that we've offered you. We

$12,088 The average amount of merit-based aid given to full-time undergraduates in the 2022–2023 academic year. (USNews.com)[80]

think it's fair, and we hope you'll come.' That's the end of it," Salisbury says. "If you want to be an empowered consumer, do it. You have nothing to lose."

Q *Does not succeeding pose any risks?*
A These negotiations can make the difference between affording a school and not. That's a big deal, especially considering how emotional the decision can become and how long the process takes.

Q *How do you do it?*
A Use the Net Price Calculator at all the schools that you're considering seriously. Federal law requires schools that offer federal financial aid to provide these calculators, which help students estimate the real cost of attending that school, including federal aid, state aid, and institutional aid, meaning given by the school itself. Calculators can vary by school, but expect to enter information about your dependency status; income, assets, and other financial data about your parents or guardians; and more. These calculators provide only estimates, though. They never guarantee aid, nor are they always entirely accurate, but they can give you a ballpark idea of real costs beyond tuition.

You can receive two types of financial aid from a school, need-based aid and merit-based, and the approach you take and your chances of successfully negotiating the amount will vary based on which type.

Your family's financial needs drive need-based aid, as the name indicates. Schools typically determine need using the information that you provide in the Department of Education's Free Application for Federal Student Aid (FAFSA) or the CSS Profile, run by the College Board. The FAFSA—again, free—establishes eligibility for federal aid, while the CSS Profile, which costs a small fee each time you send it, typically helps colleges decide eligibility for institutional grants and scholarships. The FAFSA includes tax return information and detailed information on investments, account balances, and more, while the CSS Profile can contain even more extensive detail. Your best chance of a financial-aid office reconsidering and perhaps increasing a need-based offer, experts say, is if your financial circumstances have worsened significantly since you applied. If that's the case, tell your story. Schools will listen and take it into consideration. If your child received acceptance packages from several schools, it may be possible to leverage those offers to secure a better deal from your first-choice school, says Ron Lieber, author of *The Price You Pay for College: An Entirely New Road Map for the Biggest Financial Decision Your Family Will Ever Make*. He suggests "a posture of humility" rather than entitlement. "Go to the school where the price is highest and say, 'Hey, here are the other schools that I got into. My price is going to be lower for each of them. Is it possible that I made a mistake when applying for aid? Did I do something wrong? Because I'm sort of scratching my head here, trying to figure out why your price is the highest.'" You're not being pushy or combative. You're not accusing the school of anything. You're looking for information and hoping for a little more help along the way.

Merit-based aid pertains to what you've done rather than what you have. As with need-based aid, your chances for success may look best if your circumstances have changed significantly since you applied, such as improving your SAT score by 50 or more points, raising $5,000 for a local charity, or graduating as valedictorian. Even without those accomplishments, you may have more room for negotiation than you think, and your success rate may look better than with need-based aid. Again, if you have acceptances from multiple schools, use those offers to frame the conversation. Salisbury says that the key is being genuine. Tell them how excited you and/or your child are about the school but also say that you have financial concerns. "'We're having a hard time justifying whether we can make that work and feel comfortable with it because we don't want to send our student to your school for one semester. We want to send them there for eight and a commencement ceremony,'" Salisbury suggests. Talking concrete numbers can help make your point further, he says. "'You're $4,000 more expensive than that other school. That might not seem like a lot to you. For us, that's $16,000 in difference. We might like you better, but we're having a hard time justifying that you're $16,000 better.'"

If you don't have multiple offers, you still can ask about lower costs.

There's never been more information available about the money that colleges are giving out than there is now. Elaine Rubin, director of corporate communications for Edvisor, who also worked for seven years with the US Department of Education's Office of Federal Student Aid, says that schools usually post on their websites the average amount of financial need that they cover per student. "If they say they meet 65 percent of need and you're getting only 20 to 30 percent, that could be a negotiation tool to say, 'Well, is there anything else?'"

Lieber recommends searching for Common Data Set information for the school by Googling "common data set" plus the name of the school. Common Data, a standardized collection of information provided by colleges and universities, includes the average need-based and non-need-based aid given by that school in that year, among other details. Not all schools make the information available, but most do. For example, Section H of the Common Data Set for the University of Missouri for 2021–2022 says that the school covered 64 percent of need for students with financial need, an average of $12,822.[81] If Mizzou accepts you or your child and the aid you receive falls below either or both of those numbers, consider contacting the financial-aid office and asking them to reconsider. You have no guarantee of extra help, but there's too much at stake not to ask.

PRO TIP: DON'T CALL IT NEGOTIATION

You can negotiate with many institutions. You won't always get your way—and with elite universities, you almost certainly won't—but you absolutely can do it. But never call the ongoing conversation a negotiation or haggling. You haggle for a used Buick from the lot on the corner but not for tutelage from one of America's bastions of higher learning. They use a fancier term: filing an appeal for aid. "They will never use the word *haggle*, and they'll never use the word *negotiate* because historically colleges position themselves next to the church and the monastery," says Salisbury. " 'We don't negotiate with the peasants, but we'll hear your *appeal for more aid*.'"

SCRIPTS

When asking for increased need-based aid

> "Thank you so much for the financial-aid package that you've offered. We're so excited about the possibility of my child attending your fantastic school. But we've had a change in our financial situation. I'm letting you know about it, in hopes that you might consider increasing the aid you're willing to provide."

From here, tell your story. You don't have to give every single detail, but you have to make sure that they understand your situation, so don't be afraid of vulnerability. For the most part, those involved in the college admissions process want to help you, but they can't if they don't know what you're going through.

OR

> "Thank you so much for the financial-aid package that you offered. I want to follow up with you about that. My child got into _____ [other schools], and your price is the highest among them. Might I have made a mistake or done something wrong when applying for aid? I'm trying to understand why your price would be the highest. What can you tell me about this?"

OR

> "Thank you so much for the financial-aid package that you offered. I want to follow up with you about that. I saw in the Common Data Set that the average percentage of need that you typically covered last year was _____ percent, but your offer was less than that for me. Might I have made a mistake or done something wrong when applying for aid? I'm trying to understand why my aid would be lower. What can you tell me about this?"

When asking for increased merit-based aid

> "Thank you so much for the financial-aid package. We're so excited about the possibility of my child attending your fantastic school, but a lot has happened in the last few months, which we want to share with you."

From here, tell your story. If your kid has achieved some amazing accomplishments, don't be shy. That story could unlock extra money.

OR

> "Thank you so much for the financial-aid package. A few other schools also accepted my child, but your price is the highest. You're our first choice for the next four years, but the price difference is a big deal for us. What can we do to work together on this?"

If you can, list specifics. If you're choosing between two similar schools and the difference in price, including financial-aid packages, is $5,000 a year, tell them. Framing it in concrete amounts can make a real impact.

OR

> "Thank you so much for the financial-aid package. The Common Data Set indicates that the average amount of merit-based aid that you gave last year was _____ [amount]. I'm trying to understand why my aid would be lower. Can you tell me more about these numbers, and do you have flexibility with the amount?"

If they make an acceptable offer . . .

> "Thank you very much. This means a lot to us. We're so excited that _____ [name of child] will be coming to your campus. It's going to be great. Please send a confirmation of the new offer to me at [your email address]."

If they make an offer that you're not sure about . . .

> "Thank you very much for working with us. That's an interesting option. It's a big decision, though, and I'd like to take some time to think about it. We'll discuss it as a family and let you know our decision. When would you need to hear back from us?"

If they're unwilling to work with you . . .

> "That's disappointing. Thank you for your time, though. We'll discuss this conversation as a family and let you know our decision."

Q *What if they deny your request?*

A It's not over till it's over, as the old saying goes. Even after classes have started, you still may have an opportunity to procure additional aid. Rubin explains, "A school offers financial aid to prospective students but some students won't attend, which means unclaimed scholarship or grant funds could be available when the school determines enrollment. If students still need additional funds to help cover the cost, they can ask for additional funds after the semester has begun. The students should research available scholarships and ensure that they meet eligibility criteria. When asking for additional aid, it's best to be specific. This is a very specific ask, but many students don't know that they can ask."

If the school isn't willing to work with you, factor their reluctance into your decision. If extra aid is nice to have, maybe the rejection doesn't matter. If it means more than that and the school is the top choice, not receiving extra aid may mean scrambling for scholarships, loans, or even a side hustle to cover the balance. Worst-case scenario: It could put that school out of reach financially, which can make for a tough pill to swallow.

SUCCESS STORY

In the late 1990s, Selena Rezvani had just finished her freshman year at New York University. "I loved the school," she says. "I loved year one. It was amazing." It also provided a welcome escape from suddenly losing her father a few years earlier. That devastating loss forced her family to wrestle not only with the enormity of their grief but also the financial chaos caused by his absence. Rezvani and her family received enough financial aid for her to attend one of the nation's most prestigious universities, but financial-aid packages change, year to year.

The financial-aid package for her second year dropped so much lower than the first that it threatened to derail her education at NYU. "My mom sat me down and said, 'Honey, I can't swing it. I can't send you back.'" Rezvani's mother had never negotiated financial aid with a college and had no idea how. Without that aid, they couldn't make NYU work. "I realized in that moment, *If anything's going to change where this is headed, I have to do something,*" so she did.

Rezvani wrote to the admissions office, pleading her case and outlining a plan. "I said, 'Please keep me! Here are the ways I want to contribute to the community. Here are the 5 million jobs I'll do to make it worth it to you. They changed the financial-aid package, they kept me there, *and* they gave me all those jobs, too—not just for year two but for year three and year four also."

Rezvani graduated from NYU and earned a master's from Johns Hopkins en route to becoming a best-selling author, highly sought-after speaker, and successful consultant for some of the world's biggest companies. Since Rezvani's days on campus, college costs have shot into the stratosphere, so trying this approach today might feel too daunting, given the numbers, or yield a very different response. But she still sees that moment as seminal in her life and incontrovertible proof of the power of asking. "That went against everything I had ever learned growing up—to make a fuss, to ask for what felt like a favor—and it changed the direction of my life."

A RAISE OR PROMOTION

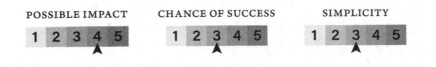

POSSIBLE IMPACT
1 2 3 **4** 5

CHANCE OF SUCCESS
1 2 **3** 4 5

SIMPLICITY
1 2 **3** 4 5

Q *What are you asking?*
A You're requesting more money, a higher title, or other forms of compensation at your job.

Q *How big a deal is it?*
A When living paycheck to paycheck or on a tight budget, even a small salary increase can make a big difference. A few extra vacation days could help with your mental health and bring additional flexibility to your life. A better title could change the way you feel about yourself and how others view and treat you. Plus, the higher your pay and the better your title now, the more you can ask when looking for future jobs.

It all won't be sunshine and rainbows, though. As a wise man once said, "With great power comes great responsibility." More money and clout may bring more stress, more pressure, and longer hours, so consider all the ramifications before you ask.

Q *How likely is it that you will succeed?*
A A million variables can influence the outcome, many beyond your control. For example, if you smashed your yearly goals and took on extra responsibilities but your company's stock lost 80 percent of its value in the past year, a raise may not be in the cards. That doesn't mean that you shouldn't ask, though. That hypothetical scenario could put you in a powerful position because a floundering company doesn't want star players sprinting for the exit. But read the room, formulate your approach accordingly—preparing to answer why you should make more while the company is struggling— and manage your expectations.

37 percent

of workers have asked their current employer for a raise. (Payscale)[82]

Q *Does asking pose any risks?*

A Higher-ups could see you as ungrateful, greedy, or unreasonable for asking. ("You know how bad a year we had" or "I thought you were a team player. We all have to do more around here because of the company's financial situation.") Conversations like those can make any working atmosphere uncomfortable. But if you make a reasonable request, that type of reaction could raise a giant red flag: proof that your company doesn't appreciate you, in which case you should consider looking elsewhere.

Q *Does not succeeding pose any risks?*

A It's primarily about relationships. Even in the best financial times, you could overplay your hand and ask for too much. Overreaching could create friction with your supervisor and slowly poison your work environment. That's why you need to do your homework before you ask. It's one thing to make reasonable request for a raise or promotion, based on substantial research and solid data. Don't make wild salary demands based only on your own wants. Still, career coach Mandi Woodruff-Santos, cohost of the *Brown Ambition* podcast, says the bigger risk lies in doing nothing. "It's about the risk of missing out on the opportunity to catch up, to build wealth, and to reinvest in yourself by having a job that pays you a reasonable salary so that you're able to do those things and have financial stability," she says. "That's the bigger risk of not asking, and the pros of asking definitely outweigh those cons."

Q *How do you do it?*

A "You can't just walk in and say, 'Hey, I want a raise because I think I deserve it,'" says Mori Taheripour, a negotiation expert who has worked with the NFL, Google, Goldman Sachs, and other clients.[83] "Maybe it's your lucky day, and maybe that just happens to work, but by and large, this is the act of persuasion."

Persuasion begins with information. Visit Glassdoor, Indeed, Salary .com, and other websites to find out what people with your title typically earn in your area and around the nation. Research the latest trends in your industry regarding paid time off, remote work, tuition reimbursement, equity grants, and other perks that you might want. If you have a mentor (page 171) or trusted confidante in your office or industry, request advice. Even if you don't have someone like that, talk to colleagues, friends, or relatives about their experiences and what they're seeing and hearing. "I always recommend that people speak to their peers or speak to other people in hiring positions in their industry or in their niche to get a sense of what their market value is for their skills and for the type of role," Woodruff-Santos says. Ultimately, however, the source that may serve you best is *you*.

Michela Allocca, financial analyst and author of *Own Your Money: Practical Strategies to Budget Better, Earn More, and Reach Your 6-Figure Savings Goals*, suggests tracking your work accomplishments monthly. That way, when the time comes for a review or to ask for a raise or promotion, you don't have to worry about remembering all the details about everything that you've achieved over the past year. You'll have a fresh, running list of what you've done and how it benefited the company. Allocca suggests organizing it this way:

- **Priorities and other regular responsibilities:** Include meetings that you lead, reports that you generate, content that you create, "tasks to keep the lights on," she says.
- **Additional work outside your typical duties:** "Somebody asking me for a favor, a new project, a last-minute request. 'Hey, can you run this quick analysis for me, or could you jump in this meeting?' Everything asked of me outside my normal role, I would write down and track for examples of how I'm going above and beyond," Allocca says.

- **Accomplishments on a weekly basis:** "They could be small, they could be large. It could be leading a meeting, presenting to an executive, wrapping a project, onboarding an intern, or whatever. Anything that's bringing value to your team and moving the needle forward in the company, whether quantifiable or not."

It may seem like overkill to track all that on an ongoing basis, especially when we all have mile-long to-do lists, but these records create an invaluable tool. "You're proving your value," says Lindsay Goldwert, author of *Bow Down: Lessons from Dominatrixes on How to Get Everything You Want.* "If you leave, they're [screwed], and that's the real power."

You need more than just bullet points, data, and lists of accomplishments, though. Timing matters, too. If you go into your boss's office at 4:45 p.m. on Friday and say, "Hey, can we talk about getting me a raise?" you probably won't get anywhere. If you want any of your colleagues to help you, never ambush, blindside, or overwhelm them. Allocca suggests planting the seeds for the ask subtly and long before asking. You can pose questions such as "What's the trajectory of this role?" or "How do promotions work here?" Allocca says, "You can approach it from a very casual standpoint and just plant it in their brain."

Finally, don't apologize for asking. A good manager won't take umbrage at your request. (If yours does, consider that a red flag.) Also, the company might have had a tough year, but if you performed above and beyond expectations, you *should* ask for a promotion or extra compensation. A rough financial time could serve as one of the best times to ask because struggling companies need to keep their best performers onboard to right the ship.

PRO TIP: ASK FOR TIME TO DECIDE

Career coach Carlota Zimmerman says that one of the most powerful underused steps when negotiating a raise or a job offer is to ask for time to decide. "You have the right to say, 'I need some time to think about this,'" Zimmerman says. This request allows you to make a less-rushed, more thoughtful decision, and it even can alter the power dynamic in the conversation.

That's exactly what happened with one of Zimmerman's clients. "She needed a $10,000 raise. They offered her $5,000. What was that going to do? She had two children going to college. She was like, 'Well, I really need to think about that.' They called her the next morning and offered her $20,000. They were worried that she was going to leave."

It can help to have a strong personal story and a powerful reason for the ask, like the one that Zimmerman's client had, but that's not necessary. It doesn't even matter whether you do need the time to think about the offer or you just want to use the time as leverage. Anyone can use the power tactic of asking for time. It takes courage and nerve, but it can prove quite successful, which Zimmerman's client demonstrated. "She was just a very good poker-hand player," Zimmerman says.

SCRIPTS

Set up the initial meeting about the raise or promotion.

> "Hi there, I'd like to speak with you about my performance and compensation. I've blown away my goals for the past year and made a real difference for the company. Could you let me know some days and times when you're available to chat?"

If they agree to the conversation . . .

> "Great, thank you so much. Before we talk, I'm sharing a document I've prepared, detailing my accomplishments since my last review and a few other points. If you have any questions or need anything else before our conversation, please let me know."

If they say that the company isn't in a position financially to give raises . . .

> "I understand, and I know it's been a challenging year. But I also know that I'm one of the top performers here, and my research shows that other people with my experience and title make more than I do. When would be a good time to talk about this?"

Consider mentioning perks other than salary increases: remote work, additional paid time off, a better title, tuition reimbursement, stock options, a bonus—anything that you would value if a raise definitely isn't going to happen. If you really want a salary increase, though, don't abandon that too quickly in favor of other forms of compensation.

If they say that the company does raises or promotions only during a certain time of year . . .

> "Thanks for letting me know. Let's revisit the conversation then. Meanwhile, could we have a quick chat about how the process works? I want to understand all the parameters. Please let me know some days and times that work for you."

At this point, you could share the rundown of your recent accomplishments and above-and-beyond work. ("While I have you, I'm sharing a document listing some of my key accomplishments since my last review. Please let me know if you have questions about any of it.")

If they refuse to engage in any discussion about compensation . . .

> "That's disappointing. Given my recent performance, how my work has benefited the company, and my research that shows that others in this role are making more than me, I think it's reasonable to have a conversation about my compensation. Could we revisit this topic in a month or so?"

Again, you could consider mentioning non-salary compensation, but don't give up on a higher salary too quickly. You also could mention the possibility of looking elsewhere or just leaving the company, but that's a dangerous game to play. If you make that threat and other jobs don't materialize, you might create an intensely uncomfortable situation at your current workplace.

In the meeting itself

> "Thank you so much for taking the time to speak with me. I enjoy working here, but my research shows that others with my experience and title earn more than I do. I also had a really good year, achieving all my goals and contributing a lot to the company, as you saw in the document I sent you. With all that in mind, what can we do to increase my salary?"

Have a target in mind as either a percentage or an amount. That target should come from your research and conversations with colleagues, mentors, and others. You can float the number yourself or wait for your supervisor to ask. Either way, prepare to have that conversation and don't start with your target number. Go slightly higher, with the goal of negotiating down to your target. But don't make the starting number so high that it short-circuits the conversation before negotiations begin.

If they ask you for a number . . .

> "Based on my research, along with my experience and accomplishments from the past year, I'd like a(n) _____ [percentage] increase."

OR

> "Based on my research, along with my experience and accomplishments from the past year, I'd like a(n) _____ [amount] increase."

If they give you an acceptable number in an initial offer or counteroffer . . .

> "Thank you so much. It means a lot that you worked with me on this."

Then confirm when the raise will begin, ask if you need to provide any additional information, and request confirmation of the raise in writing. Consider pushing your luck to ask for additional forms of compensation, such as extra time off, tuition reimbursement, or a title increase. Read the room first, however, so you don't overplay your hand.

If they give you an unacceptable initial offer or counteroffer . . .

> "I appreciate you working with me on this, but based on my research and all that I've accomplished for the company, I think it's reasonable to ask for more than that. Is there any wiggle room here?"

If they say no, consider bringing up additional perks such as a title change or extra time off.

If they say that the company isn't in a position financially to give raises right now . . .

> "I understand. It's been a challenging year. But I know that I'm one of the top performers here, and my research shows that others with my experience and title make more than I do. Do you have any wiggle room to make something work?"

Again, consider mentioning perks other than salary increases: remote work, additional paid time off, a better title, tuition reimbursement, stock options, a bonus. If you want a higher salary, don't abandon that too quickly for other possibilities.

If they say that the company does raises and promotions only during a certain time of year . . .

> "Thanks for letting me know. I'd like to revisit this conversation at the right time. I'll send an invite to get some time on our calendars around then. Meanwhile, could you tell me more about how the process works?"

If they refuse to have any discussion about compensation . . .

> "That's disappointing. Given my performance, how I've helped the company, and my research, which shows that others in this role make more than me, I think my request is reasonable. Could we revisit this conversation in a month or two?"

Again, consider non-salary compensation but don't give up on salary too quickly. Consider mentioning the possibility of leaving. But if you make that threat, prepare to live with the consequences.

Q *What if they deny your request?*
A If you felt heard and respected but forces beyond your control such as a bad financial quarter stood in the way, thank your supervisor and revisit the topic in a few months. If the entire experience left you feeling unheard and unappreciated, consider looking elsewhere. Either way, don't badger your supervisor about it, sulk, slack off, or trash-talk the company. Take the high road—because you don't want to burn a bridge you may need to use later—and look for your next job on your own time.

A HIGHER SALARY OR BETTER BENEFITS WITH A JOB OFFER

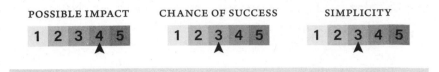

POSSIBLE IMPACT   CHANCE OF SUCCESS   SIMPLICITY

1 2 3 4 5   1 2 3 4 5   1 2 3 4 5

Q *What are you asking?*
A You're requesting more money or other types of compensation at the end of a successful job interview.

Q *How big a deal is it?*
A Your ability to negotiate salary and other compensation can make or break an interview. Striking out can kill your chances of getting the job or your interest in the position. But doing it right could mean more money in your pocket, more days off, newfound clout, and more. Every successful hiring negotiation determines what you'll earn in that job, so it sets the bar for future interviews. The more successful your negotiations, the higher your floor for future earnings, which is good!

Q *How likely is it that you will succeed?*
A If you just graduated, your chances may not look great. If, as an industry veteran, you have a ton of connections, a sparkling reputation, and an impressive arsenal of skills, you may be able to name your price. For most of us, reality lies somewhere between those poles.

Q *Does asking pose any risks?*
A While relatively rare, some companies have revoked job offers or otherwise retaliated because someone tried to negotiate, says Stefanie O'Connell Rodriguez, host of Real Simple's *Money Confidential* podcast and creator of the *Too Ambitious* newsletter, which covers how ambition affects women's lives.[85] These stories shouldn't keep you from attempting to negotiate, she

says, but you should acknowledge the possibility of negative outcomes. So many people have heard over and over: If you ask, the worst thing that can happen is that someone says "no," which can lead to feeling blindsided when that kind of retaliation happens. A higher salary can bring more pressure and greater expectations, too.

Q *Does not succeeding pose any risks?*

A Along with the above, you may not be able to take the position if the compensation doesn't measure up. It can be heartbreaking to get that close to a job that then slips away.

Why Applicants Offered a Job Didn't Ask for More Money

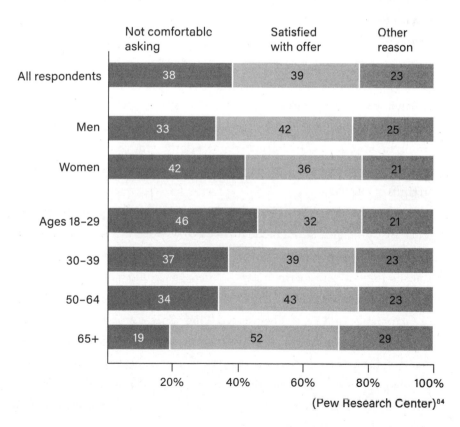

(Pew Research Center)[84]

Q   *How do you do it?*

A   "You absolutely have to be prepared going in," says career coach Carlota Zimmerman. "Take the time and do your research." That research includes understanding what people in that kind of position typically earn, which you can aggregate from sites such as Glassdoor and Salary.com as well as from talking to colleagues, coworkers, and friends. Look into the job market as a whole and other trends in your industry regarding time off, remote or hybrid work, 401(k) matching, tuition reimbursement, and so on to get a feel for what seems reasonable to ask.

With that research in mind, determine a realistic salary range and what you would accept for other kinds of compensation, such as paid time off. Job interviews are stressful enough. Don't put yourself in a position to make crucial decisions on the fly. Also don't let your salary range rest on what you've earned in the past. It should reflect salaries typical for the job you're trying to land now. In some instances, you'll know the salary range when going into the interview. Multiple states have enacted transparency laws, which require companies with more than a certain number of employees to list salary ranges on job listings. That transparency is far from universal, though, and some companies like to play with absurdly high maximums to grab attention, so accurate ranges will remain a mystery for many positions. In those cases, Zimmerman suggests letting the company guide when the money conversation happens, even if that means going through a few rounds of interviews.

When the topic arises, be enthusiastic but direct: " 'I'm glad you brought that up,' and take a minute to talk about why you're so excited to work for this company, what this company means to you, what this opportunity means to you," Zimmerman says. "Then you could say something like, 'With that in mind and given my experience and expertise, I'm looking for a salary range of XYZ.' " Then stop talking. That last part can prove challenging because most of us don't deal with silences well, but you must put the ball in their court while exuding confidence. "Make eye contact with the decision maker," Zimmerman says. "Say you've got several people interviewing you, but someone's senior. Make confident eye contact with that person." Then let them make the next move.

This strategy goes against the old saw: Whoever gives the first number "loses." Experts say that, no matter who gives a salary number first, applicants must recognize and appreciate their own value and walk away if the offers don't match their perceived worth. Career coach Mandi Woodruff-Santos, cohost of the *Brown Ambition* podcast, puts it this way: "It's about telling yourself that you're worthy and recognizing that the companies have the budget" to offer what you're worth.

Laura Adams, host of the *Money Girl* podcast, also points out that "by the time they've made an offer, they've chosen you. They want you. So that's when you have the most leverage, but that's when people are most scared. They feel like, 'Oh my gosh, if I don't just take this offer right away, I'm going to lose this opportunity.' They're not taking advantage of that moment to push the envelope a little bit and figure out what they're worth." Companies often start with a purposefully low offer to start the negotiations, and "in a lot of cases, the company would have paid higher salaries than what they were offering and what people immediately would accept." That's good reason to stand firm, even if doing that feels incredibly scary.

Finally, don't feel pressured to decide then and there. It's perfectly acceptable to say that you need some time, regardless of whether you do need it or you want to flex and make them sweat a bit. For an example, see the pro tip on page 193.

SCRIPTS

If you're comfortable giving a salary range . . .

> "The possibility of working here is exciting. The people I've met and what they've said have impressed me. It feels like a great fit, and I know that I can make a positive contribution to the company. With that in mind and given my experience and expertise, I'm looking for a salary between _____ [minimum] and _____ [maximum]."

Then stop talking.

If they respond positively to your range . . .

> "That's great to hear. What else can you tell me about the benefits and compensation for this role?"

Ask about perks that matter most to you, such as paid time off, tuition reimbursement, stock grants, and so on.

If they respond with a number lower than your range . . .

> "Thanks for sharing that with me. That's lower than what I'm looking for, and based on my research, experience, and expertise, I think the range I gave is reasonable. What flexibility do you have?"

If they say there's no flexibility, don't panic or give up hope. They may be engaging in gamesmanship with you. If the job requires negotiating with vendors, clients, or others, they may want to see how you handle the process in a real-life situation. Stand firm with your range and use the rest of the interview to continue emphasizing your value. The rest of the compensation package—paid time off, stock grants, 401(k) matching, tuition reimbursement, bonuses, and more—could make up for a disappointing salary range, so understand the complete offer before dismissing it solely based on salary.

If you don't want to give a salary range . . .

> "The possibility of working here is exciting. The people I've met and what they've said have impressed me. It feels like a great fit, and I know that I can make a positive contribution to the company. With that in mind, I'm looking for fair compensation based on my experience and expertise. What's the salary range for this position?"

If they provide an acceptable range . . .

> "Thank you for letting me know. What else can you tell me about the benefits and compensation package?"

Keep your poker face going. If you seem too excited, they could hold steady at the minimum because they think you'll take it.

If they respond with a range lower than what you want . . .

> "Thanks for sharing that with me. That's lower than what I'm looking for, and based on my research, experience, and expertise, I think the range I gave is reasonable. What flexibility do you have?"

Consider countering with a specific range of your own but don't undermine your value by presenting a lower range than you planned because you feel afraid. If they say there's no flexibility, remain calm. They may be testing how you react under pressure. Hold steady and keep highlighting the value you're offering to their company. The rest of the package could compensate for the range, so gather all the details before making your next move.

If they won't provide a range . . .

> "That's interesting. Many companies post salary ranges in job listings, which is great, so it's disappointing that you seem unwilling to share that information. What *can* you tell me about the compensation for this role?"

If they continue not to engage, consider it a major red flag that potentially hints at an overall lack of transparency within the company. Knowing that, if they corner you into providing a salary range, give one above what you initially planned to request. That red flag likely means that you won't be joining the company in the future, so you have nothing to lose by testing the boundaries of your salary range. That information can prove useful in future interviews with other companies.

Once a number is on the table . . .
If they refuse to negotiate . . .

> "That's disappointing. I'm interested in this job, and I know I would be a tremendous asset to the company. But my research indicates that my compensation range is reasonable. What can we do to move toward a resolution that will satisfy both sides?"

If you need more time to consider the offer . . .

> "I appreciate the offer. I'm going to need some time to think about it. When would you need to hear back from me?"

Q   *What if they deny your request?*

A   If the offer is so low that you can't live on it, thank them for their time and move on. (If the money doesn't matter, congrats! For the rest of us, it does.) Most of the time, though, the next steps don't look so cut-and-dried, and you have a lot of variables to consider, including:

- How unhappy are you in your current role?
- How strong is the rest of the compensation package?
- Is the new company flexible about remote work?
- Did you click with the people you met?
- Did you feel respected and heard in the interview?
- Does the new company excite you?
- Does the new company clearly value diversity and inclusion?
- Would you take pride in telling people that you work there?

Ultimately, we all want to work where we feel valued and respected, where we can make a positive contribution—maybe even feel challenged and inspired—and where we can make a good living. If the offer from a new employer checks those boxes but falls short of your salary demands, it still can make a great fit. But you can't make that decision without knowing your worth first.

FEAR OF THE WORST-CASE SCENARIO

Freaking out about that job interview? Amanda Abella, founder and CEO of sales training and marketing company Make Money Your Honey, counsels her clients to remember that, even though anxious minds dwell on everything that could go wrong, those worst-case scenarios usually don't happen. "Oftentimes the story they've created in their minds about how something is going to go is far worse than the reality of taking the action. If we remember that our brains are trying to keep us safe and that we're not being chased by lions or in any actual physical danger, that helps with confidence. Then we do the thing, and the anxiety immediately subsides because the thought of doing it was worse than doing it. Often the remedy to anxiety and lack of confidence is just doing it and realizing that it wasn't so bad after all."

A BETTER SEVERANCE PACKAGE

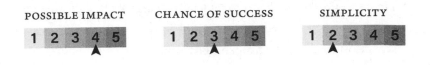

POSSIBLE IMPACT   CHANCE OF SUCCESS   SIMPLICITY
1 2 3 4 5   1 2 3 4 5   1 2 3 4 5

Q *What are you asking?*
A You're requesting more favorable exit benefits when parting ways with your employer.

Q *How big a deal is it?*
A No matter how hot or cold the job market, a good severance package can make a big difference. Any extra money, every extra week of insurance coverage, and anything else you can squeeze from the company can help you better pad your safety net or weather the hardships of unemployment. But from a company's perspective the severance paperwork typically requires that you waive the right to make future claims related to your employment. That could include blocking you from revealing confidential or proprietary information, making defamatory statements, or working for a competitor. Depending on your circumstances, this could be a very big deal and likely would require the services of an employment lawyer before you sign.

Q *How likely is it that you will succeed?*
A On your own, not very likely, experts say, but with professional help, somewhat more likely. The pros all recommend working with an employment lawyer, which doesn't make financial sense for most people. Even if it does, retaining a good lawyer doesn't guarantee success. Your odds may vary for many reasons, including why you're leaving.

Q *Does asking pose any risks?*

A What are they going to do? *Fire* you? Seriously, though, it shouldn't hurt to ask. If a company does reduce your severance package because you asked for a better deal, contact a lawyer, pronto.

Q *Does not succeeding pose any risks?*

A Worst case, you keep the original package.

Q *How do you do it?*

A First, take a deep breath. Leaving a job—whether being let go, quitting, or for another reason—can unleash a stampede of emotions. I know from firsthand experience. To borrow from Taylor Swift, "I've been there, too, a few times." You may think, *Just give me the paper. I'll sign whatever you want to get outta here*, which is exactly the reaction that the company wants. Signing makes their jobs easier, but it may not serve your best interests. Even if it does, you may not have the mental clarity to make that judgment. A slow-motion bomb is dropping on your life, after all. That's why saying that you need more time is such an important step. More time can allow you to get your feet under you emotionally, to read the termination agreement with a clear head, and perhaps to contact a lawyer. Companies always prefer that you sign before walking or ending the call, but they typically will give you a window of time to sign the document or risk losing the offer, so asking for a little extra time likely won't pose a problem.

Again, experts recommend working with an employment lawyer familiar with the laws of your state, province, or jurisdiction, especially if you think that you have legitimate and actionable claims of wrongdoing against your company. Asking relatives or friends for recommendations is one of the best ways to start, as is contacting your local bar association, but even a simple Internet search for "employment lawyers near me" can help. If you do look online, also read reviews of the firms to check for red flags.

Many lawyers offer a free or reduced-rate consultation in which you can tell them about your circumstances and get an initial take on how to consider proceeding. (You don't have to work with the first firm you contact.

Even if their services are free, they still need to respond promptly, communicate with respect, and otherwise behave professionally. If that first interaction doesn't feel right, move on.) Sometimes the slightest involvement of a lawyer can prompt action. According to career coach Carlota Zimmerman, "Sometimes just having a solid attorney contact them, they suddenly will say, 'Oh, that was a misunderstanding. Let's work this through,' because they don't want to deal with it."

Severance packages include more than just salary. Will you receive your payout in a lump sum or as regular payments over time? Are you being paid for unused vacation? How long will the company's insurance plan cover you? What happens to your equity or pension plan? Do they intend to contest your application for unemployment insurance? Does it include a noncompete clause, restricting your ability to work for certain companies for a set time? These packages contain a lot of information that you and/or your lawyer need to review carefully before you make any decisions. From there, follow your lawyer's lead in communicating with your former employer. Above all, "take your time," Zimmerman says. "Once that legally binding contract is signed, it's too late to say, 'Wait, I can't work in this industry for the next five years?'"

SCRIPTS

"Thank you for this offer. I'd like to take a little time to read it thoroughly and perhaps have a lawyer review it. When do I need to give you a response?"

If they push you to sign immediately . . .

"I hear you, but I need to give the document the attention it deserves, read it with a clear head, and potentially speak with a lawyer about it. When do I need to give you a response?"

If they push back about speaking with a lawyer . . .

"This is an important document. I'm not a lawyer, so a professional looking out for my best interests should review it before I feel confident moving forward."

Q *What if they deny your request?*

A If they insist that you need to sign right away or risk losing the deal, thank them for the offer, tell them that your lawyer will contact them soon, and leave or end the call. Retain a lawyer as soon as possible.

If you're trying to negotiate a better deal but aren't getting anywhere, you may have to leave well enough alone. That's especially true if you've hired a lawyer because the longer the negotiations run, the more legal fees you probably will have to pay. The last thing you need after leaving a job is running up unnecessary costs, so decide when to fight or when to cut your losses and move on.

FIVE KEY POINTS ABOUT DEADLINES FOR SIGNING SEVERANCE AGREEMENTS

- No federal or state law requires companies to provide severance to all terminated employees.
- If the organization offers severance, it must follow certain rules, and those rules can vary by state.
- Federal law requires companies to give employees age 40 or older at least 21 days to consider the severance agreement. In a group layoff, that number jumps to 45 days.
- Federal law makes no requirement for people younger than 40, but experts say that many companies typically allow a short window, usually 7 to 10 days, to review the document.
- Once you sign the document, you typically have 7 days to change your mind.

No federal or state law requires companies to provide severance on termination, but if they do, federal law requires that employees age 40 or older have at least 21 days to consider a severance agreement.

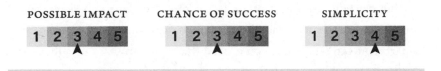

COMPANY MATCHING FOR CHARITABLE DONATIONS

POSSIBLE IMPACT	CHANCE OF SUCCESS	SIMPLICITY
1 2 **3** 4 5	1 2 **3** 4 5	1 2 3 **4** 5

Q *What are you asking?*
A You're requesting that your employer contribute some of or the same amount of a donation that you made to a charity.

Q *How big a deal is it?*
A For charities, it's a game-changer. According to Double the Donation, a company that helps businesses run their donation-match programs, more than 26 million Americans work at companies with charitable-matching programs.[86] That includes 65 percent of Fortune 500 companies. These programs donate $2 to $3 billion yearly, but that amount represents just the tip of the iceberg. Double the Donation estimates that anywhere from $4 to $7 billion in matching contributions go unused every year, an enormous missed opportunity for charities.

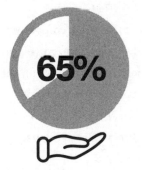

65% of Fortune 500 companies have a matching program for charitable donations, and 84 percent of donors say they're more likely to give if the donation is matched. (Double the Donation)

Q *How likely is it that you will succeed?*
A If your company already has a program in place, you only need to confirm that your company will match donations to your organization of

choice. If you're giving to massive charities, such as the American Cancer Society, Habitat for Humanity, or United Way, that likely won't pose a problem. Some companies may not match contributions going to charities supporting reproductive rights or addiction recovery, for example, and most companies have limits on how much they match, which your HR person or department can tell you. If you exceed that number, that's usually it—no additional matching.

Q *Does asking pose any risks?*
A Your supervisor might not like that you asked or counter that you're not focusing on what matters most to the company. But if they respond too harshly, that reaction may signal that you're working for folks who don't share your values. It could be time to think about working elsewhere.

Q *Does not succeeding pose any risks?*
A Again, the main risk would be learning something negative about your company that makes you reconsider working there. For example, their rejection of your request—whether related to a specific donation or to the idea of a donation-matching program—could indicate that the company's views contradict your own, including that they potentially don't value charitable contributions or community service.

Q *How do you do it?*
A If you've made the donation already and just want your company to match it, you'll need to provide documentation for the donation. Before you start, make sure you have a receipt showing the charity name, date, and donation amount. You also could need the organization's tax identification number, which may or may not appear on the receipt. After you submit that information, you should receive a notification within a day or two, usually by email, about whether the company granted a match.

For many businesses, particularly larger ones, you often can make the initial donation through an HR portal or dedicated website. In that case, search for the charitable organization and follow the prompts to complete the donation, which may include the option to request that your company match the amount. If you do that, the request will happen immediately, and, again, you should find out in a day or two.

If your company doesn't have a matching program, contact your HR person or department. They should tell you whether your company is willing to match charitable contributions and the process to do so. If they're willing, provide all the information outlined previously (receipt, tax ID, and so on). If they don't, ask them to change their policy. Consider scheduling a meeting to discuss the idea, and when the time comes, remember that businesses aren't philanthropic enterprises. Sell them on why that kind of program will benefit the business.

FIVE REASONS THAT YOUR COMPANY NEEDS A DONATION-MATCH PROGRAM

- Matches often are tax-deductible, which improves the bottom line.[87]
- This feel-good benefit can help recruit new employees.
- It can serve as positive PR for the business.
- Third-party vendor tools, such as Bright Funds, Double the Donation, and YourCause, can run it with minimal effort.[88]
- It can help people in need.

SCRIPTS

If the company has a program, you probably don't need a script for matching a donation. It usually happens online. The scripts below cover initial outreach to determine whether your company has a program and conversations if your employer doesn't have one.

> "Does the company match charitable donations made by employees? I [have made/am considering making] a donation to _____ [organization or cause], and I'd like the company to match what I'm doing. Who can I speak with about this?"

Be prepared to give details about the donation, including the name of the organization and the amount. If you think it will help, share details about why this donation matters to you.

If your employer doesn't match charitable contributions...

> "I understand. I'd like to talk with you about starting something. My research shows that having a matching program could bring real value to the company for a variety of reasons. Can we arrange a time to talk more about this?"

When pitching the idea of starting a program...

> "Thank you for taking the time to consider this idea. I'm passionate about helping others, and other employees here feel the same way. A program that matches charitable donations would benefit the organization for a number of reasons." Possible reasons include:

> "These donations usually have a tax benefit, which can help improve the bottom line."

> "HR can use the program to attract prospective employees. Two-thirds of Fortune 500 companies offer it, including Apple, GE, Microsoft, and others, and our competitors do, too."

> "It can generate feel-good PR for the company, which can strengthen customer approval and loyalty."

> "With third-party tools that I've researched, it can be up and running quickly and with minimal effort."

> "It's great for morale. So many folks here are passionate about various causes, and it would mean a lot to them for the company to support those organizations."

Q *What if they deny your request?*

A Follow up with someone in your company and ask them to reconsider. You may need to share more information about the charity or details of why the charity matters to you and merits the match, especially if it's a smaller, less well-known organization. From there, it's up to you to determine how much the rejection matters. Is it merely annoying or a sign that your company doesn't share your values and that you should consider working elsewhere?

SUCCESS STORY

After a two-year battle with multiple forms of cancer, my father passed away in October 2020. The following September, on what would have been his 75th birthday, I created a GoFundMe page to raise money for the American Cancer Society in honor of his memory. I had never crowdsourced charitable donations, so I just reached out to relatives, friends, colleagues, and acquaintances. Their outpouring of support pushed past my $500 goal quickly, but I wasn't going to stop there.

I vaguely remembered hearing that LendingTree, my employer, matched employees' charitable donations up to a certain amount each year, but I didn't know anything beyond that. I sent a quick email asking for details, and the HR team replied that they offered $1,500 in charitable matching each year if requested. That amount surprised me, as did learning that some other large companies have yearly maximums of $10,000 or more.[89] That kind of money can do enormous good for a lot of charities that desperately need funding.

Armed with that knowledge, I was determined to spread the word about these campaign matches. When contacting my network to donate, I reminded everyone to ask if their employers matched donations and, if so, to take advantage of that benefit. As a result, we raised at least an extra $790 in donations for the American Cancer Society (just for the matches I learned about), which helped push the fundraiser's total to more than $5,000, which wouldn't have happened if I hadn't sent that initial email to my HR department.

7. RELATIONSHIPS

Navigate Finances with Family and Friends

How to ask for:

INFORMATION ABOUT YOUR PARENTS' FINANCIAL SITUATION

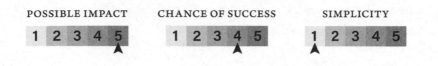

POSSIBLE IMPACT	CHANCE OF SUCCESS	SIMPLICITY
1 2 3 4 **5** ▲	1 2 3 **4** 5 ▲	**1** 2 3 4 5 ▲

Q *What are you asking?*

A You're requesting that your caregivers discuss their finances with you, including their goals and wishes.

Q *How big a deal is it?*

A "It's important to understand your parents' financial situation as they get older because you'll likely have to get involved with their financial lives," says Cameron Huddleston, author of *Mom and Dad, We Need to Talk: How to Have Essential Conversations with Your Parents about Their Finances.* "You might have to help a parent stay on top of household finances after the death of a spouse. You might have to help care for one or both parents if they have health issues or cognitive decline, such as dementia, and you'll likely have to deal with what's left behind after both of your parents have died. The more information you have about their finances, estate planning, and wishes, the easier it will be to handle any of these monumental tasks."

Retirement Savings in 2022		
Age	**Median**	**Average**
45–54	$61,500	$179,200
55–64	$89,700	$256,200
65+	$87,700	$280,000

For people age 55 and older, average retirement savings look OK, but remember that the median separates the higher half of a set from the lower half. That number paints a very different picture and gives you even more reason to speak with your parents about their financial situation. (Vanguard)[90]

Q *How likely is it that you will succeed?*

A More likely than you think, Huddleston says. "A lot of people are surprised when they discover that their parents are willing to have this conversation. A lot of financial advisors have said that their older clients want to have these conversations. Kids just need to ask."

Q *Does asking pose any risks?*

A If you don't approach the topic carefully, your parents might ignore your efforts or accuse you of nosiness. If you have siblings, ask them first whether they want to participate in these conversations; if you don't, you risk upsetting them, too. You also may learn upsetting details about your parents or their financial situation. For example, you could find out that your parents have no savings and/or huge debts, feel embarrassed to say so, and don't have any kind of financial plan. Maybe they do have plenty of money, and they've decided to leave it all to the cat. But none of that should keep you from asking. There's too much at stake.

Q *Does not succeeding pose any risks?*

A If you don't have the discussion, you may not be able to help your parents as they age. If they won't communicate with you, it's impossible to know everything they need or to honor their wishes. If they suddenly die and you have to handle their finances, you might feel blindsided or helpless.

Q *How do you do it?*

A Every family behaves differently. For some, you'll need to have many separate conversations before you even approach your parents. For example, if you have siblings and you all have good relationships, the first step is determining who wants to join the discussion and to what degree. These conversations sometimes can prove more difficult than talking to your parents. But you need to keep your siblings in the loop about what you want to do, otherwise you risk fostering resentment and bitterness, making an already awkward or challenging activity worse. If your relationship with a sibling or a sibling's relationship with your parents has fractured so badly that a constructive conversation looks impossible, you may want to sidestep the sibling. Ideally, however, all your parents' kids should know that you're going to have the talk.

For the main conversation itself, experts suggest approaching it from a place of love and caring. It's not about numbers, paperwork, passwords, or account balances. It's about preparing to take care of loved ones when they can't do it for themselves. Huddleston says, "If money isn't a taboo topic in your family, you've talked about it openly, and you have a good relationship with your parents, there's nothing wrong with simply saying, 'Mom and Dad, I want to be able to help you as you get older if you ever need help. But to do that, I need some information, so I'd like to carve out some time to have some conversations.'"

Many families don't talk openly about money, though, or friction exists among children and parents. In cases like those, a less-direct approach might work best. Asking, "How've you been feeling lately?" or "How's retirement treating you?" can open the door to a conversation, as can mentioning a TV show or recent news report or playing a "spontaneous" game of What If? "If you could retire today and money was no option, what would you do?"

Behavioral scientist Jeff Kreisler suggests using other people's stories as an entry point to a larger discussion. "'Hey, Mom and Dad, do you remember my friend Jonathan? His parents retired, and they just had to sell their house because they didn't diversify. How can we make sure that you avoid that situation?'" Telling a story that way—how parents, to motivate a grown child, might mention a classmate who became a successful lawyer or doctor—can make a point more subtly. "If you avoid making it 'Let me tell you what to do' as much as 'Let's figure out what's important to you and how we can help,' that's going to be the best way to get there," Kreisler says.

To start the conversation, you also can share your own experiences. Maybe you maxed out your 401(k) contribution, met with a financial planner, or wrote a will for the first time. Tell your parents, then use that information as a diving board to ask whether they ever have done the same. From there, steer the conversation to other topics regarding their finances.

It's OK to let them know that the conversation feels awkward for you, too. Yvonne Thomas, PhD, a psychologist in Los Angeles, suggests telling them, "I don't want to think about this either, but we have to because I love you and want to honor what you want. We have to be prepared." Also, you're not going to resolve everything in the initial conversation. Honestly, you may not resolve anything beyond determining whether your parents will speak with you about these topics—and in some cases, you won't settle even that question fully. Consider these the first steps of a marathon, not the whole race.

SCRIPTS

For speaking with siblings before approaching your parents

> "Do you have a few minutes to talk about _____ [what you call your parents]? I want to speak with them about their financial situation, so I'm checking with you first. I'm not sure how they'll react, but they're getting older, so we need to start the conversation. We don't need to ask for all the details right away, but we may have to help them stay on top of their finances as they age, which will be easier if we start now rather than scrambling in the middle of a health crisis or after they're gone. When in the next week or two looks good to talk about this?"

If one or more of your siblings doesn't want to have the conversation . . .

> "I hear you, but it's important. I've heard stories from _____ [source(s)] about how they wished they'd spoken to their parents about it sooner. This first [call/meeting] is just about starting the conversation. We're not asking them for bank balances, passwords, or anything like that. I want to know what their financial plans and goals are and what they're doing to work toward those. With other stuff, we can cross those bridges later. Would you like to [be on the call/join the meeting]? It's fine if you don't, but it's time to get the ball rolling."

If they're afraid of how your parents will react . . .

> "Yeah, I'm nervous about that, too, but this is important, so we can't let nerves keep us from having the conversation. Plus, I've read that parents often are OK with talking with their kids about this stuff, so hope-

fully ours will feel the same way. When's a good time to talk more about this with me?"

If they question your motives . . .

> "This isn't about me. It's about making sure that they're in a good place financially as they get older. It's also about knowing their wishes, goals, and plans. So many people never talk to their parents about these things but wish they had. You should be as involved in these conversations as you want, which is why I reached out to you first rather than going directly to them. The whole family should have this discussion."

If they refuse to participate . . .

> "I'm sorry to hear that, but I understand. I'll speak with them about it and let you know how it goes. Even if you don't want to be involved, you should know what they say."

If they support having the conversation but don't want to participate . . .

> "I understand. I'll speak with them about it and let you know how it goes, including any decisions or next steps. If you change your mind, just let me know."

If they want to join the conversation . . .

> "Great, I'm glad to hear that. Let's talk about how best to make this work. Do you want to talk about that now, or would you prefer to do it later?"

For starting the conversation with your parents
The direct route . . .

> "Can we set aside some time soon to talk about your financial situation? I want to be able to help as you get older, but to do that, we need to talk

> about a few things. I'm not going to interrogate you, I promise, and you can share as much or as little information as you like. I've heard too many stories about folks who never had these conversations with their parents but, when an emergency happens, wish they had. I don't want that to happen to us. You have the ultimate say over what happens with your money, and talking about that now can ensure that happens. When's a good time to talk about this?"

For an indirect route, you have lots of options, including:

Leveraging your experience:

> "I just maxed out my 401(k) contribution for the year. How are your savings going?"

> "I just had my first-ever meeting with a financial planner. Have you ever met with one?"

> "An article I read said that most people don't have enough money saved for retirement, which is scary. I'm nervous about that for myself. How are you feeling about your own savings?"

> "I [just made/am thinking about making] a will for the first time. Do you have one?"

Leveraging someone else's experience:

> "A coworker told me that her parents had to sell their home because they burned through their retirement so quickly. How do you feel about your savings?"

> "A friend told me that his dad died of a heart attack but didn't leave a will, so everything is crazy for him now. That kind of freaked me out. Do you have an up-to-date will?"

"My boss was telling me that her mom passed away and it's been a nightmare because they never talked about her finances. She's having a really hard time trying to figure out what accounts and documents exist and where. That made me think of you. Do you have someplace where you keep a current record of all your accounts and stuff like that?"

What If? "party game" questions:

"If you won the lottery tomorrow, what would you do with your winnings?"

"What's your idea of a perfect retirement?"

"If you could do any job for the rest of your life, what would it be?"

"If you could live anywhere, where would you choose?"

If they don't feel comfortable talking about money . . .

"I hear you, but it's important. So many people scramble to help their parents as they get older and wish they'd spoken about it sooner. It's your money, and you should do whatever you want with it. If we talk about it now, it'll be easier to make sure that everything gets handled the way you want if there's ever an emergency."

If they say it's none of your business . . .

"I can understand why you'd say that. Your money is your business, I get it. But the best way for you to make sure that it goes where you want is to say so now. Otherwise, we won't know. So many people never have this conversation with their parents, but after it was too late, they wished they had. This is just about starting a conversation. If you don't want to talk about your money, you don't have to, but talking about it now will make it easier to ensure that what you want happens. I just want to get a feeling for what your financial plans and goals are and where everything stands.

> With other stuff, we can cross those bridges later. Can we set aside a time
> to talk for a bit?"

If they question your motives . . .

> "This isn't about me. This is about you and making sure that you have as
> much control as possible over your finances as you get older. The more we
> know now about what you want, the more we can do to plan accordingly.
> So many people never talk to their parents about this but wish they had.
> It's important, so the whole family should discuss it."

If they agree to have the conversation . . .

> "Thank you for agreeing to talk. It feels weird asking you about all this, but
> it really is important, so I appreciate your willingness. What's a good day
> and time for you?"

Q *What if they deny your request?*
A If siblings refuse to take part, consider mentioning the idea again in a
few days. With time for reflection, that decision might change. If it doesn't,
take the high road. Thank them for considering it and tell them that you're
moving forward with the conversation and will let them know how it goes.

The same goes for your parents. If they don't want to talk, try again in
a few days—and maybe even a third or fourth time. Consider enlisting the
help of a third party, such as another family member, family friends, a member of the clergy, or a financial professional whom your parents trust. If your
best attempts don't bear fruit, there's only so much you can do. It's their
money, after all. "If they want to tell you, that's fine," Huddleston says. "If
they don't, then you're going to have to live with that."

SUCCESS STORY

In 2017, Yanely Espinal's grandfather died unexpectedly. Her whole family scrambled to process their heartbreak and manage costs, including the funeral. The chaos after his passing, which countless families face every day, profoundly affected Espinal. She never wanted her own family to face that sort of turmoil. She also knew that she and her eight siblings needed to act, and soon.

"We're already stressed and sad and grieving," says Espinal. "Why add another layer of stress to that? We want to prevent that from happening with Dad and Mom, so let's talk now about a plan."

That talk started with a WhatsApp chat called "Parents' Retirement," in which Espinal and her siblings talked about their parents' ongoing financial needs, their eventual retirement, and other topics. A sibling Zoom call followed. Ultimately, they decided on two primary goals: covering their parents' monthly expenses and building a one-year emergency fund.

All the siblings agreed that Espinal, a financial educator with a social media platform called MissBeHelpful, should oversee their efforts. Because their income levels varied widely, it was less obvious how much each sibling would contribute. The discussion settled on a sliding scale, she says, which allowed all of them to help "without completely throwing off their financial situation." They decided that each sibling would give what he or she felt comfortable contributing. Espinal offered to keep the amounts secret, but her siblings unanimously agreed that was unnecessary. Ultimately, the group realized that "this isn't about us, our petty egos, and our financial whatevers. Put that aside. We're here to figure it out for Mom and Dad."

That's exactly what they've done. They haven't reached all their goals—"The only way to be truly on pace is to go back in time and begin investing for their retirement when I was still in elementary school"—but they contribute enough monthly, when combined

with their parents' Social Security payments, to cover their housing, food, and other essential bills.

It was more than about money, too. They learned details about
their parents' wishes that they "never would have guessed," including that their mom wanted to be buried in her native Dominican
Republic rather than in Brooklyn, New York, where they lived for 30
years. The kids never would have known if they hadn't asked.

A CONVERSATION WITH YOUR SIGNIFICANT OTHER ABOUT MONEY

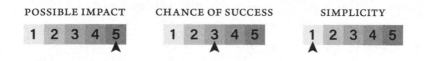

POSSIBLE IMPACT	CHANCE OF SUCCESS	SIMPLICITY
1 2 3 4 **5** ▲	1 2 **3** 4 5 ▲	**1** 2 3 4 5 ▲

Q *What are you asking?*
A You're talking with your partner about your finances.

Q *How big a deal is it?*
A Money issues can wreck relationships, and lack of communication often lies at the heart of the problem. A 2022 Personal Capital report said that 39 percent of adults avoid talking about money with their romantic partner—a number that rises to 44 percent for Millennials—and those figures add up to a recipe for disaster.[91] For a healthy relationship, it's crucial that you both share your beliefs, dreams, fears, goals, hang-ups, and thoughts about money. You don't have to agree on everything, which is good because you probably won't. But by being open and honest with each other and having those sometimes-uncomfortable discussions, you can develop a deeper understanding of your partner and possibly even prevent future troubles. Have these discussions long before you say, "I do."

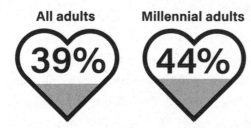

All adults
39%

Millennial adults
44%

Almost 4 in 10 adults avoid talking about money with their significant other, a rate that increases among Millennials. (Personal Capital)

Q *How likely is it that you will succeed?*

A Given how much some people hate talking about money, prepare for pushback. A little reluctance or nervousness is fine, but brick-wall unwillingness to talk also happens. "If they just say, 'That's an off-limit topic,' that's a red flag," says relationship expert Marni Feuerman, PsyD.[92]

Q *Does asking pose any risks?*

A Your loved one could get upset with you for asking. You also could find out information that troubles you, such as crippling debt, terrible credit, or no savings. Revelations like that could cast doubt on whether you want to continue the relationship. But better to know sooner than later, so start the conversation.

Q *Does not succeeding pose any risks?*

A If your loved one flies off the handle because you asked or, worse, refuses to talk about money at all, that could hoist a major red flag. If you're serious enough about the relationship to talk about money, don't give up just because the first conversation doesn't go well.

Q *How do you do it?*

A Do it early (not on the first date). When you feel the relationship getting serious, broach the topic. If you're planning a honeymoon or filling out baby registries, you waited too long. "The sooner, the better," Dr. Feuerman says, "because how somebody treats money and their financial goals, determining compatibility as far as that subject goes, is critical." But don't rush it, either. If money as a topic comes up organically and you run with it, great. Don't shoehorn it into a conversation in which it doesn't fit. Instead, arrange a time in advance to talk. It may seem awkward, especially if you've never talked about your finances before, but that strategy can help.

Kara Pérez, founder of financial education site Bravely Go, used to spring money conversations on her husband, who doesn't like talking about money—"Hates it, hates it, *hates* it," she says—and of course it never went well.[93] Then she changed her approach. "I started saying, 'Hey, I would love to talk about money this week. When would be a good time for you?' That's a good, general starter because now they know, and you're also giving them the option of 'OK, well, I don't want to do it right now, but I think maybe Saturday afternoon, after I get back from walking the dog. We can do it then.' So you've given them some control over the situation." Consider providing a talk list. It doesn't have to read like a school syllabus. It can consist of short bullets, such as: earliest memory of money, best/ worst money advice from parents, and so on. That way, your partner has time to think about a response rather than having to answer on the spot. That approach can work for your first couple's conversation about money or the 101st.

For that first conversation, reassure your partner that you're not look-ing to talk about numbers. You're not performing a financial audit. You just want to hear your significant other's thoughts and feelings about money and what it means so you can get to know each other better. Experts suggest starting with a discussion of money experiences with family when grow-ing up. You can ask about first memories of money, family conversations about it, first experiences with debt, and more. You have a million options, so write some of them down before you start, just in case nerves, pressure, or tangents make you forget in the moment. All those details will give you insight into your partner's views and beliefs about money. "If you under-stand where people have been, it's a lot easier to have grace and patience with where they're at," says Logan Cohen, a marriage and family therapist in Charlotte. "If you can be patient with where someone is, the likelihood that they'll want to listen to you is a lot higher."

Aditi Shekar, founder of money management app Zeta and cohost (with her husband) of *The Money Date* podcast, suggests employing a "past, pres-ent, and future approach."[94] Begin by asking about your earlier experiences with money, continue with where you stand now financially, and then state your thoughts and goals about the future. "They're not meant to be 'Tell me what your bank account balance is,'" Shekar says. "They're meant to be more casual conversations: 'Tell me about your financial story, then tell me about where you want to go,' so it's really low pressure and low expectation." You don't need to get to the "where you want to go" part in that first discus-sion, either. Just open the door to later conversations.

Lastly, show kindness and patience. Awkward conversations rarely play out perfectly. But if you show genuine interest in learning about your loved one's financial views and beliefs, remaining as understanding and nonjudgmental as possible, the conversation could represent an important step in your relationship. It can strengthen your compatibility with this amazing person, or it can reveal details that need further discussion and work. Either way, you need to do it if you want your relationship to succeed in the long run.

TEN GREAT CONVERSATION-STARTER QUESTIONS ABOUT MONEY

- "What's your earliest memory of money?"
- "Did your parents talk with you about money when you were little?"
- "Do you consider yourself a saver or spender?"
- "If you won the lottery today, what's the first thing you'd do with the money?"
- "What's your biggest financial mistake or success?"
- "What's the best or worst piece of money advice that you've received?"
- "Did you get an allowance as a kid? If so, what did you do with it?"
- "If you could give 18-year-old you a piece of financial advice, what would it be?"
- "Did you ever do a lemonade stand, sell candy or magazine subscriptions, or anything like that as a kid?"
- "How much could your partner spend without telling you?—and vice versa."

SCRIPTS

Asking to have the conversation

> "So we've never really talked about money, and I'd love to know your thoughts on a few topics. I'm not going to ask for your bank account balances, credit score, or anything like that. I just want to know more about your experiences with money, your views, and beliefs about it, and I'm happy to answer any questions you might have for me, too. When's a good time to chat about it?" Consider planning a money date for the occasion, offering to order your partner's favorite dinner or buy a nice bottle of wine.

If they're reluctant or they reject the idea altogether . . .

> "I know talking about money isn't easy. It's awkward for me, too, but as we move forward with our relationship, it's an important topic. I don't want to know your ATM pin or go through your credit report. I just want to hear more about how you think and feel about money. How does that sound?"

If they continue to refuse to talk . . .

> "I hear you. Can you think about it for a little bit, and maybe we can revisit this in a few days? Like I said, it's an important topic, and it would mean a lot to me to have this conversation."

If they agree to schedule a talk . . .

> "Thank you. I really appreciate it. It'll be a conversation, and we might even be able to have fun with it. Either way, I think it'll be a great step in our relationship, and it means a lot to me, so thank you."

Starting the first money conversation

> "Thank you for agreeing to do this with me. I know it may feel awkward. It does for me, too, but it's important. Plus, I'm really excited to hear what you have to say." Then follow with:

"Do you want to start with anything in particular?"

OR

"I'm not going to do all the talking, but I have an idea of where to start, if that's OK with you."

If they agree, ask questions such as:

"What's your earliest money memory?"

"When you were little, did your parents talk with you about money?"

"What's the best or worst piece of money advice that a relative or friend ever gave you?"

"Did you get an allowance as a kid? If so, what did you do with it?"

"Did you ever do a lemonade stand or anything like that when you were a kid?"

If they're struggling to answer or feeling nervous . . .

"How about I start to give you time to think about your answer. Is that OK?"

When the conversation ends . . .

"Thank you so much for doing this with me. Now we know some new, interesting details about each other, which is great. This really meant a lot to me, and I'd love to do it again. Would you be up for having another one of these chats, maybe next month?" If they push back, saying that it feels like too much too fast, reply that you understand and there's no rush. Then make a note in your calendar to bring it up again in a few weeks.

Q *What if they deny your request?*

A Don't give up because the first conversation doesn't go well. People have bad days. It's entirely possible that, after a few days, your loved one will feel more receptive than the first time. After thinking about it for a few days, your significant other may even come back to you and suggest having the talk. But if you encounter anger or venom, tread lightly.

Ultimately, this isn't a "nice to have" conversation. It's non-negotiable. A long-term relationship can't work if both parties won't speak about all sorts of topics, and few topics are more important than money. If your loved one adamantly refuses to discuss it, that red flag should give you pause about the long-term viability of the relationship.

FINANCIAL HELP FROM A RELATIVE OR FRIEND

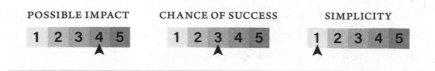

POSSIBLE IMPACT   CHANCE OF SUCCESS   SIMPLICITY

1 2 3 **4** 5   1 2 **3** 4 5   **1** 2 3 4 5

Q   *What are you asking?*
A   You're requesting a loan from a friend or family member.

Q   *How big a deal is it?*
A   Borrowed funds can offer a lifeline if you're navigating a rough patch. They can bridge the gap for a down payment on a home or a vehicle. They could make it possible for you or your child to attend college or start a small business. It's not just a big deal financially, either, because it can have a major impact on your relationship with the lender—and not always positively.

Q   *How likely is it that you will succeed?*
A   According to a Bankrate survey, 69 percent of American adults have loaned money to friends or family.[95]

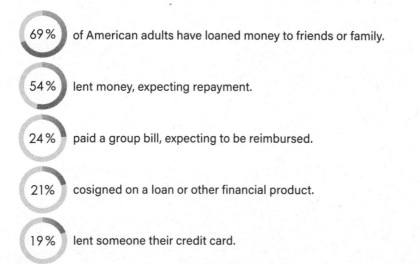

69% of American adults have loaned money to friends or family.

54% lent money, expecting repayment.

24% paid a group bill, expecting to be reimbursed.

21% cosigned on a loan or other financial product.

19% lent someone their credit card.

Q *Does asking pose any risks?*

A This request requires tremendous vulnerability, which is why it's vital to be thoughtful and selective about whom to approach. This ask isn't only about who has the financial means to help. It should be about who will have your back in a time of need or who will root for you as you work toward a milestone. On your team, you want people who can change lives by helping others. But not everyone will be willing to help. Some may judge or denigrate rather than choosing to inspire and support. You can't always tell the difference beforehand. Sometimes you have to trust your judgment and move forward.

Q *Does not succeeding pose any risks?*

A You risk not being able to accomplish what the loan would've allowed, and you risk damaging a relationship. You absolutely must consider the relationship risk first. Are you willing to risk it for money? Only you can decide.

Q *How do you do it?*

A If you're requesting financial help from a friend or relative, always offer to pay it back. In high-amount instances, such as money for a down payment on a home or vehicle, seed money for a small business, or tuition for college, it may not prove realistic to pay it back in full anytime soon—if ever. But offering to repay the amount—however long the timeline, however small the installments—sends a necessary message. If the other person says the money is a gift, push back. It's only right to repay the money, even if slowly. If the other person insists, accept that kindness graciously and offer profuse thanks. That person went above and beyond to help you. Honor that act of generosity by putting those funds to good use.

If the funds aren't a gift, Laura Adams, host of the *Money Girl* podcast, advises that you treat the request "like a business transaction."[96] That means formulating a repayment plan and putting it on paper. It doesn't need to be long, it doesn't need tables and charts, and it doesn't need fine print. But it should explain how much you need, for what purpose, your anticipated rate of repayment, the timeline, and how you'll handle a situation that prevents you from repaying in a timely manner. Depending on the lender, ballpark estimates should suffice. Even some creativity may help: Perhaps, as part of the repayment plan, you could do some cleaning, painting, yard-work, or other tasks for the person. The terms on that first document may change—because you should work with the lender on mutually agreeable terms—but they still matter. You're showing your commitment to repaying the loan and explaining how that process will go. "If you've got it all tidy and in a written document, that can salvage the relationship," Adams says. "But if you go into it in a very casual way, that's where things crumble and fall apart." Smaller transactions may not require as much documentation or any. This process may seem excessive if you're borrowing $50 because you forgot your wallet when grabbing drinks or dinner. But whatever assures your potential lender that you're serious about repayment is worth doing.

Successful business transactions build numbers, contracts, and fine print atop mutually beneficial relationships. Both sides win. Both parties move toward a better future. These transactions require vulnerability and empathy. If the other person doesn't know your situation, be open and hon-est, tell your story, share your experience *and* what you're trying to accom-plish. It may feel awkward or uncomfortable—and sometimes it's easier to share this vulnerability with strangers than with loved ones—but it can help forge a genuine connection that can strengthen with time.

INCLUDE IN YOUR REPAYMENT PLAN

- the amount you want
- the purpose of the money
- how much you'll repay, how often, and the repayment window
- what you'll do if you can't repay as outlined above

SCRIPTS

> "I'd like to chat about whether you'd be willing to lend me some money. I understand if you're reluctant, so as a show of good faith, I've written down the amount, why I need it, how I'd repay you, and other details. You'd be taking the risk, so everything's negotiable. If you agree, I want you to feel comfortable helping me and to know that I understand how serious this is because I value our relationship. Are you open to talking about it?"

If they're uncertain or reject the idea altogether . . .

> "I totally get it, and I don't feel great about having to ask. Are you at least willing to talk about it? What questions can I answer for you?"

Some questions that might arise:

> "Why did you ask me?"
>
> *Possible answer:* "Like I said, this is hard for me, but you and I always have been able to talk about important life stuff. I figured that you'd be willing to listen and be understanding about my situation, so I thought it was worth taking the chance."
>
> "Why do you need the money?"
>
> *Possible answer:* Tell your story. Maybe you lost your job or a major source of income. Maybe you need help with medical costs. Maybe you want to start a small business or go back to school. Whatever the story, share it. If the reason was important enough to ask for help, chances should look good that others will see that.
>
> "What guarantees do I have that you'll pay me back?" or "What happens if you don't pay me back?"

> *Possible answers:* "I give you my word that I'll pay you back, and I'll write in the document what will happen if I can't. Again, I know you're taking a risk, so I want you to feel comfortable doing that."
>
> "I promise that I'll communicate about this as often as possible. It's a tough time, so something might happen that could delay part of the repayment. If that does happen, I'll let you know as soon as possible so it isn't a surprise. That's only fair."

If they agree to lend you the money . . .

> "Thank you so much for helping me. It really means a lot. I'll update the document to add the details that we've discussed so everything's clear. I promise to do everything I can to honor your willingness to help me and repay you as soon as possible."
>
> **OR**

If they say they'd prefer to give the money as a gift . . .

> "That's incredibly generous of you. Thank you so much. But it's only right that I pay you back. Let's talk about the terms I drafted."

If they continue to insist on gifting the money to you . . .

> "Thank you so much. This really means so much to me. I promise I'll put this money to good use."

Q   *What if they deny your request?*

A   You could try again with the same friend or relative, but keep in mind the old saw that there's no use in beating a dead horse. If others might be willing to help, move on. Otherwise, think about crowdsourcing funds, a credit card, or a personal loan.

REPAYMENT OF MONEY LENT TO A FRIEND OR RELATIVE

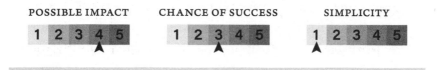

POSSIBLE IMPACT	CHANCE OF SUCCESS	SIMPLICITY
1 2 3 **4** 5	1 2 **3** 4 5	**1** 2 3 4 5

Q *What are you asking?*
A You're requesting that a family member or friend repay money that you loaned.

Q *How big a deal is it?*
A Potentially a big deal, depending on the amount you lent and your relationship with the borrower.

"GET CLEAR WITH YOURSELF"

Anyone can ask to borrow money, says clinical psychologist Lauren Cook. "What's harder is for the person being asked because they've got all their emotional stuff going on. 'Is this person going to be angry with me if I don't support them?' Especially if someone in the family has people-pleasing tendencies, which is often the person getting asked for $500 because sometimes the person will know, 'I'm not even going to ask that [other] person because they're going to say no to me. They have boundaries.' But if you were that person who's getting asked, you have to get clear with yourself: 'All right, what are my boundaries here? Am I going to give this as an act of help? Will I have resentment if I give this and don't get this money back?' Play the tape and ask yourself, 'How will I feel after giving?' If the feeling is relief, there's probably some people-pleasing going on. If there's resentment, maybe there's some lack of boundary-setting happening. That's where I'd start."

Q *How likely is it that you will succeed?*

A Your experience may vary, but this ask sometimes won't go according to plan. A Bankrate survey reported that 44 percent of people who loaned cash or a credit card to a friend or relative or cosigned on a financial product said that they had suffered a negative consequence as a result, such as losing money, hurting their credit score, or even damaging their relationship with the borrower.[97]

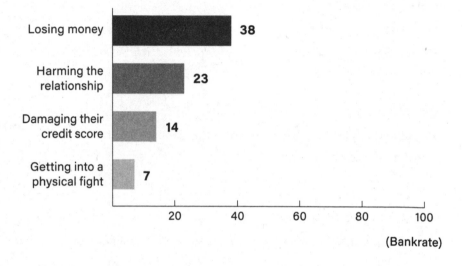

(Bankrate)

Q *Does asking pose any risks?*

A Any situation in which relationships and money mix can get dicey fast. It can become so toxic that many people give money to friends or family only as a gift, with no expectation of repayment. "I'm a big believer in making every loan a gift," says Lindsay Goldwert, author of *Bow Down: Lessons from Dominatrixes on How to Get Everything You Want.* "Otherwise, you're going to jeopardize the friendship." You as a prospective lender need to establish the plan as soon as possible. It's one thing to ask a borrower about repayment discussed when you made the loan. It's something else entirely if you didn't make repayment details clear from the outset.

Q *Does not succeeding pose any risks?*

A Your relationship can sustain irreversible damage, and not being repaid can cause headaches when bills come due.

Q *How do you do it?*

A If you laid out the loan with expectations and consequences, ask the borrower calmly and politely about the (next) payment. It can help to emphasize the importance of communication. Make sure that the other person knows that you understand that life happens. When it does, he or she should text, email, or call you to say that the (next) payment may come late and why. You're a friend or relative, not a loan shark, but if missed payments become commonplace, the talk will have to get tougher. It also can help to explain your own financial situation. If you have a tight budget and that missing payment means putting expenses on a credit card rather than paying cash, say so.

If you didn't discuss repayment details, proceed with caution. Coming in hot, with anger or accusations, will make the situation worse. Instead, approach evenhandedly: "We never talked about how you'd repay me, but I'd like to discuss it now." Emphasize that you'll work with the other person to come up with a plan that works for you both. Again, showing vulnerability and compassion makes sense. The borrower is going through a difficult stretch already; intimating that the person is a deadbeat likely will make it worse. But be firm. If the money didn't matter to you, you wouldn't be going through the headache and stress of asking for it back. Request repayment calmly and politely.

In either situation, "transparency and communication have to go hand in hand," says Cook. "Otherwise, the volcano will explode, and it won't be a pretty picture."

SCRIPTS

If you have a detailed repayment agreement in place . . .

> "Hey there, I haven't received a payment from you [lately]. Can we talk about when you'll be able to get that to me?"

If they'll pay you today or within a specific and reasonable timeframe . . .

> "That's great. Thanks so much. If something comes up in the future and you're going to be late, just let me know. The more we communicate about this, the better."

If they need more time but don't give a time frame . . .

> "I hear you, but let's nail down a time when you expect to be able to pay. If you know you're going to be late, let me know. Life happens, I understand, but the more we communicate, the better. When will you be able to get that to me?"

If they refuse to speak with you about it . . .

> "I know things are tough. The best way to handle this, though, is to talk to each other. I'm happy to help, but if we don't communicate, that becomes impossible. When do you think you might be able to pay?"

At this point, you could offer to tweak the existing agreement. Tread lightly, however. You could set a precedent that you're willing to change the terms of the deal.

If this is your first time talking about repayment . . .

> "We never talked about how you'd repay me, but I'd like to discuss it now. I'm on a tight budget, too, and that money matters to me. Do you have a plan to pay me back? Let's make one that works for both of us."

If they reply with a plan that sounds good to you . . .

> "That sounds great. Thanks for working with me on this. If something happens where you need a little extra time, let me know. Life happens, I know, but if we communicate with each other, that'll make everything easier for us both."

If they're willing to work with you on a plan . . .

> "Great, thanks so much. I know it's awkward to talk about this, but our relationship matters to me, so the best way to handle it is to be open and honest with each other. If we do that, we can figure out something that works for both of us."

Make sure that the borrower feels empowered. The more empowered the other person feels, the more fruitful the conversation. You don't have to agree to unacceptable terms, but listen and remain open to what the borrower says. For example, you can ask:

> "How much do you feel comfortable paying each _____ [week, month, year]?"

> "Is a certain time of the _____ [week, month, year] easier for you to pay?"

> "What's the easiest way for you to pay? Cash, check, app, something else?"

If they refuse to speak with you about repayment . . .

> "I know you're in a tough spot, and I was happy to help you, but, again, my budget's tight, too. I should've brought this up sooner, but I also never said that this was a gift, so let's figure out a plan that works for us both."

If they agree to talk it through, go back to "If they're willing to work with you on a plan," above.

Q *What if they deny your request?*
A You have a few options, none of them great. You could approach the borrower again in a few days, but it isn't likely that the person will prove any more willing than before. Depending on how the conversation ended, it may be worth a try. (For example, if the person had a bad day or a lot going on, consider giving it another go. But if the conversation ended with animosity, steer clear or at least wait a bit longer.) Also consider enlisting help. Speaking with a mutual relative or friend about the situation could lead to a breakthrough. In extreme cases, you might need to consider hiring a lawyer. Involving others is a risky move, however, because it could make the borrower feel attacked, which could make the situation even more untenable.

The most likely option, unfortunately, is accepting that you're not getting the money back. Depending on the amount, that reality can land a devastating blow financially and emotionally, but it happens more often than you might realize. In the Bankrate survey mentioned previously, 38 percent said they'd lost money lent to family or friends, and 23 percent reported experiencing a damaged relationship. That's why your best choices, when it comes to lending money, are, if you can afford it, to gift it, as Lindsay Goldwert recommends, or simply to say no.

EMOTIONAL HELP MATTERS, TOO

You don't have to lend money to help someone financially. Offering advice, helping a person avoid temptation, and even just cheerleading can make a real difference. Ashley Feinstein Gerstley, founder of the Fiscal Femme and author of *The 30-Day Money Cleanse,* calls people who help that way your "financial dream team." That informal team could include friends, family, coworkers, neighbors, whomever. It's about surrounding yourself with people who will help you move toward your goals. But of course, they can't help if they don't know what you're trying to do, so it all begins with opening up about your struggles and asking for support.

"It's the same as with a health challenge," Gerstley says. "If your friends know that you're trying to not eat sugar, they're not going to bake you cookies and bring them to the office. But if they didn't know, they might do that because they thought it might make you happy."

Money vulnerability can feel scary, though, even with those closest to you. "A great place to start is to say, 'I'm looking to save money' or 'I'm trying to pay down my debt.' You don't have to share the number if that feels too much for you at the time," she says. Sharing the "why" can help connect others with your journey, which can make it easier for them to help you.

LOWERING WEDDING PARTY COSTS

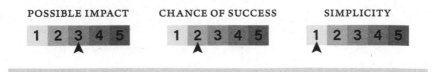

POSSIBLE IMPACT	CHANCE OF SUCCESS	SIMPLICITY
1 2 **3** 4 5	1 **2** 3 4 5	**1** 2 3 4 **5**
▲	▲	▲

Q *What are you asking?*
A You're requesting lower costs for participating in a friend's or relative's marriage ceremony.

Q *How big a deal is it?*
A Potentially big on multiple levels. Weddings can cost a lot of money. Reducing or controlling the costs of joining the wedding party can save you thousands. But you run the risk that asking might damage your relationship with the bride or groom.

Q *How likely is it that you will succeed?*
A Every relationship is different, and it can depend on the nature and magnitude of the request. But a true friend will understand. Data also offers some hopeful signs. A 2023 LendingTree survey found that nearly half of

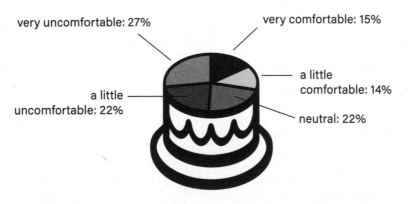

very uncomfortable: 27%
very comfortable: 15%
a little comfortable: 14%
a little uncomfortable: 22%
neutral: 22%

Are you OK if your wedding guests go into debt to attend your wedding? (LendingTree)

those surveyed said they'd feel at least somewhat uncomfortable knowing that friends and family took on debt to attend their wedding.[98] "Real friends don't want to find out later that you went broke going to their wedding," says friendship coach Danielle Bayard Jackson, author of *Fighting for Our Friendships*. "A real friend wouldn't want you to do that to yourself." Most of us would agree with that idea in theory, but the reality could look messy or turn into an absolute train wreck.

Q *Does asking pose any risks?*
A Just beginning this conversation poses a risk. The bride or groom, feeling angry or hurt, might take umbrage at the request. Before you speak with someone, think through what probably will happen and plan accordingly if the chat goes badly. But know that many brides and grooms will empathize. They're spending a lot of money, too. A good friend or relative will work with you to plan for you to participate in a way that won't send you to the poorhouse.

Q *Does not succeeding pose any risks?*
A The financial risks can prove significant, as can the emotional and social risks. These sorts of conversations can end relationships, which is tough music to face. "A lot of us are friends with people who, we know deep down, aren't truly our friends," Jackson says, "and we're scared to have these conversations because it would reveal what we already secretly know." But that doesn't mean that these talks shouldn't happen.

Q *How do you do it?*
A First, decide whether the reward is worth the risk. If the bride or groom won't take the request well and the savings look relatively small, maybe your best move is no move at all. On the other hand, if your friend or relative will understand and if enduring the awkwardness of the conversation can save you hundreds or thousands, then having that talk is a no-brainer. Most situations won't look nearly so cut-and-dried, though, so take the time to consider what will happen, as stressful and nerve-wracking as it may feel.

When you've decided to move forward, enter the conversation with a plan rather than an ultimatum. "We never say 'no,'" Jackson says. "It's 'What can I offer?'" If you can afford only one or two nights of the bachelor/ette trip, say so. You could skip that trip, the rehearsal dinner, or other prewedding events to ensure that you can attend the ceremony itself. Flexibility is key. You're asking the bride or groom to compromise, so prepare to do the same. Listen to the person's point of view and work toward a solution that makes everyone comfortable. Brides and grooms have different priorities. For some, bachelor/ette parties seriously matter, while others may not care. Some may place a big emphasis on the rehearsal dinner, wedding reception, or other related event. Understanding what matters most can help guide the discussion.

Happy compromise is the best-case scenario, but in the real world, that isn't always possible. You're bringing this concern to your friend or relative because it matters to *you*. Don't be afraid to be vulnerable and share your story. The other person may not know your situation, and learning details may inspire willingness to work with you. The discussion should operate as a two-way street, but if it doesn't, you ultimately need to do what's right for you, even if that means upsetting that friend or relative.

"It's OK to set boundaries," says clinical psychologist Lauren Cook. "You don't need to feel guilty about that. If you're going to feel resentment and not enjoy being at the bachelorette party, for example, or it's going to cause you so much stress that you're losing sleep and having to sacrifice basic necessities, you need to assert yourself and say, 'Hey, I just can't swing this.'"

SCRIPTS

"I'm so honored that you invited me to participate in your wedding. I want to be there for you, but I'm conflicted because my bank account isn't going to let me do everything I want. With that in mind, I want to work with you on a plan. I have a few ideas, but first I want to hear what you think and what's most important to you. That way, if I can't make everything work, I'll be there for what matters most to you."

From there, if you like, you can share details about your financial situation, such as:

> "I haven't told many people, but I have a lot of _____ [kind] debt, and I've had to make sacrifices to pay that down. I'll put money aside to take part in your wedding, but I can't afford everything."

> "This is hard for me, but I don't make a ton of money, so I have to watch what I spend. I carved out space in my budget to make sure I can be there for you, but I can't spend as much as everyone else."

If they're agreeable to your request, be flexible and be grateful . . .

> "Thank you so much for listening. It means a lot to me. Your willingness to work with me on something as important as your wedding shows how much our relationship matters. We're going to have an amazing time."

If they react negatively to your request, stay calm but remain firm . . .

> "I hear you. I wish I didn't need to talk with you about this. I'd love to participate in every part of your amazing wedding, but I hope you'll understand that my financial situation just won't allow me to do that. That's why I came to you. I want us to talk so we can figure out what matters most to you so I can plan to attend the most important events."

Q *What if they deny your request?*

A This discussion might prove too volatile to have more than once. If so, consider speaking with other members of the wedding party to canvas whether they can help you reduce costs. That could mean sharing a hotel room, splitting a rental car, helping you shop for bachelor/ette supplies, and more. Chances are good that you're not alone in struggling with the cost. Sharing that burden can make a huge difference.

THE BRIDE OR GROOM SHOULD ASK QUESTIONS, TOO.

Poor communication can make challenging situations worse. Lauren Byrne, who runs Millennial personal finance and travel site HelloHenrys.com with her sister, Kelda, found out the hard way. "I had come back from a bachelorette party for a friend, and at the end of the trip, I got an additional charge for all the bride's expenses. That plan hadn't been shared or communicated beforehand. In some groups, it's common to pay for the friend, but I had no idea, when we were going on this big trip, that I would be expected to pay for the bride's flight, housing, food, and everything. Getting that at the end from one of the other bridesmaids was a shock."

When it came time for Lauren to plan her own wedding, she wanted her wedding party to have a different experience. She and her sister surveyed their guests about the bachelorette trip as well as wedding-day expenses using Google Forms, which respondents filled out anonymously. That anonymity, the sisters reasoned, made people feel more comfortable about answering openly and truthfully. The bachelorette-trip form asked about their budget for the trip, among other details. The wedding-day form offered bridesmaids a variety of dress options in a wide range of prices. Bridesmaids also learned that they didn't have to get their hair or makeup done professionally.

Those responses made a difference in the planning. Kelda, who planned Lauren's bachelorette trip and served as her maid of honor, says, "People listed a lower accommodation budget than we initially expected [for the bachelorette trip]. This changed what we were planning in terms of an Airbnb and made it so that women shared beds versus each having her own."

When Kelda married a few years later, she used the same approach, with Lauren returning the favor as bachelorette-trip planner and maid of honor. After that, the sisters' friends asked them to share their forms to help plan their own weddings. You can find ready-made templates online, too. In 2021, Talia Morales went viral on TikTok for talking about one that she created for her wedding.[99] Where you find one doesn't matter, but taking the time to think about your guests does. You may be sparing a loved one the awkward, uncomfortable experience of triaging the costs of participating in your wedding, and that's a big deal.

SPLITTING THE BILL FAIRLY AT A GROUP GATHERING

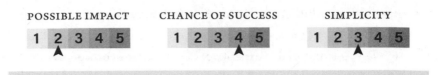

POSSIBLE IMPACT	CHANCE OF SUCCESS	SIMPLICITY
1 **2** 3 4 **5**	1 2 **3** 4 **5**	1 **2** **3** 4 **5**

Q   *What are you asking?*
A   You're seeking to split the check at a restaurant, bar, or other venue in a way that works best for you.

Q   *How big a deal is it?*
A   Potentially quite big for your wallet and your relationships. Meals or drinks with family, friends, or coworkers can get expensive quickly. Those gatherings also can cause serious awkwardness when the time comes to divvy the bill because people may have different views on how it should happen. A recent GoBankingRates survey showed an even split in people's preferences for how to handle paying for a group dinner, with 41 percent preferring to split the bill based on each individual's order and the same percentage wanting to split the total evenly among the group.[100] The remaining 18 percent preferred taking turns, trusting friends or family to return the

18% would rather take turns paying the whole bill.

41% prefer splitting it by each person's order.

41% say split it evenly among the group.

(GoBankingRates)

favor next time. Whichever direction the group chooses, if you don't communicate how you want to approach the bill, you could end up paying for far
more than what you ate or drank. Sometimes it's OK to pay a little extra—or
even cover the tab entirely—but not having a choice can feel maddening.

Q *How likely is it that you will succeed?*
A Every instance is different. Is it an expensive meal? How big is the
group? How long have you known most of them? Are the people easy-going
or more intense? Do you see these folks regularly? Are you comfortable
being vulnerable with them? Do their financial situations all look relatively
similar? Did you organize the gathering, or did someone invite you? Is it a
special occasion? These questions and more affect your likelihood of success and your approach for asking.

Q *Does asking pose any risks?*
A No one is going to make you pay more to retaliate against your request.
(If they do, walk out the door and find new friends.) But your relationship(s)
could experience consequences. Anytime you mix money with friends or
family, feelings can get hurt, so proceed with caution. Still, in most cases,
the risks shouldn't prevent you from making the ask.

Q *Does not succeeding pose any risks?*
A Your $20 meal of salad and sparkling water could turn into a $100
check share because everyone else ordered appetizers, bottles of wine, and
steak and the group decided to split the bill equally among everyone.

Q *How do you do it?*
A Timing is crucial. "Frontload that conversation as soon as possible
because the pressure rises when you're carrying that uncertainty from
drinks to appetizers to dessert," says Danielle Bayard Jackson, author of
Fighting for Our Friendships. Ideally, you should do it in the group text,
DM, email, or call that arranges the dinner. That way, by the time the food
or drinks start flowing, everyone knows where everyone stands. Anyone
with a major issue can adjust plans accordingly and even bow out of the

gathering altogether. Also, restaurants and bars have different policies when it comes to splitting a big bill. If you're not sure, call ahead and, you guessed it, ask.

The next best option is to do it as soon as the whole party has gathered. If you organized the gathering, clink your glass to get everyone's attention, announce how you want to split the bill, and read the room. If everyone agrees, end with an appropriate toast thanking everyone for coming and let the festivities continue. It sounds reasonable enough, but it's not ideal because many people may not want to voice financial concerns or disagreement in a room full of people and may feel forced into paying more than their fair share. This approach puts others in exactly the situation that you're trying to avoid for yourself. To prevent that hypocrisy, consider telling the guests that, if they have concerns, they should text you or speak with you individually.

SCRIPT

"Hi everyone, I'm so excited to see you all. Before we get together, let's make sure we all are on the same page when it comes to the bill. It's easier to discuss now than when we're there and have had a glass of wine or two."

From here, mention your preferred way to divvy the check . . .

"I suggest that we split the bill equally. We all know and trust one another, so that seems like the easiest way to do it. Sound good?"

OR

"I suggest that we each pay for our own orders. The _____ [venue] has a varied menu, and this way, if someone orders big-ticket items but someone else has a tighter budget, no one's feelings get hurt. If we order anything to share or for the table, we can divvy that accordingly, but apart from that, let's keep it simple and go Dutch. The _____ [venue] confirmed that they're good with multiple checks. Sound good?"

OR

> "I love my reward points. Is it OK if I pay the bill and everyone pays me what they owe by cash, app, or whatever? If anyone's not comfortable with that, let me know, and we can figure something else out. If that sounds like a plan, let's decide now whether to split the bill equally or we each pay for own orders. Sound good?"

With the last option, you're assuming a lot more risk in the name of reward points. If people don't pay what they owe, you're stuck covering their full share of the bill.

If people push back on your suggestion . . .

> "I hear you. I'm totally fine going with what the majority wants. The most important thing is figuring out the plan now so it's not awkward when we're there. What's everyone's preference?"

When you've come to a decision . . .

> "Thanks, everyone. I'm so glad we did this. Can't wait to see you all!"

Q *What if they deny your request?*

A If it doesn't go your way the first time, don't push the envelope. Complaining or whining won't do much other than irritating everyone. The solution could be as simple as changing what you plan to order, so you can manage your costs. But if you're not comfortable with the plan, it's OK to bow out gracefully. "A friend was watching her spending," says Lindsay Goldwert, author of *Bow Down: Lessons from Dominatrixes on How to Get Everything You Want.* "We all went out for a fancy dinner one night, and she said, 'I'll meet you afterward for drinks.' No one was offended. We just wanted to see her."

You have some sneakier options, too, says Bayard Jackson. "Maybe on your way to the restroom, you stealthily take the server to the side and cover your own bill. I've seen people pretend that they have to leave early and say, 'I'm going to get my bill because I have to head out in 10 minutes.' "

The worst-case scenario is that others judge or mock you for taking your stance. In that case, consider skipping the gathering and maybe dissociate from them. Real friends won't hold it against you. If they do, they're not really your friends.

PAY IT FORWARD

CONGRATULATIONS! By reading this book, you've learned how to save or earn thousands in the near future. That money can help pay off debt, pad an emergency fund, or go into an account for a down payment, mortgage, college, or retirement. Any of those possibilities can make a real difference in your life. Depending on the circumstances, your experience will vary, but succeeding in even one of these asks ideally could pay for this book. With every additional ask, the benefits can add up!

Remember, though, that it's not about just you—or at least it shouldn't be. It's amazing to save more or earn more for yourself, but it can prove even more rewarding to help your loved ones do the same. The extra $20 per month that you help your elderly mother save on her phone bill can help stretch her fixed income further. Showing your little brother how to ask for mentoring can help him discover exciting new career opportunities. Explaining how to reduce a big medical bill can allow your best friend to put some extra money into her kid's college fund.

Money is a big deal, but how it improves someone's life or perspective matters most. Seeing you make one of these requests and succeed may make your loved ones think, *You know, that didn't seem so hard. Maybe I should try.* Then—powering through the sweaty palms, racing heart, and trembling voice to their own successes—they may think, *That wasn't so bad. I should do more of this!* Next time, the palms will feel drier, the voice steadier, the request easier. It all starts with someone serving as an example, though. People don't know what they don't know, and often the only way to find out is for someone to show them. Be that example to your family, friends, and community, even if you don't feel qualified.

For Maribel Francisco, it started when, as a kid, she helped her parents in ways that so many children of immigrants must. "We as children are translators for legal documents for our Spanish-speaking parents. We don't know legalese, and we sometimes will translate something verbatim, and our parents will be like, 'What does that mean?' Then they'll get mad at us because we understand the language, so we should understand what this document says and be able to explain it." Those experiences of helping her parents, though frustrating at times, helped inspire her to do what she does today. A money coach, she founded Our Wealth Matters, dedicated to helping the immigrant community navigate the financial world. That confusing world can prove maddening for native speakers of English and downright impossible for people learning the language as adults.

In her TED Talk, Aja McClanahan, author of *How a Mother Should Talk about Money with Her Daughter: A Step-by-Step Guide to Budgeting, Saving, Investing, and Other Important Lessons*, explains how a largely self-inflicted financial meltdown led to moving in with her grandmother, feeling broke and embarrassed. McClanahan talks about the transformative power of her grandmother's transparency about money and the accountability that she forced on her not-always-focused granddaughter. McClanahan said her grandmother focused on solving problems, not just complaining about money. "She would talk about money, but then she would also have solutions. She's just like, 'Hey, don't spend as much money as you make, make sure you pay your bills first,' things like that." McClanahan has made a point of passing what she learned to her daughters and trying to help other parents do the same.

It took Chris Browning, founder and host of the *Popcorn Finance* podcast, a while to grasp his influence. "It started to dawn on me, *Oh, there's not a lot of black men doing what I do,* so when younger black men see me, I'm an example. When I was younger, I didn't have a lot of people at all in the financial space that I would say, 'Oh, look at that. There's a person who kind of looks like me who's out there doing this.' I never had that type of representation that I can remember seeing, so I really did start to take it much more seriously that the role I play, regardless of whether I'm doing it intentionally, is representation for other people."

Author of *Financially Responsible* and host of the *Overcoming Financial Trauma* podcast, Rahkim Sabree mentioned a conversation with a friend that had a significant impact on him. "I said, 'Hey, you know, this last month or so has been kind of crazy for me financially. I'm thinking about getting a job.' He said, 'Why?' and I said, 'Well, I need money.' 'So go get some more money.' 'Well, it's easy for you to say that. You have a job.' But the conversation was so impactful because following those statements was: You don't realize how much of an inspiration you are to other people in that your success is the success of other people. People are looking to you as an example. So keep going. If anybody can make this happen, it's you. That's the biggest compliment to me, when somebody says, 'If anybody can do this, it's you.' All right, you believe in me.'"

You don't have to have a big social media presence or host a popular podcast to make a difference. What you do and how you act matters to many people in your life. Your parents, siblings, or significant other care about what you do and say. If you have them, your kids always watch and learn from you. You can influence coworkers, the people in your rec league, and that networking group. The list goes on. Every one of them could learn something from this book, so don't keep it a secret. The next time you get together with colleagues, friends, or family, tell them how you saved or made more money with one of the asks. When they do the same, you're going to be a hero. Encouraging people to take that first step helps them open the door to new, exciting possibilities. When you fully embrace that you have more power over your money than you realize, you can help improve others' lives, too. "If you're wondering, 'How on earth can I be somebody's money role model when I'm barely making it myself?' my advice to you is 'Just be you and strive to be a better you tomorrow,'" McClanahan says in her TED Talk. "And don't forget to tell someone else about your journey along the way."

SCORECARD

HOW MUCH YOU'VE SAVED

You've worked hard to improve your financial life. Celebrate those efforts by tracking what you've done and how much you've saved or earned in the process. Even if you can't assign a monetary value to what you did— speaking to your parents about money for the first time or having a negative item removed from your credit report, for example—record it here anyway. Seeing the victories stack up on the page can motivate you to make another request and another. Before you know it, this book will have paid for itself many times over.

If you have a great success story to share, let me know at success@ mattschulz.com. I'd love to hear it!

What I asked	What I saved or earned	Date

What I asked	What I saved or earned	Date

What I asked	What I saved or earned	Date

ACKNOWLEDGMENTS

To my wife, Shannon Schulz, and my son, Will, thank you for your encouragement and support throughout this process and for being OK with me disappearing into my office every night after work and on a whole lot of weekends for months on end. I love you both.

To my mom, Ellen Schulz, and my sister, Erin Rosenfeldt, thank you for a lifetime of supporting my love of reading and writing and always being there for me. I love you.

To my amazing agent, Sarah Smith with the David Black Literary Agency, your passion and enthusiasm for this project were crystal clear from that first phone call. Thank you for believing in me and for everything that you've done to make my dream of becoming a published author come true. Bobbi Rebell, thank you for being kind enough to introduce me to Sarah. That email changed my life. Thank you to Gary Morris for pinch-hitting while Sarah was away.

To my incredible editor, James Jayo with Countryman Press, thank you for your patience with the new guy. Your thoughtfulness, insights, and humor have blown me away. Thank you to Maya Goldfarb and the rest of the Countryman team, too. I couldn't imagine the book in better hands.

To my work family at LendingTree—Doug Lebda, Megan Grueling, Brian Karimzad, Morgan Lanier, Tony Berlin, Brianna Wright, Kali

McFadden, Vita DeCeglio, Ismat Mangla, Dan Shepard, Nelson Garcia, Frankie Rendon, Nancy Jones, Jacob Channel, Nick Clements, Diyva Sangameshwar, and others—I'm so proud to be a part of this team. Thank you for making this the best job I've ever had.

To my previous work family at Bankrate—Dan Ray, Jody Farmer, Julie Sherrier, Chris Speltz, Ben Woolsey, Bruce Zanca, Greg McBride, Mark Hamrick, Katie Yates, Ryan Feldman, and Ted Rossman—thank you for taking a chance on me all those years ago. The opportunity for me to write this book never would have arisen if you hadn't. You changed my life forever.

To Kathryn Tuggle, this book is what it is because of your guidance in its formative stages. I'll always be grateful.

To Jeremy Wallace, Gene and Karen Menez, Vicky Nguyen, David Paredes, Yanely Espinal, Laura Adams, Selena Rezvani, Sharon Epperson, Beth Pinsker, Lauren Cook, Mindee Aamodt, Trae Bodge, Annie Nova, Tiffiny Williams, Lisa Rowan, Virgie Bright Ellington, Richard Kerr, Erika Leone, Cameron Huddleston, Kimberly Palmer, Beverly Harzog, Alison Morris Roslyn, Kristin McGrath, Catey Hill, Stefanie O'Connell Rodriguez, Jennifer Barrett, Carlota Zimmerman, Gerri Detweiler, Ron Lieber, Betsey Sorensen, Marshall Allen, Victoria Araj, Jenn Jones, Kristin Marcum, Barbara Sloan, Rob. Nylund, Sara Glakas, Mandi Woodruff-Santos, Jean Chatzky, Beth Waldron, Lindsey Stanberry, Miranda Marquit, Niccole Kunshek, and so many others, thank you for all you've done in helping me get this boulder up the hill. Your help proved invaluable from when this was just an idea all the way to today. I couldn't have done this without you.

To Dr Pepper, Zoom, and the transcription service Rev.com, you three are the real MVPs.

Finally, to my dad, Paul Schulz, this is for you. I love you and miss you every day.

NOTES

1. Matt Schulz, "Despite Federal Reserve Rate Hikes, 76% of Lower Credit Card APR Requests Were Granted in Past Year," LendingTree, April 24, 2023, www.lendingtree.com/credit-cards/study/lower-apr-requests.
2. Alexandria White, "Here's Our Most up-to-Date List of Credit Card Financial Assistance Programs during Coronavirus," CNBC Select, July 8, 2021, www.cnbc.com/select/credit-card-issuers-offer-customer-assistance-amid-corona virus-financial-hardship/; "Q&A: Larry Cordell on Recent Mortgage Forbearance and Delinquency Data," Federal Reserve Bank of Philadelphia, March 3, 2022; www.philadelphiafed.org/consumer-finance/mortgage-markets/larry -cordell-on-recent-mortgage-forbearance-and-delinquency-data.
3. Denitsa Tsekova, "Banks Are Closing Credit Cards and Slashing Credit Limits amid the Pandemic, Survey Finds," Yahoo Finance, July 22, 2020, www .yahoo.com/video/banks-close-credit-cards-and-slash-credit-limits-amid -the-pandemic-survey-finds-170739834.html.
4. www.moritaheripour.com/about
5. www.amandaclayman.com
6. www.drlaurencook.com
7. www.confidentgirlhotline.com/about
8. www.selenarezvani.com/about
9. www.tippedfinance.com
10. www.wealthparatodos.com/about
11. www.affordanything.com/team-afford-anything
12. www.linkedin.com/in/kristin-mcgrath-5b8a0523
13. www.samanthaobrochta.com
14. www.truetrae.com/about
15. www.bravelygo.co/about

16. All calculations in this paragraph use the Discover credit card payoff calculator: www.discover.com/credit-cards/calculator/credit-card-interest-calculator.

17. Matt Schulz, "Despite Federal Reserve Rate Hikes, 76% of Lower Credit Card APR Requests Were Granted in Past Year," LendingTree, April 24, 2023, www.lendingtree.com/credit-cards/study/lower-apr-requests.

18. Tom Anderson, "Asking Credit Card Companies to Lower Rates and Fees Works 80% of the Time," CNBC.com, March 17, 2017, www.cnbc .com/2017/03/27/asking-credit-card-companies-to-lower-rates-and-fees -works-80-of-the-time.html.

19. www.sarahapotter.com/podcast

20. Security.org Team, "2023 Credit Card Fraud Report," Security.org, January 31, 2023, www.security.org/digital-safety/credit-card-fraud-report.

21. "Lost or Stolen Credit, ATM and Debit Cards," Federal Trade Commission Consumer Advice, January 2022, consumer.ftc.gov/articles/lost-or-stolen -credit-atm-debit-cards.

22. Amy Loftsgordon, "Your Liability for Unauthorized Credit and Debit Card Charges," Nolo.com, www.nolo.com/legal-encyclopedia/unauthorized-credit -debit-card-charges-29654.html.

23. "How Long Can the Card Issuer Take to Resolve My Credit Card Billing Error Dispute," Consumer Financial Protection Bureau, September 23, 2022, www.consumerfinance.gov/ask-cfpb/how-long-can-the-card-issuer-take-to -resolve-my-billing-error-or-dispute-en-64.

24. "How Do I Get My Money Back after I Discovered an Unauthorized Trans-action or Money Missing from My Bank Account?" Consumer Financial Pro-tection Bureau, August 25, 2020, www.consumerfinance.gov/ask-cfpb/how -do-i-get-my-money-back-after-i-discovered-an-unauthorized-transaction -or-money-missing-from-my-bank-account-en-1017.

25. AnnaMaria Andriotis, "Millions of Americans Skip Credit Card and Car Pay-ments," *Wall Street Journal*, May 20, 2020, www.wsj.com/articles/millions-of -americans-skip-credit-card-and-car-payments-11589985381.

26. www.nfcc.org/who-we-are

27. "Consumer Reports Investigation Finds More Than One-Third of Consum-ers Found Errors in Their Credit Reports," *Consumer Reports*, June 10, 2021, www.consumerreports.org/media-room/press-releases/2021/06/consumer -reports-investigation-finds-more-than-one-third-of-consumers-found -errors-in-their-credit-reports.

28. "How Credit Actions Impact Credit Scores," MyFICO.com, www.myfico .com/credit-education/faq/affects-of-credit-actions.

29. www.experian.com/disputes/main.html; www.equifax.com/personal/credit-report-services/credit-dispute; www.transunion.com/credit-disputes/dispute-your-credit

30. "If a Credit Reporting Error Is Corrected, How Long Will It Take before I Find Out the Results," Consumer Financial Protection Bureau, September 1, 2020, www.consumerfinance.gov/ask-cfpb/if-a-credit-reporting-error-is-corrected-how-long-will-it-take-before-i-find-out-the-results-en-1339.

31. www.experian.com/blogs/ask-experian/author/rod-griffin

32. "What's in My FICO Scores?" MyFICO.com, www.myfico.com/credit-education/whats-in-your-credit-score.

33. "The Complete Guide to Your VantageScore," VantageScore, October 11, 2019, vantagescore.com/press_releases/the-complete-guide-to-your-vantagescore.

34. LaToya Irby, "What Is an Adverse Action Notice?" *The Balance*, September 23, 2022, www.thebalancemoney.com/what-s-an-adverse-action-notice-959985.

35. Matt Schulz, "Despite Federal Reserve Rate Hikes, 76% of Lower Credit Card APR Requests Were Granted in Past Year," LendingTree, April 24, 2023, www.lendingtree.com/credit-cards/study/lower-apr-requests.

36. www.meredithmediationandcoaching.com

37. www.bravelygo.co/about

38. "CFPB Proposes Rule to Rein in Excessive Credit Card Late Fees," Consumer Financial Protection Bureau, February 1, 2023, www.consumerfinance.gov/about-us/newsroom/cfpb-proposes-rule-to-rein-in-excessive-credit-card-late-fees.

39. www.jeffkreisler.com/moneybook.html; www.linkedin.com/in/jeffkreisler

40. www.marshallallen.com

41. www.medicare.gov/procedure-price-lookup; www.cms.gov/medicare/physician-fee-schedule/search

42. www.patientadvocate.org

43. The Associated Press, "New Laws Allow Pharmacists to Disclose Cheaper Options," AARP.org, October 11, 2018, www.aarp.org/health/drugs-supplements/info-2018/gag-rules-pharmacists.html.

44. A 2018 Schaeffer Center study found that commercially insured patients' copayments for a generic prescription exceeded the total cost of the medicine more than a quarter of the time (28 percent), with an average overpayment of $7.32. Erin Trish, PhD, Karen Van Nuys, PhD, and Robert Popovian, PharmD, "U.S. Consumers Overpay for Generic Drugs," Leonard D. Schaeffer Center for Health Policy & Economics, University of Southern

California, May 31, 2022, healthpolicy.usc.edu/research/u-s-consumers-overpay-for-generic-drugs.

45. www.ghlf.org/about-us/team/team-robert-bio

46. www.truthrx.org

47. Health Information Privacy Division, "Individuals' Right Under HIPAA to Access Their Health Information 45 CFR § 164.524," US Department of Health and Human Services, October 20, 2022, www.hhs.gov/hipaa/for-professionals/privacy/guidance/access/index.html.

48. Dounia Marbouh, Iman Khaleel, Khawla al Shanqiti, Maryam al Tamimi, Mecit Can Emre Simsekler, Samer Ellahham, Deniz Alibazoglu, and Haluk Alibazoglu, "Evaluating the Impact of Patient No-Shows on Service Quality," National Library of Medicine, June 4, 2020, www.ncbi.nlm.nih.gov/pmc/articles/PMC7280239.

49. Chris Harrop, "Patient No-Shows Pose Concern amid Medical Practice Staffing Challenges, Consumer Price Hikes," Medical Group Management Association, August 3, 2022, www.mgma.com/data/data-stories/patient-no-shows-pose-concern-amid-medical-practic.

50. ibid.

51. www.financialbestlife.com

52. "Breaking Down Reissue & Substitution Rates," SnapClose, www.snapclose.com/reissue-and-substitution-rates.

53. Stephen Brobeck, "Hidden Real Estate Commissions: Consumer Costs and Improved Transparency," Consumer Federation of America, October 2019, consumerfed.org/wp-content/uploads/2019/10/Real-Estate-Commissioner-Report.pdf.

54. "Discrimination When Buying a Car," National Fair Housing Alliance, https://nationalfairhousing.org/wp-content/uploads/2018/01/Discrimination-When-Buying-a-Car-FINAL-1-11-2018.pdf.

55. Lena Borrelli, "Average Funeral Cost," Bankrate, July 3, 2023, www.bankrate.com/insurance/life-insurance/average-funeral-cost.

56. www.glenvillefuneralhome.com/6/Our-Staff.html

57. Jessica Hall, "Do You Want Your Funeral to Be a Porsche or a Hyundai? Funeral Homes May Have to Post Prices Online for the First Time," MarketWatch, December 3, 2022, www.marketwatch.com/story/how-much-does-a-funeral-cost-funeral-homes-may-have-to-post-prices-online-for-the-first-time-11669738565.

58. Stephanie Bolling, "Cremation Is Gaining Popularity as Funeral Costs Rise,"

Forbes, January 11, 2023, www.forbes.com/advisor/personal-finance/cost -of-cremation.

59. Ethan Darby, "Grave Liners vs. Burial Vaults: What's the Difference?" Trigard, February 13, 2020, www.trigard.com/blog/grave-liners-vs-burial-vaults.

60. www.benefits.va.gov/compensation/claims-special-burial.asp

61. "Should You Prepay for Your Funeral? Safer Ways to Plan Ahead," Funeral Consumers Alliance, funerals.org/?consumers=should-you-prepay-for-your -funeral.

62. "The Best Time of Year to Buy Things for Your Home," HouseLogic by Realtors, www.houselogic.com/remodel/budgeting-contracting/best-time-of-year-to-buy-things-for-your-home.

63. www.girlscouts.org/en/footer/faq/parenting-faq.html

64. www.brooklynyouthsportsclub.org/staff; www.brooklynyouthsportsclub.org/conrad; www.theroseclassic.com/index.cfm?page=modPages&sec=view&pageid=13

65. www.lisarowan.com/pop-fashion-podcast

66. www.tiktok.com/@pricelesstay?lang=en

67. "Air Travel Consumer Report: December 2022, Full Year 2022 Numbers," US Department of Transportation, March 16, 2023, www.transportation .gov/briefing-room/air-travel-consumer-report-december-2022-full-year -2022-numbers.

68. rppa-appr.ca/eng/compensation-flight-delays-and-cancellations

69. www.choice.com.au/travel/on-holidays/airlines/articles/flight-delays-and -cancellations-compensation

70. www.caa.co.uk/passengers/resolving-travel-problems/delays-and-cancellations /cancellations

71. "More Than $600 Million in Refunds Returned to Airline Passengers under DOT Rules Backed by New Enforcement Actions Issued Today," US Department of Transportation, November 14, 2022, www.transportation .gov/briefing-room/more-600-million-refunds-returned-airline-passengers -under-dot-rules-backed-new.

72. www.transportation.gov/airconsumer/file-consumer-complaint

73. www.nerdwallet.com/article/travel/airbnb-pricing-statistics

74. Sally French and Sam Kemmis, "Airbnb Pricing Statistics: 2023," NerdWallet, January 30, 2023, www.nerdwallet.com/article/travel/is-it-cheaper-to -rent-a-car-at-the-airport.

75. Jacqueline DeMarco and Poonkulali Thangavelu, "A Guide to Foreign Trans-

action Fees," Bankrate, February 24, 2023, www.bankrate.com/finance/credit
-cards/a-guide-to-foreign-transaction-fees.

76. Matt Schulz, "Despite Federal Reserve Rate Hikes, 76% Of Lower Credit Card APR Requests Were Granted in Past Year," LendingTree, April 24, 2023, www.lendingtree.com/credit-cards/study/lower-apr-requests.

77. Gracey Cantalupo, Forbes Communication Council, "Does Mentoring Still Matter for Fortune 500 Companies?" Forbes, May 19, 2022, www.forbes .com/sites/forbescommunicationscouncil/2022/05/19/does-mentoring -still-matter-for-fortune-500-companies.

78. "SHRM Releases 2022 Employee Benefits Survey," SHRM, June 12, 2022, www.shrm.org/about-shrm/press-room/press-releases/pages/shrm -releases-2022-employee-benefits-survey--healthcare-retirement-savings -and-leave-benefits-emerge-as-the-top-ranked-be.aspx.

79. "Publication 15-B (2023), Employer's Tax Guide to Fringe Benefits," Internal Revenue Service, January 10, 2023, www.irs.gov/publications/p15b.

80. Emma Kerr and Sarah Wood, "13 Things to Know about Merit-Aid Scholarships," USNews.com, April 26, 2023, www.usnews.com/education/best -colleges/paying-for-college/slideshows/things-to-know-about-merit-aid -scholarships.

81. mailmissouri.sharepoint.com/:b:/s/IRQI-Website-Ogrp/EfX6IwEox1FE vDiojv4kK0ABLWmRYeEWXlTQgPJ8Kk5hAw?e=HAwsRw (Pg 22 of PDF)

82. "Raise Anatomy: How to Ask for a Raise and Get It," Payscale, www.payscale .com/research-and-insights/how-to-ask-for-a-raise.

83. www.moritaheripour.com/about

84. Kim Parker, "When Negotiating Starting Salaries, Most U.S. Women and Men Don't Ask for Higher Pay," Pew Research Center, April 5, 2023, www .pewresearch.org/short-reads/2023/04/05/when-negotiating-starting -salaries-most-us-women-and-men-dont-ask-for-higher-pay.

85. www.stefanieoconnell.com

86. "Corporate Giving and Matching Gift Statistics," Double the Donation, www. doublethedonation.com/matching-gift-statistics.

87. Adam Weinger, "Tax Benefits of Corporate Matching Gifts: The Basics," Double the Donation, www.doublethedonation.com/tax-benefits-of-corporate -matching-gifts/#companies.

88. hello.brightfunds.org; www.doublethedonation.com; solutions.yourcause.com

89. "Top Matching Gift Companies," Double the Donation, www.doublethe donation.com/list-matching-gifts-companies.

90. Cheyenne DeVon, "Here's How Much Americans Have Saved for Retirement at

EveryAge,"CNBC.com,July30,2022,www.cnbc.com/2022/07/30/vanguard
-how-much-americans-have-saved-for-retirement-by-age.html.

91. Sigrid Forberg, "Discussing Finances Is More Taboo Than Sex These Days—
    But It's Time for Couples to Have 'the Talk,'" Moneywise, February 22, 2022,
    moneywise.com/managing-money/budgeting/couple-finances-taboo-talk.
    References a Personal Capital report no longer available following Personal
    Capital's acquisition by Empower but previously available at: www.personal
    capital.com/blog/whitepapers/2022-love-money-report.

92. www.drmarnionline.com

93. www.bravelygo.co/about

94. www.aditishekar.com/zeta

95. Allie Johnson, "Poll: Lending Money Goes Wrong Nearly Half the Time,"
    Bankrate, December 13, 2021, www.bankrate.com/finance/credit-cards/
    lending-money-survey.

96. www.lauradadams.com/podcast

97. Allie Johnson, "Poll: Lending Money Goes Wrong Nearly Half the Time,"
    Bankrate, December 13, 2021, www.bankrate.com/finance/credit-cards/
    lending-money-survey.

98. Maggie Davis, "62% of Bridal Party Members Have Taken On Debt to Cover
    Wedding Costs," LendingTree, April 10, 2023, www.lendingtree.com/debt
    -consolidation/bridal-party-wedding-survey.

99. Kirstie Renae, "A Bride-to-Be on TikTok Is Sharing the 'Genius' Way She's
    Organizing Her Bridesmaids Using Google Forms," Insider.com, July 15,
    2021, www.insider.com/woman-sent-bridesmaids-google-form-to-organize
    -wedding-2021-7.

100 Casey Bond, "Here's the Best Way to Handle Splitting the Check," GoBank-
    ingRates, October 20, 2022, www.gobankingrates.com/money/financial
    -planning/modern-money-etiquette-whats-really-best-way-handle-splitting
    -check.

INDEX